architect, *verb*

architect, *verb*

The New Language of Building

Reinier de Graaf

VERSO
London • New York

This paperback edition first published by Verso 2024
First published by Verso 2023
© Reinier de Graaf 2023

1 3 5 7 9 10 8 6 4 2

Verso
UK: 6 Meard Street, London W1F 0EG
US: 388 Atlantic Avenue, Brooklyn, NY 11217
versobooks.com

Verso is the imprint of New Left Books

ISBN-13: 978-1-83976-192-8
ISBN-13: 978-1-83976-194-2 (US EBK)
ISBN-13: 978-1-83976-193-5 (UK EBK)

British Library Cataloguing in Publication Data
A catalogue record for this book is available from the British Library

Library of Congress Cataloging-in-Publication Data
A catalog record for this book is available from the Library of Congress

Typeset in Sabon by MJ & N Gavan, Truro, Cornwall
Printed and bound by CPI Group (UK) Ltd, Croydon, CR0 4YY

Contents

Introduction

What makes good architecture? Ask any architect and you will likely get a lengthy exposé on the all-importance of his or her work, their passion matched only by the passionate indifference from society at large. Architecture, it seems, has landed itself on the wrong side of history. Admittedly, confronted with the most pressing issues of our time—economic inequality, climate change and universally dwindling human rights—the discipline has not made a good showing: complicit in escalating house prices, an integral part of the largest CO_2-emitting industry, and all too oblivious to the political machinations it helps perpetuate.

Elitist in the 1970s, forgotten in the 1980s, rediscovered in the 1990s, idolized for much of the 2000s and 2010s, architecture today mostly registers as a cause for concern—a discipline insufficiently aware of its consequences, therefore one to be scrutinized and kept in check. Gone are the days of splendid isolation and privileged deliberations among peers. Architecture has caught the attention of both the public and the private sector in no uncertain terms, and there is *one* thing the two wholeheartedly agree on: too much is at stake to leave architecture to architects.

Valued at US$280 trillion, buildings represent the largest global asset class: triple global GDP, worth twice the world's oil reserves and thirty times its gold stock.[1] Construction is arguably the most important pillar of our financial system and, as our most recent global crisis demonstrated, also a potential source of its collapse.

What is true in financial terms equally applies to environmental issues. Buildings produce 30 per cent of all global greenhouse gas emissions while their construction accounts for 40 per cent of the world's energy use.[2] 'The built environment affects us all!' is the mantra of virtually every conference discussing the relevance of architecture. And the 'affecting' isn't limited to the economy or the environment. Witness the growing number of publications and online lectures on the subject, the built environment also profoundly affects us emotionally. 'Happiness', 'wellbeing', 'liveability' and 'the sense of place' are but a few examples of the increasingly emotive terms in which our built environment is being discussed, their prolific use indicative of the apparent lack of each.

In the age of big data, everything is quantifiable, even feelings. At long last, the elusive profession of architecture can be held accountable: good architecture makes people feel good, bad architecture does not. The logic is hard to argue with. But even if less technocratic evaluations of buildings ought to be welcomed, a problem arises when one tries to establish a basis for such evaluations. How does one measure happiness, wellbeing, liveability or place? While the economic or environmental impacts of the built environment tend to manifest in the form of certain hard facts, the same does not apply to its presumed emotional effects. Sure, one can hold polls, issue questionnaires, rely on internet data, but no matter how large or detailed the number of liveability rankings, wellbeing ratings or happiness indices produced in the wake of such efforts, a nagging contrast persists—between the immeasurable value attributed to each of these properties, on the one hand, and their inherently unmeasurable nature on the other. The immeasurable cannot be measured. Any attempt to do so only means that the very subjectivity which the numbers sought to exorcise from their subject re-enters through the back door.

Efforts to hold the creative disciplines to objective standards tend to leave a dubious taste—be it the Nazi's concept of degenerate art, Stalin's Socialist Realism, China's ban on weird buildings or, more recently, the British government's fraught attempts to monopolize the notion of beauty. One could argue that to measure something represents the first step in removing it from the realm of free will. Once things are measured, they can be classified, compared and, if needed, encouraged to change in order to compare more favorably. What is measured is forced to comply. It becomes *vectorized*. Ironically, it is the global system of free competition that has escalated this process to the extreme.

Global indices now exist for almost any aspect of our lives, professional or personal, factual or emotional, real or imagined. In subjecting an ever-larger number of segments of our lives to quantification, the world of free global competition increasingly exposes itself as a source of un-freedom. No longer is 'life, liberty and the pursuit of happiness' each individual's free choice; it is instead an imperative to which to conform and strive.

Nothing succeeds like success. We can only go further, forward, up. Competition permits no challenge, quite simply because it internalizes all challenge. Its whole principle *is* to challenge, everything, all the time, everywhere … until only a perpetual contest is left. Not to strive for *something*, but to strive, pure and simple. The aim equals the means. Values do not serve to be adhered to, but to mobilize. There are no truths, only aspirations. No absolutes, only comparisons, promoted in the form of endless benchmarks, references, precedents, touchstones, best-in-class examples. The principle has consumed the economy as much as it has consumed political ideology, the world of science as much as that of art and culture. It pervades our language as it pervades our thinking. It operates through words and numbers, most commonly a combination of the two, relying on commonplaces as a substitute for ideals and measurement as a substitute for logic. The more foregone the conclusions, the more extensive the numerical evidence presented in their support. Amateur philosophy meets pseudo-science, practised by an army of thought leaders, strategy consultants, content specialists and subject matter experts.

Architecture, arguably a mix of amateur philosophy and pseudo-science in its own right, has proven particularly vulnerable to this trend. Neither an art nor a science, it is left without the defence mechanism of either, condemned to fighting a war on two fronts: against unsubstantiated commonplaces and the arbitrary measurement systems that sustain them, against words which do not permit an antonym—which architect, in their right mind, would not wish for people to be happy, want to design unliveable buildings, or oppose a sense of wellbeing? —and against numbers which do not permit questioning. There is no arguing with people's feelings, not when expressed in hard figures.

From architects trying to explain to the world what they are doing, we increasingly witness a world in which architects are told what they *ought* to be doing. Once a discipline of ideas—a domain that helped formulate standards—architecture is progressively expected to comply to standards imposed by others: a besieged profession, forced to adopt ever-more extreme postures of virtue, held to account by the world of finance, the social sciences and recently even the medical sector, each with less disputable evidence at their disposal.

But how good is good? What would remain of architecture if it did exactly what it is told? What kind of environment ensues when all expectations, however unreasonable, incompatible or contradictory, are met?

If *Four Walls and a Roof* was about debunking myths projected *by* architects, **architect**, *verb* aims to debunk myths projected *onto* architecture by the outside world—a rebuttal of doctrines which have been applied to architecture over the last twenty years. It recounts the transformation of the architecture profession over the past twenty years, starting in post-Guggenheim Bilbao and ending in Silicon Valley: from the architect as miracle worker to the nerds plotting his redundancy. Knowing the first was never true and assuming the latter will never happen, the chapters of this book primarily dwell on the stages between, in which architecture progressively finds itself at the mercy of extraneous quests which it is neither able to resist nor capable of fulfilling. In order of appearance: starchitecture (1), world-class (2), excellence (3), sustainability (4), wellbeing (5), liveability (6), placemaking (7), creativity (8), beauty (9) and innovation (10).

Yet, the overriding quest of this book inevitably comes from within—a quest for architecture to be architecture again, written in the sincere hope that, in ridding it of unsolicited baggage, our profession might one day re-emerge as an independent and critical discipline.

starchitecture

noun [U]

UK /ˈstɑːkɪtɛktʃə/ US /ˈstɑːkɪtɛktʃə/

the work of architects whose celebrity and critical acclaim have transformed them into idols of the architecture world:

There are signs that the era of starchitecture is coming to an end.

1

Tears and Love

'Without embarrassing Frank, tell me what you think of the building?'

Frank's hands are behind his back. Visibly uneasy with the turn of the conversation, he edges away from the other two men speaking. 'I'm gonna leave,' he chuckles.

But Frank should stay; it's important he hears this.

The two men continue their conversation: 'Just … tell me. Just tell me what you think of the building.'

'Well … I'm like Muschamp in the *New York Times* … that all you can do is say "wow!"'

'Wow?'

'It's just too bad, there's no words. Architecture's not about words. It's about tears. And love…'

'About tears and love…?'

'I get the same feeling in the nave of … Chartres cathedral.'

'Same feeling in Chartres…?'

'The same tears!'

'It overwhelms…?'

'Mm-hm.'

'Because of its…?'

It never becomes clear what '…' is. The conversation is cut short. Talk of tears has sparked real tears. There is no point in extracting further comments from this man. The beauty of the space is simply too much, even for his trained eye. Pushing him to rationalize his feelings would amount to nothing short of bad taste. An arm around his frail shoulders is the only elegant way out. A photo flash goes off.

It is May 1998: *Charlie Rose* is paying tribute to the Guggenheim Bilbao and to its architect Frank Gehry [Frank]. The man breaking into tears is Philip Johnson: the 'Nestor' of American Architecture, first-ever winner of the prestigious Pritzker Architecture Prize and with an oeuvre spanning seven decades. If appreciation of one's peers is a measure of success, it is hard to trump that of Philip Johnson—even when, at his age, his emotions might get the better of him.

Johnson has been moved by many things in his life. Particularly by things which contradict each other. Having cultivated a passion for classical architecture as a student, he evolved into an early promoter of modern architecture after graduation. An ardent supporter of the Nazi movement in the 1930s, he enlisted in the US Army upon the outbreak of World War II. A power broker for progressive architecture during the '50s, '60s and '70s, he abruptly converted to postmodernism in the 1980s, only to shift back in the 1990s after the political tide had shifted again.

What *does* one make of the tears shed by a man whose convictions have proven so volatile? Charlie and Frank, his companions in the atrium of the Guggenheim, seem to wonder that as well. Asking Philip Johnson to comment on the work of a fellow architect on a TV show proves a risk. The old man declines to comment. 'Tears and love.' He is lost for further words. Even the word 'wow!' gets stuck somewhere halfway in his throat. The extent of his adulation leaves him no other option *than* to embarrass Frank. It is best gone unheard.

We will never know what '…' is.

A Lourdes for a crippled culture

The article Johnson refers to is a review by Herbert Muchamp, the then-architecture critic of the *New York Times*. Muchamp's article had been published about half a year earlier, at the time of the Guggenheim's completion.[1] Even if the word 'wow' is conspicuously absent from the article's text, the reviewer very much shares Johnson's unconditional veneration of the museum. The opening line—'The word is out that miracles still occur!'—is reprinted on the *NYT Magazine's* cover and serves as a warning of what's to come. 'Wow' is practically the only word to go unused in his extensive, rhapsodic homage to Gehry's creation: 'Stone, glass, titanium, curves, straight lines, opacity, transparency, openness and enclosure are brought into sensuous conjunction. You may think, as you stand within this space, that the Tower of Babel story was a myth concocted by people who were afraid of diversity', he gushes. 'Here you see that many languages can not only coexist but also babble around within a broad and vibrant vista of the world.'

The same space that brought Johnson to tears inspires Muchamp to imagine the alternative ending to a biblical scene. Muchamp sees Gehry's hand everywhere. Even a nearby zebra crossing is endowed with meaning: 'Even the dotted line painted down the middle of the street and the stripes of the pedestrian crosswalk at the corner look somehow Gehry-fied, an accidental version of the lines Renaissance artists used with such precision in architectural drawings to highlight the new laws of visual perspective.'

Renaissance drawing and biblical scenes are not the only things Muchamp reads into Gehry's building: 'And that the building I'd just come from was the reincarnation of Marilyn Monroe. What twins the actress and the building in my memory is that both stand for an American style of freedom. That style is voluptuous, emotional, intuitive and exhibitionist.' He adds, 'it is mobile, fluid, material, mercurial, fearless, radiant and as fragile as a newborn child. It can't resist doing a dance with all the voices that say "No." It wants to take up a lot of space. And when the impulse strikes, it likes to let its dress fly up in the air.'

Gehry's creation—'a sanctuary to free association'—clearly also sets Muchamp free. It provides him the artistic licence to make the review his own—no longer about the work of the architect, but about that of the critic. He confesses as much: 'upon leaving his Guggenheim, a 49-year-old architecture critic might suddenly find himself speaking in the voice of Marilyn Monroe. Her presence in Bilbao is totally my projection.' It is a curious admission at the end of the (nearly 5,000-word) article, which his last fragile attempt at explaining the building's larger significance—'a Lourdes for a crippled culture'—does little to mitigate: 'Fools give you reasons; wise men never try. An architecture critic has no choice but to be foolish on this occasion.'

Sometimes, having too many words is the same as having none.

Something more daring, please

Rumour has it that Gehry's first atrium proposal was a box but that the idea did not quite crack it. At the time of his commissioning, rectangular plans had already become an anomaly in his architecture and so he was asked to come up with something more daring, something more 'Gehry'.[2] Only a radical proposition, something that 'pushed the limits', would help the city which was to be its future home.[3]

Bilbao was hardly the Guggenheim's first choice.[4] In the early 1990s, Bilbao was an economic and cultural backwater. Competition from ports in Southeast Asia had all but spelled the end of local shipyards and plunged the city, once one of Spain's wealthiest, into a deep recession. Its debts were mounting, and unemployment ranked at 25 per cent. On top of that, Bilbao routinely suffered from terrorist attacks by the Basque separatist movement, ETA.

Having missed out on the first Spanish regeneration wave, which saw Barcelona host the Olympics and Seville the World Expo, the Basque regional government embarked on the 'Revitalization Plan for Metropolitan Bilbao'. Its objective: to elevate the economic and cultural standing of Bilbao to a level comparable to other major cities in the EU.

A cultural institution had been part of the revitalization plan from the moment of its inception and the first contacts between the Basque administration and the Guggenheim Foundation date back to February 1991. At the time, the economic situation of the Guggenheim Foundation was not dissimilar to that of Bilbao: budget overruns on the extension of its museum on Fifth Avenue and expensive art acquisitions had left the foundation short of cash and with rising debts. Recouping these debts was further complicated by the fact that 95 per cent of the museum's artwork was left undisplayed, stocked in the basement of its Fifth Avenue branch and miscellaneous other storage facilities.

Like Bilbao, the Guggenheim badly needed a regeneration plan. In 1988, the directorship of the Guggenheim had been handed from Thomas Messer, an art professional, to Thomas Krens, somebody with a background in business, with an MBA from Yale. Krens launched a daring plan to mobilize the museum's idle art stock, creating an international franchise system which allowed cities around the world to build satellite museums—at their own risk and expense.

Bilbao was the first city to take up the idea. As part of the EU's regional development programme, the Basque region had been the recipient of ample EU funding. From the US$1.5 billion revitalization plan, the Basque administration reserved US$100 million for the new museum building, US$50 million for art acquisition, US$12 million annually to operate the museum (for a seventy-five-year period) and another US$20 million for use of the Guggenheim's name. To be paid up front.

In return, the Guggenheim promised to provide Bilbao with three exhibitions a year, grant the Basques exclusive rights to profits from tickets and merchandise sales, strengthen the collaborative relationship with the Guggenheim's Venice branch, ensure that the Guggenheim Bilbao was made an integral part of all Guggenheim PR campaigns worldwide and grant the Basques majority voting rights in a new consortium to be formed at the time of the museum's opening. And, most importantly, it conceded that all further Guggenheim satellites in Europe required Basque approval—a concession that prompted Krens to declare that the Guggenheim was, from here on, 'a Basque Institution'.

Basque or not, the investment in the museum was recouped within the first year of its opening. And that was hardly the end of things. In its first three years, the museum attracted more than 3.5 million visitors, of which more than 80 per cent came to Bilbao exclusively to see the museum. Their total spending amounted to more than 100,000 million pesetas (€600 million at today's Euro rate), equalling an average spending per visitor of approximately 30,000 pesetas (€175). More than a third went to restaurants, bars and cafeterias, roughly a quarter to the hotel branch, another quarter to shops and stores, about 5 per cent was spent on transport costs and another 5 per cent on tickets for the museum itself.

The direct added value to the economy of the Basque Country amounted to more than 80,000 million pesetas (€480 million) of GDP, implying the maintenance of an annual average of 4,000 jobs. For the Basque treasury departments, the additional economic activity generated by the museum represented more than 15,000 million pesetas (€90 million) of additional revenue in the form of value-added tax, company tax and income tax.[5]

The impact of the museum was huge and continued to be so during the years to come. In 2002, one year after 9/11, the museum received another 930,000 visitors, bringing in a further €149 million to the local economy and another €27 million to the Basque treasury in taxes. The permanent collection received 250,000 visitors, 239,000 people participated in educational programmes, 14,000 paid to be individual members and 140 companies signed up to be corporate members. By 2002, nearly 75 per cent of the museum's expenditures were self-funded.[6]

Just before the opening, a terrorist plot was foiled. Three Basque separatists disguised as gardeners had tried to plant explosives on Jeff Koons's flower puppy. A shootout ensued and a policeman was killed. The killing had 250,000 people all over Spain marching in protest. It was not the last the world heard of the Basque separatists—a ceasefire was not properly sealed until 2006—but it curiously marked a turning point in the public perception of the extent to which the city of Bilbao was at risk from terrorism: research of news items published between 1997 and 2010 demonstrated that for every 10 per cent increase in news coverage of the ETA, visitor numbers to the museum dropped by 0.76 per cent, but that for every 10 per cent increase in coverage of the museum, visitor numbers increased by 1.71 per cent. It's estimated that 8.4 million of the 13 million visitors to the museum during its first thirteen years came because of the international press about the museum, implying that media coverage of the Guggenheim Museum Bilbao generated an economic value of around €2 million per year.[7]

Bilbao is not Paris

Until the opening of the Guggenheim Bilbao, the only buildings in recent history to have attracted a similar level of attention were the Sydney Opera House (1973) and the Centre Pompidou (1976). The Pompidou, too, contains a museum: the Musée National d'Art Moderne. But one needs to be reminded of that. Since its opening, the Centre Pompidou—or Beaubourg, as it is popularly called—has mainly registered as a piece of public infrastructure. (Something to which its appearance has done its best to contribute.) Built for the people, to be enjoyed *by* the people, the exact function of the Pompidou is at best 'incidental' to its existence. Designed in sharp contrast to its surroundings—another thing it has in common with the Guggenheim—its (visual) impact inevitably trumps that of any collection on display. 'Tourists came in the millions to gawp—not at the paintings but at the pipes.'[8] Twenty years on, those same tourists flock to Bilbao to gawp at the Guggenheim—not at its contents but at its curves.

Yet, there is one important difference. Bilbao is *not* Paris. While Paris, as one of the most iconic capitals in the world, could boast large tourist numbers well before the opening of the Pompidou, Bilbao, prior to the Guggenheim opening, was a city with no tourist infrastructure to speak of. When asked about their reasons for visiting Bilbao, 85 per cent of all respondents cited the museum as a reason, in fact *the only* reason for visiting the city. While no similar survey had ever been carried out at the time of the Pompidou's opening, it is unlikely that Paris saw the same increase in tourist numbers and even less likely that anyone ever attributed their reasons for visiting Paris to just one reason. Paris was 'on the map' well before the Centre Pompidou.

What is different about Bilbao is that it takes the importance that can be attributed to a single work of architecture to a whole other level. Even if Bilbao's metropolitan regeneration plan entailed projects of multiple internationally renowned architects—Norman Foster to design the Bilbao Metro Railway, Michael Wilford the Abando Passenger Interchange and Santiago Calatrava the new Bilbao airport terminal and Nervion footbridge (even the Guggenheim itself had been an international competition)—its legacy will forever be equated with one: that of Frank Gehry's Guggenheim Museum. If it was not for the Guggenheim, the city's revival would never have happened. Bilbao exists *because of* the museum. However unfair, that is the perception which has come to endure.

And if a single building can change the fortunes of an entire city, then all one needs to change a city's fortunes is a single building. It is a simplification, but if there is such a thing as a Bilbao Effect, it is mostly a temporary suspension of conventional wisdom. Cities are invariably larger than buildings, costlier to build and more difficult to plan. And yet the Bilbao Effect offers a window of opportunity to bypass all the complicated and time-consuming procedures usually associated with city planning as a public task. Post-Guggenheim Bilbao becomes the living proof that cities can be radically altered on the back of a single construction project, taking five years at most —less than half a decade.

Coffee for everyone

The Bilbao Effect called for emulation, not least in Spain itself. After accession to the EU in 1986, as a result of the EU's cohesion policy, Spain came to enjoy a substantial net inflow of money. By the 1990s, Spain had one of the strongest economies in Europe. In addition, as part of its transition to democracy after the death of Franco, Spain's governance structure has been substantially altered. Power, formerly centralized in Madrid, has been devolved to seventeen autonomous regions—a policy which went by the popular name of 'café para todos' (coffee for everyone). Some regions, most notably the Basque Country, Catalunya and Galicia—each with their own language—were given the institutional infrastructure to go with it, including their own parliaments.

Spain's economic upturn, in combination with a more decentralized political system, sparked stark competition between regions and cities which registered directly on the international stage. Seville was awarded the World Expo in 1982, Barcelona the Olympics in 1986. It was in these cities that the importance of architecture manifested: the permanent legacy of (what otherwise might be) passing fortunes. Architecture made solid all that melts into air. The central position architecture projects were given within the Bilbao metropolitan regeneration plan was directly inspired by the approach taken earlier in Barcelona and Seville.

Bilbao went on to inspire other cities in Spain. Two years after the opening of Gehry's Guggenheim Bilbao, San Sebastian, the region's second city, opened its Kursaal Congress Centre designed by Raphael Moneo. After the Basque Country, it was Galicia's turn. When La Coruna launched its Museum of Mankind by Isozaki, neighbouring Vigo soon followed suit with a maritime museum designed by Aldo Rossi. In the region of Asturias, Brazilian master Oscar Niemeyer was 'brought back from the dead' to design the International Cultural Centre of the town of Avilés, hoping his involvement might spark its own Niemeyer Effect.[9] The number of foreign architects involved prompted Richard Rogers (a quarter of whose work is in Spain) to label Spain 'Europe's architectural hothouse'.

It is hardly surprising that the regions which, under the devolution of political power, moved forward most aggressively with formalizing their autonomy (Catalunya, the Basque Country and Galicia) were also the first to manifest that autonomy in the form of architectural projects. Europe's architectural hothouse was ultimately driven by local interests. In that context, Kenneth Frampton's notion of 'critical regionalism' acquired an interesting twist: more than the description of an approach to architecture, it became a reflection on Spain's political situation at the time.

Emulation

The effect was hardly limited to Spain. 'The miracle in Bilbao' sparked considerable attention elsewhere around the world— not least in the United States, where the first five years after the opening of the Guggenheim Bilbao saw at least fifty new museum projects launched.[10] Perhaps not surprisingly, most of these were in cities whose local economy stood to gain significantly from the raised profile such projects might bring. Competition between cities—in the US traditionally played out in sports such as baseball or football—acquired a new dimension in the field of culture.

What had been branded a project of American cultural imperialism by some—'McGuggenheim'—found its most prolific, and perhaps most successful, application in its country of origin. Just as in Bilbao, the Sydney Opera House was invariably invoked as a reference for towns eager to project their image in the face of the world: 'a world-class building to help create a world-class city'. Even the process was copied: a competition between famous architects (generally three) judged by evaluation committees made up of municipal officials, museum curators and donors. (Architects were conspicuously absent from such groups.)

In Cincinnati, Ohio—home of the Major League's Cincinnati Reds—Zaha Hadid triumphed over Bernard Tschumi and Daniel Libeskind to design the city's Center for Contemporary Art (2003). In the 'mile high', skiing, hiking and climbing city of Denver, Libeskind got to design the Denver Art Museum (2006). (He got his revenge by beating Isozaki—not 'wow' enough in the eyes of the selection committee, or Thom Mayne—whose explanation nobody could understand.)

But by far the most resounding victory was won by Santiago Calatrava because of the way he gained the right to design the Art Museum of the blue-collar, beer-brewing town of Milwaukee (2001). When Walter Annenberg, a Milwaukee-born businessman, donated $1 million for a selection process involving more than fifty architects, Calatrava withdrew, only to be coaxed back and given the commission on a silver platter. Calatrava's contribution did a great deal to delight the city. 'We've never had that one icon—except for maybe a bratwurst—that we can say is most reflective of Milwaukee as a world-class city and destination', said William A. Hanbury, executive director of the Greater Milwaukee Convention and Visitors Bureau.

Calatrava was hardly the only museum architect to receive such praise: according to Raymond Buse of the Cincinnati

Chamber of Commerce, 'larger than life Zaha Hadid had put the Queen City at the epicenter of the architectural universe', and for Wellington Webb, mayor of Denver, Daniel Libeskind had put Denver 'on the map as a world-class destination city'. Even the rhetoric mirrored that of Bilbao. When it comes to lyrical praise, however, the ultimate prizewinner was Libeskind's own quote, claiming to have been 'inspired by the light and geology of the Rockies, but most of all by the wide-open faces of the people of Denver'.

Notwithstanding such praise, the economic successes proved more elusive than expected. Even if the Milwaukee Art Museum received 500,000 visitors in its first year, a substantial overrun on its construction budget left it short of funds to operate and maintain the building. By 2011 the museum had a deficit of US$4.6 million.[11] Of the million visitors expected in the first year of the Denver Art Museum, only 650,000 came, causing a decision to lay off 14 per cent of the staff.[12] In 2015, facing calls for a more 'comfortable, hospitable and social space', the Cincinnati Art Museum spent US$1.1 million in the redesign of its signature lobby, furnishing Hadid's streamlined forms with lounge seating, plush carpets and ample outlets to keep electronic devices charged. The investment seemed to pay off, upping the museum's sluggish visitor numbers to a record 136,879. Hadid was not consulted on the redesign, however. CAM board members had concluded that involving her would be too difficult and expensive.[13]

By 2010, budget overruns, negative balance sheets and waning visitor numbers had become commonplace in many new American museums. Museum directors came and went, often within a year after the new museums had been completed.[14] The effect on their surroundings, too, had proved minimal. Neither Cincinnati, Milwaukee nor Denver suffered any discernable upward economic effects after the openings of respective museums. Ten years into the new millennium, the Bilbao Effect was already proving a myth.

The orphaned museum

The downward spiral that started in America continued in Europe. In Europe, more than mere city marketing, the Bilbao Effect was the much-hoped-for panacea for ailing industrial towns. Having witnessed the transformation of a run-down Basque port, culture seemed the obvious choice for a second lease of life for many post-industrial cities. Contrary to the US, however, museums in Europe did not boast the same tradition of private wealthy benefactors. In Europe, museum financing depended mainly on the public sector. Art collections either gifted to or owned by the public were a rarity. The American version of the Bilbao Effect—prominent icons for insignificant towns—was given a distinct European twist—prominent museums for questionable content, in some cases content hardly worthy of a museum.

Increasing faith was put in the architecture to do the museum's job for it. In Britain, Tony Blair encouraged architects to 'delight' people and urged the public sector to consider the 'wow factor' in addition to just cost or functionality when reviewing building designs.[15] The same cast that designed museums in the US were the architects of choice for European museum projects. Daniel Libeskind designed the Imperial War Museum North in Manchester, Zaha Hadid was responsible for the Phaeno Science Centre, Wolfsburg, and Calatrava went on to produce museums for Valencia and Tenerife in his native Spain. There were others, too. Coop Himmelb(l)au—runner up for the Guggenheim Bilbao—got to design the Musée des Confluences in Lyon and in West Bromwich Will Alsop created The Public.

The selection of a star cast of architects, however, did little to obscure the often flimsy raison d'être of the buildings they designed. Libeskind's Imperial War Museum, built in the run-up to the 2002 Commonwealth Games in Manchester, was the fifth in a series of Imperial War Museums in the UK. It was also the first purpose-built one. And while its content begged the question if that was warranted—the first four Imperial War Museums were in a former hospital, a former aerodrome, in Churchill's former command centre and on a warship—that did little to discourage the architect from taking inspiration. The Museum's 'interlocking shards representing the nature of conflict on land, in the air and on water'.[16] For budget reasons, they were built not of titanium but of aluminum.

Wolfsburg, home to Germany's Volkswagen, planned to create an art museum until Dr. Wolfgang Guthardt, the city's director for culture, sports and education, visited Technorama in Switzerland and convinced the city that building a science centre was a better idea. 'Since VW was shifting more of its production overseas, the town was trying to reinvent itself as an entertainment and tourism destination.' After an international competition, Zaha Hadid was commissioned to design Phaeno. Notwithstanding rave reviews for the building—'one of the dozen most important modern works of architecture in the world'—describing its actual function remained a challenge. According to the centre's website: 'People are naturally curious. They enjoy unlocking secrets, solving mysteries and constantly discovering new things. From frozen shadows to the fire tornado, you'll find an incredible number of possibilities to give free rein to this curiosity at Phaeno in Wolfsburg and to embark on an adventure tour through the world of phenomena.'[17]

A similar fate affected the Musée des Confluences, designed by Coop Himmelb(l)au in Lyon. The museum, the brainchild of then-mayoral candidate Michel Mercier, was due to open in 2005 but suffered severe delays when Mercier was not elected. In 2008, contractor BEC walked off the project, complaining that it had to redo all the architects' drawings because of their 'lack of definition'. BEC was compensated €3.6 million and a new tender was issued, which was won by Vinci in 2010. However, it was only after the city council sold shares from the Compagnie Nationale du Rhône (CNR) and two motorway companies (ASF and APRR) in 2012 that the project could be further financed. The museum, conceived as Lyon's answer to Bilbao—'a museum like none other anywhere in the world', in the words of its first director, Michel Côté—was eventually finished in 2014 as a science centre and anthropology museum.[18] The associated costs—more than four times the original budget—provoked a significant public outcry over the waste of taxpayer money.

The trend of the 'orphaned museum' reached its apex in West Bromwich, England. In 2003, as part of a plan to reinvigorate the former industrial borough of Sandwell, the town commissioned Will Alsop to design The Public, a multipurpose venue inspired by Cedric Price's Fun Palace. Although officially referred to as an 'arts centre' (for its display of interactive digital art), the building's ultimate reason for being was as open-ended as its name. In 2004, a few months after the start of construction, Will Alsop was removed from the project. In 2009, the Arts Council, which had initiated the project, pulled out and the city took over. In 2013, having cost £1.5 million annually to run it, The Public was closed to the public.

Full circle

Perhaps not surprisingly, the Bilbao Effect found its Waterloo in Spain. Ten years into the new millennium, the country that bred the phenomenon also became its burial ground. Spain was among the countries in Europe worst hit by the 2008 financial crisis and continued to feel the aftershocks long after. The economically adverse conditions caused its regional governments to fall victim to increasing political squabbling. Spain, the land of great opportunity for local and foreign architects alike, transformed into the land of unfinished buildings, aborted projects and shelved plans. Europe's architectural hothouse, showcase of architecture's unlimited powers, became the shop window of its failings.

A poignant case of 'sand in the engine' presented itself in Galicia, involving Frank Gehry's colleague and long-time rival, Peter Eisenman. In 1999, Manuel Fraga, president of the regional government, member of the right-wing People's Party and the former minister of information and tourism under Franco, launched the idea of building a City of Culture of Galicia in the region's capital, Santiago de Compostela. An international competition was organized featuring an all-star cast of twelve architects: Ricardo Bofill, Peter Eisenman, Manuel Gallego Jorreto, Annette Gigon and Mike Guyer, Steven Holl, Rem Koolhaas, Daniel Libeskind, Santiago Calatrava, Juan Navarro Baldeweg, Jean Nouvel, Dominique Perrault and César Portela. Calatrava pulled out, but this time the tactic did not work; Eisenman won.

Eisenman's project consisted of six buildings, each with a specifically defined use: library, newspaper library, music theatre, museum of the history of Galicia, a central services building and a building to showcase new technologies. Its complex design —a computer-generated artificial landscape intersected by five cracks—was matched by an equally complex explanation: 'The project in Santiago is neither synthetic nor a single dialogue. It is not a dialectic between grid and bearing wall. Rather, it is ceiling becoming volume and curtain-wall becoming volume.'[19]

When the socialists won the regional elections in 2005, the complex was substantially redefined. Certain uses were scrapped, others added and whatever uses remained were opportunistically reshuffled among the various buildings. The overhaul did little to temper Eisenman's conviction about the project: 'The idea of the project was always to offer a framework for new cultural ideas that are constantly emerging.'

In 2010, with the People's Party back in power, another reshuffle took place: the Museum of Galicia was renamed Gaiás Centre Museum to host temporary exhibitions; the Heritage Research Centre became the Centre for Cultural Innovation and the archive was integrated into the library, allowing the vacated archive building to become the Centre for Creative Entrepreneurship.

When the library and the archive eventually opened in 2011, the event was hailed as a great victory for the People's Party— 'another obligatory stop on the main itineraries of the world', as Alberto Núñez Feijóo, president of the regional government of Galicia, put it.[20] However, in 2013, after a more than €300 million cost increase and faced with a maintenance bill of over €60 million per year, the Galician parliament voted to stop the project. The International Art Centre and the Workshop Resource Centre would remain unbuilt. The architect, however, remained unfazed: 'The scale and the ambition of the job probably make the City of Culture unique in the world. There is no way that it can be considered a waste of money. It is a serious investment in the welfare of Galicia and of future generations.'[21]

The political machinations at work in Galicia's City of Culture were modest in comparison to those surrounding Valencia's City of Arts and Sciences, launched and built at about the same time. This time Spanish architects were at the forefront. In 1989, the president of the Valencian Autonomous government, Joan Lerma (of the Spanish Socialist Workers' Party), visited the new Cité des Sciences et de l'Industrie in Paris and commissioned scientist Antonio Ten Ros to draft a proposal for a City of Science and Technology for Valencia. A project to this effect, designed by Santiago Calatrava and Félix Candela, was presented to the local government in 1991, where the conservative People's Party criticized it for 'inflating the ego of socialists', only to embrace it in an even more ambitious form once they came to power.

Upon completion, twenty years after its launch, the complex ended up being home to an IMAX cinema, a planetarium, an interactive museum of science, an open-air oceanographic park, an opera house and performing arts centre, and a covered plaza. Yet serious problems remained. The science museum was built with no fire escapes or elevators for the disabled. The opera house had 150 seats with obstructed views and shortly after its opening its skin began to wrinkle. These manifest shortcomings, in combination with a budget overrun of approximately €600 million, brought the Valencia branch of left-wing party Esquerra Unida to set up a website called Calatravatelaclava [Calatrava bleeds you dry].[22] Only once Calatrava sued and claimed €30,000 in reparations was the website removed. The court ruled that its name was unnecessarily 'insulting and degrading', but that only triggered a new site—'Calatrava no nos calla' [Calatrava won't silence us]—to go live almost immediately after.[23]

Shortly after the verdict, Calatrava delivered a conspiracy theory not unworthy of later US president Donald Trump: 'It is a political maneuver by the communists. They are not attacking the Alhambra in Granada. They are not attacking the cathedral in Santiago de Compostela. They are not attacking the Prado in Madrid.'[24]

The irony is hard to miss. More even than Frank Gehry, Calatrava is a global brand: he is the architect who, almost singlehandedly, made sure that Spain had as much of an effect on the world as the world had on Spain. Calatrava has built in New York City, Toronto, Lyon, Basel, Berlin, Malmö, Dallas, Rio, Dubai and Jerusalem, to name a few cities. If the Bilbao Effect were to have a signature, it would be not Gehry's, but Calatrava's. In Valencia, however, fifteen years on from the opening of the Guggenheim in Bilbao, the controversy surrounding the construction of a high-profile, high-priced public icon had become an exclusively Spanish affair, with the Spanish architect viewing the attack on his work as an attack on a Spanish tradition in which he firmly places himself. The Bilbao Effect might be less global than thought.

Architecture after Bilbao

'Art in its most expansive form can truly effect change in the world!' The prophetic line is from the Guggenheim's founding charter. After Bilbao, one wonders if the same can be said for architecture. The trajectory of museum architecture closely followed that of the museum boom of the 1990s: boosting the profile of the art world, only to evaporate in the subsequent decade and be reduced to nothing after 2008. The fate of the two seems intimately tied. Some architects have relished the relation, others have abhorred it. Frank Gehry himself has been ambivalent, playing the wilful artist on certain occasions, the dedicated craftsman on others: 'There is not a straight line or right angle in the building. It's not artistry, it's precision!'[25] He appeared on *The Simpsons* to mock his own creative process, only to 'really, really regret it after'.[26]

Why *shouldn't* architecture rival art? It seems the central thesis of Gehry's museum, finding face in the photographic love affair between the building's interior and Richard Serra's *Snake* on display during its opening. 'If the art can't compete, then perhaps it's simply not good enough', said filmmaker Julian Schnabel in the documentary *Sketches of Frank Gehry*. His words echo those of Muchamp, that 'by exercising their imagination, artists can inspire others to use their own'. In this case, the artist is Gehry. And 'Gehry's language is architecture, not words.' Like art, architecture exists in his own right and thus reserves the right to remain unexplained.

The debate whether architecture is (an) art is as old as it is inconclusive, and it is hardly worth engaging in. But if there is one thing the museum boom of the 1990s and 2000s has demonstrated, it is the impossibility for museums to survive without the art to fill them. The autonomy of museum architecture only goes as far as the art it accommodates. Ultimately, art and architecture inhabit very different commercial realities. Record valuations at auctions aside, the 'value of art' will always remain elusive. As a value proposition, architecture is subject to a very different dynamic. Where art *defies* value, architecture must *deliver* it.

Whether Frank Gehry, or any other architect, thinks architecture equals art is ultimately of no importance. The point is the difference in *expectations*. Art enters the economic cycle with a disclaimer—that it is art—while architecture can never enter the cycle without its engrained obligations: the building's function, its effect on the city, public opinion and so on. The more these obligations can be measured in commercial terms, the more inescapable they become. When it comes to numbers, architecture can be held to account in a way art never can. Ironically, the Bilbao Effect—the ultimate allegiance between art and architecture—has only exacerbated that difference.

The Guggenheim Bilbao was hardly the first iconic building, but it was the first to be credited with a measurable economic spin-off. And while that temporarily elevated the status of architects to near deities, it proved detrimental in the long run. After the Guggenheim, architecture was never quite the same. A single building had defied all expectation, only for expectations to defy all of architecture ever since. Economic success became the measure of architecture's quality, to which architecture, in turn, had no choice but to apply itself. Architecture found itself in debt to promises it didn't make and ultimately can't fulfil. After Bilbao, ambitious museum projects could only fail. And they did. In New York, Abu Dhabi, Helsinki, Taichung and Rio de Janeiro. In the end, even the Guggenheim itself was unable to replicate its success.

Bilbao marks a rift in time. There is the time *before*—when we did not realize the transformative powers of architecture—and there is the time *after*—when we now supposedly do. The most important report to substantiate the Bilbao Effect, the KPMG report, was commissioned by the Guggenheim itself, who had a vested interest in claiming that there *was* an effect.[27] Its conclusions stand, and with them the perception of what architecture can accomplish.

After Bilbao, the world will never be able to look at architecture in the same way. When, in 2013, the KPMG report on the Guggenheim sparked a similar report by Deloitte on the economic impact of the Sydney Opera House, we had no option but to take its word. Forty years after its opening, the building was concluded to have contributed US$775 million annually to the Australian economy, to support 8,439 full-time equivalent jobs and to represent a total worth of US$4.6 billion to Australia. The Sydney Opera House did not just change the image of Sydney; it affected an entire continent. Where do architects go from here?

Postscript

Philip Johnson died in 2005; *Charlie Rose* got axed by PBS in 2017 over #MeToo allegations and Frank Gehry, despite numerous attempts, is yet to build another Guggenheim. The city of Bilbao has moved on, meanwhile. It overcame the financial crisis of 2008; the average wealth of its citizens trumps that of Spain; ETA has disarmed; its mayor has been awarded the World Mayor Prize; eighteen Michelin Star restaurants adorn the city and Athletic Bilbao has managed to defeat Barcelona to win the Copa de España. Effect or no, Bilbao seems to be doing just fine.

At over 828 metres (2,716.5 feet) and more than 160 stories, **Burj Khalifa (Dubai, 2010)** is the **tallest building in the world**—twice the Empire State Building, and almost three times the size of the Eiffel Tower. Burj Khalifa holds the highest occupied floor in the world; has the highest outdoor observation deck in the world; boasts the elevator with the longest travel distance in the world; is equipped with the tallest service elevator in the world; and has the world's tallest LED-illuminated façade, as well as the largest LED-illuminated façade.[1] In the Guinness Book of Records, Burj Khalifa is linked to yet another set of extremes: an exterior cladding of 26,000 hand-cut glass panels; three months to clean the structure from the top to the bottom, the highest fireworks ever created on a building, the highest BASE jump from a building and the fastest time to climb a building by bicycle. Burj Khalifa became the tallest building in the world in 2007 at the expense of Taipei 101, which, in 2004, had taken over this position from Petronas Twin Towers (Kuala Lumpur, 1996), which still hold the record for Tallest twin towers. Recently completed on Manhattan's Billionaires' Row, Steinway Tower (NYC, 2022) currently holds the distinction of being the world's skinniest skyscraper. At 1,428 feet high, containing ninety-one storeys, Steinway Tower has only one residence on each floor and is twenty-four times as tall as it is wide.[2] **Clement Canopy buildings (2019)** in Singapore holds the record for being the **tallest building with modular construction.** Consisting of two towers, measuring 459 feet and holding 40 floors each, Clement Canopy is the tallest tower project ever to be built in modular concrete—made up of 1,899 off-site manufactured modules to hold 505 luxury residential apartments.[3] Mini Sky City (Changsha, 2015) holds the record of being the **fastest tall building ever constructed.** After four and a half months of pre-fabricating the building's 2,736 modules, the 57-storey skyscraper itself was put together with a speed of three floors a day, in a total construction time of less than three weeks—the fastest speed ever recorded in the construction industry.[4] Traveling with a rated speed of 1,260 m/min, connecting from the 1st to the 95th floor in approx. 42sec, Guangzhou CTF Finance Center (Guangdong, 2009) **officially** holds the Guinness World Record as the **skyscraper with the world's fastest elevator.**[5] Memorial Necrópole Ecumênica (Santos, 1983) is the **world's tallest vertical cemetery**, holding crypts, rooms to hold services, a crematorium, a mausoleum 'for families who want to preserve their legacy in a more personal and private way'. There is also a tropical garden with a waterfall, a small rooftop cafe to take in the view and a classic cars museum on the property.[6] When completed, La Sagrada Família Basílica (Barcelona) will be the **world's tallest church building.** 4 towers along each of its 3 façades represent the 12 apostles; another 4 towers represent the 4 evangelists. Jointly, these towers will surround the largest tower, which will be 170 metres high and be dedicated to Jesus Christ.[7] At 478 m (1,568 ft 2.8 in), the **highest glass-floor observation deck** is in Lotte World Tower (Seoul, 2017)[8], while Ping An Finance Center (Shenzen, 2019) holds the **highest glass floor cantilevered observation deck**, measuring 547.60 m (1,796 ft 7 in). 45 mm (1.7 in) thick glass makes up floor capable of supporting over 500 kg per square metre.[9] When it opened, the Eiffel Tower (Paris, 1889) was **the world's tallest structure**, nearly double the height of the world's previous tallest structure—the 555-foot Washington Monument – only to be surpassed by the 1,046-foot Chrysler Building in New York in 1930. Even if the Eiffel Tower eventually eclipsed the Chrysler Building again with the addition of an antenna in 1957, it still trailed behind another Gotham skyscraper, the Empire State Building.[10] Just as Burj Khalifa may one day have to concede its position as the **world's tallest building to Kingdom Tower (Jeddah)**, set to contain 168 floors and measure a total of 1008 meters in height. 1,640 feet long by 1,312 feet wide the **New Century Global Center (Chengdu, 2013)** is **the building with the largest floor area** in the world, twenty times the size of Sydney's legendary Opera House, four times the size of Vatican City, and three times the size of the Pentagon. Its 420 acres of floor space nearly equal the area of Monaco (499 acres).[11] Boeing Everett Factory (Everett, 1967), is the world's **largest building by volume.** Designed by Boeing, the Everett Factory produces the 747, 767, 777, the 787 Dreamliner, the 747-8 and the popular 777X airplanes. The building encloses 472 million cubic feet of space over 98.3 acres and is visited by thousands of people every year.[12] Envisioned by Steve Jobs as a center for creativity and collaboration, Apple Park (Cupertino, 2017) is transforming miles of asphalt sprawl into a haven of green space in the heart of the Santa Clara Valley. The ring-shaped, 2.8 million-square-foot campus is the world's **largest naturally ventilated building**, projected to require no heating or air conditioning for nine months of the year. It is also the **building with the largest curved glass panels** in the world. Spanning over 20,000 square meters (215,278 square feet), Tropicalia (Opal Coast, France, 2024) will be the world's **largest** *single-domed greenhouse*. The gigantic, energy self-sufficient structure is set to be completed in 2024.[13] Costing over US$37 million, MGM Cotai (Macau, 2019) is the **building with the largest free span grid-shell glazed roof**, *covering 8,073.1 m²—the equivalent of 30 tennis courts*.[14] With a surface area of 3,947.22 m² (42,487.35 ft²), the façade of the Al Rostamani Maze Tower (Dubai, 2019), standing at 9.5 meters tall with an area of 640 square meters.[17] The **longest building** in the world is Prora (Rugen 1939). Built between 1936 and 1939, Prora consists of several identical connected six-storey buildings, which, added up, measure 4500 metres. Inspired by UK seaside resort chain Butlin's, Robert Ley, head of the German Labour Front, envisaged Prora as a means to provide affordable holidays for the ordinary worker in the context of the Nazi's Strength Through Joy programme.[18] 2,400 meters beneath the peak of Jinping Mountain lies the **China Jinping Underground Laboratory (Sichuan, 2015), the deepest underground laboratory in the world**. Embedded in a thick rock cover that prevents the penetration of cosmic rays, the lab is able to conduct research of the elusive substance, 'Dark Matter', estimated to account for about 85% of all matter in the universe. Its intricate tunnel system maximizes the use of space and allows the research to proceed without outside interference.[19] 310 feet below existing grade, Salesforce Tower (San Francisco, 2018) is the **building with the deepest foundation in the world**.[20] An incredible 60.02 meters (197 feet) deep, Deep Dive Dubai (Dubai, 2021) is the world's **deepest pool**, holding 14 million liters (3.7 million gallons) of wate—the equivalent of six Olympic-sized swimming pools.[21] **The world's heaviest building** is the Palace of the parliament (Bucharest, 1984), constructed from 700,000 tonnes (1.5 billion lb) of steel and bronze combined with 1 million m³ (35.3 million ft³) of marble, 3,500 tonnes (7.7 million lb) of crystal glass and 900,000 m³ (31.7 million ft³) of wood.[22] At a construction cost of US$ 15 billion, Abraj Al Bait (Mecca, 2012), also known as the Makkah Royal Clock Tower, is the world's **most expensive building**. At a height of 601 metres, Abraj Al Bait is the tallest hotel in the world, with a floor area of 1,500,000 square metres and a 100,000-person capacity. Measuring 43 metres in diameter, standing at a height of 530 metres, the building also features the world's **tallest and largest clock**, said to be visible from over 30km away. The upper portion of the clock tower features a 23-metre-high crescent constructed of fibreglass-backed mosaic gold.[23] The Venetian Resort (Las Vegas, 1999) is the **building with the largest floor area of polished marble tiles**. Cream, brown and black marble tiles shipped over from Italy and Spain cover a floor area of 139,354 m²—equivalent to 535 tennis courts. West Edmonton Mall (Edmonton, 1981) is the **building with most parking spots**, with a capacity to hold 20,000 vehicles and overflow facilities on an adjoining lot for 10,000 more cars.[24] Wembley Stadium (London, 2007) is the **building with most toilets**—2,618, to be exact—more than any other building in the world. Bloomberg European HQ (London, 2017) is the world's **most sustainable office building**. Designed by Foster + Partners, the office complex has been awarded an Outstanding BREEAM rating, attaining a 98.5% score—the highest design-stage score ever achieved by any major office development.[25] The Edge (Amsterdam, 2014) is the **smartest office** building in the world. The Edge sheds new light on real estate in the future: buildings that generate more energy than they consume. With a BREEAM score of 99.48%, NewLogic III building (Tilburg, 2019) is the world's **greenest industrial building**,[26] while the greenest parliament in the world is the Knesset (Jerusalem, 2015), boasting a 4,560-square-meter (50,000 square feet) solar field on its roof and 13 other ecologically conscious projects at a cost of NIS 7 million ($1.8 million).[27] New York (2013) is the **most instagrammed city**, while the Palace of Versailles (1661) is crowd-ranked as **the most beautiful building**. Although later rebranded as 'one of the', Medibank Building (Melbourne, 2014) is the **healthiest workplace**. Featuring bright colors and curved stairways to create a positive work environment, the design keeps employees moving, engaged with one another, and happy in the office.[28] But the **happiest house on earth** is Happy Rizzi House (Melbourne, 2002), a day-glow masterpiece of cartoon-inspired architecture set smack in the heart of a staid German historic neighbourhood. Standing in stark contrast to its old-world surroundings, the Happy Rizzi House is the vision of New York pop artist James Rizzi, best known for designing the cover for Tom Club's 1981 debut album, and architect Konrad Kloster. Representative of Rizzi's style, the structures are decorated in wild shapes and faces coloured in bright pinks, yellows, and greens reminiscent of an 80s music video.[29]

world-class
adjective
UK /wɜːldˈklɑːs/ US /wɝːldˈklæs/
among the best in the world:
  a world-class athlete/performance/building

2

Officially Amazing

According to the Guinness World Records list, 'the farthest man-made leaning building in the world' is the Capital Gate in Abu Dhabi, a thirty-five-storey, 160-metre-high building conceived as the centrepiece of the Abu Dhabi National Exhibition Centre's (ADNEC's) development. Capital Gate boasts an impressive inclination of eighteen degrees, fourteen degrees more than the Tower of Pisa. More than 50 per cent of Capital Gate's 50,000 square metres counts as usable floor space, which means it qualifies as 'a building rather than a tower'.[1] A seemingly futile distinction, but evidently one important enough to mention.

The 'farthest man-made leaning tower', it turns out, is in Canada. It is the observation tower of the Montreal Olympic Stadium, with a curved angle of forty-five degrees. Only its top three floors are occupied, and therefore it doesn't meet the criteria of being a building.

The term 'man-made' is intriguing. Given that buildings are man-made by definition, this qualification must inevitably refer to the leaning, not the building. The campanile in Pisa is a leaning tower, but Capital Gate a *man-made* leaning tower (sorry, building); what makes the two different is the cause of the lean. Leaning buildings have become so by the forces of nature, while man-made leaning buildings have become so by human force and ingenuity. The Tower of Pisa, incidentally, does not feature in the Guinness World Records list. The world's most leaning tower is the bell tower of the fourteenth-century protestant church of Suurhusen in former East Germany with an angle of inclination of 5.1939 degrees (as measured on 17 January 2007).[2]

The first Guinness List (then Book) of Records was published in 1955. In addition to records such as the tallest man alive or the oldest living woman, the list featured just two building categories: the world's tallest skyscraper (then the Empire State Building) and the world's largest office building (then the Pentagon). In 2021, the list has come to include the world's largest mirrored building, the world's fastest automated parking facility, the world's most slender tower, the largest television building in the world (record held by author's firm), the highest outdoor infinity pool in a building, the largest roof in the shape of a star, the largest building in the shape of a shoe, the largest building in the shape of a bird, the largest building in the shape of a picture frame as well as the world's first artificial fog building.

The Guinness World Record List validates otherwise meaningless efforts, even if only in the form of a (meaningless) superlative. As the competition intensifies, the number of categories proliferates. And Capital Gate finds itself in good company, neatly ranked along other 'Officially Amazing' efforts, such as the largest human playing card, cycling backward with a violin, most people brushing their teeth simultaneously and the largest collection of sickbags from the largest number of airlines. In the context of some of the records listed, the effort to create the world's farthest leaning building could be regarded as moderately rational behaviour.

Still, how rational is a project like Capital Gate? Admittedly, its engineering is impressive, some of its design solutions unquestionably dazzling. In retrospect, the bag of tricks at the disposal of those who contributed to the project seems inexhaustible: a precambered concrete core poured slightly off vertical to counterbalance the lean of the building, gradually 'pulled' into position as the rest of the building is erected and kept that way by an asymmetrical system of post-tensioning ... 490 foundation piles driven twenty to thirty metres underground to support the weight of the structure as well as mitigating the counter stresses caused by the overhang ... floor plates that change shape and orientation as they progress up the tower, migrating from east to west, morphing from 'curved triangular' to 'curved rectangular'. Not a single one of the building's 12,500 glass panes on the façade are the same.

The building deploys a diagrid structure, a framework of diagonal latticed beams. In fact, it deploys two: one at the building's façade and another one to support a large central atrium applied to reduce the building's overall weight. The internal diagrid is linked to the central core by eight unique pin-jointed structural members; all 8,250 steel diagrid members are different thicknesses, lengths and orientations; each of the 822 diagrid nodes (702 external and 120 internal nodes) is of a different size and angular configuration.

And the complexity did not stop at the drawing board. Eighteen months into construction, the project found its buildability further challenged by the sudden introduction of an infinity pool and a restaurant hanging one hundred metres above the ground (a new slant on high-rise living from the architects) and again, one month from completion, by the addition of a helipad on the roof—a last-minute request from the Sheikh's office.[3]

Why?

As an engineering feat, the Capital Gate project is well documented and well known (and likely only more so since being accredited a world record). Various articles have appeared in the media; the architects have written a book about the project, and the internet features multiple videos about the effort, including an episode of National Geographic's *Megastructures*.[4] Invariably—and perhaps justifiably—the effort to create the world's farthest leaning building is portrayed as a heroic effort. And yet highlighting the building's state-of-the-art engineering, even if over and over again, fails to produce a definitive answer to one pressing question: Why?

The Capital Gate project is subject to an enduring paradox: the more we get to know about its realization, the more the reasons underlying that realization become a mystery. It is one of those projects that tend to become less clear with explanation. It is a project of which the 'what' and the 'how' perpetually obscure the 'why'. What complicates matters is that there appears to be no single person whom we can ask. The website of RMJM, the project's architects, does not list individual contributors to projects. The ultimate authorship remains a mystery. The building, we must conclude, is the result of 'teamwork'.

That said, multiple faces have become associated with the project since its completion in 2010. In *Megastructures*, Neil van der Veen is seen sketching the building while being credited as one of the concept architects, while Tony Archibald, RMJM's project leader, talks about the building so eloquently that one is tempted to take him for the creative mind behind the project. The engineers beg to differ, though. In the same documentary, Mona Vasigh, RMJM's engineer on the project, makes a convincing case that the building was realized largely despite the whims of her architect colleagues. Capital Gate is not the result of inspiration but of headache. And then there is, of course, the client, His Highness Sheikh Sultan bin Tahnoon Al Nahyan, ADNEC's chairman, for whom RMJM's work simply represents the logical execution of his vision.

If *Megastructures* attributes authorship of the building by implication, the website of architect firm U+A in Dubai is more emphatic, unequivocally crediting one of its founding partners, Pierre Martin Dufresne, a former partner of RMJM, as the architect of Capital Gate. However, given that U+A was founded in 2006 and Capital Gate was completed no sooner than 2010, it is unlikely that Dufresne's involvement in the project extended beyond the initial stages. (In the world of architecture, opinions whether or not someone who didn't see a project through till the very end can be considered the author of that project tend to vary.) Dufresne is also the co-author of *18°*, a book detailing the project's history, written by Jeff Schofield, senior design architect at RMJM at the time of the building's conception.

Yet, given the distant, almost observational tone of that book, one wonders how much Dufresne's participation in it does to support his claim to fame. Somehow, the hybrid nature of *18°* simultaneously undermines the credibility of Jeff Schofield as a critical writer and that of Martin Dufresne as the believable architect of Capital Gate—Schofield because of his ongoing involvement with RMJM, Dufresne precisely because of his leaving. *Megastructures* aired in May 2010, shortly after the building's completion, while *18°* didn't get published until December 2016. It remains an open question if the book is indeed an earnest attempt to set the record straight or simply a case of belated score settling.

Equally contested as the authorship of the building is its source of inspiration. With multiple authors come multiple fancies. According to Schofield, 'the building's form is meant to represent a swirling spiral of sand, while the curved canopy, known as the "splash", which runs over the adjoining grandstand and rises on one side of the building, creates a wave-like effect, reflecting the building's proximity to the water and the city's sea-faring heritage.' That's not all, however: 'By integrating with the National Day Grandstand—one of Abu Dhabi's most historic structures—Capital Gate underscores the bond between the traditional and modern that is characteristic of Abu Dhabi's developmental approach.'[5]

The website of his co-author, Dufresne, offers a different explanation: 'The design's inspiration behind the unusual organic form stems from a figurative interpretation of a ship's hull splitting waves. The sea and maritime transportation bear an essential role in the development of the UAE ... Energy, fluidity and dynamism complement the idea of the sea throughout the architecture.'[6] Neil van der Veen's explanation seems to opt for a short compromise: 'We took this idea of wind and water which are both dynamic, fluid type of rhythms of nature and we said: How can we capture those in time?'

Sustainability

Capital Gate, naturally, is committed to the cause of sustainability. It carries all the hallmarks: metal mesh sun shading, a double skin façade, high performance glazing, a vegetated roof on the basement, low-flow water fixtures, district cooling, variable-speed air conditioning, heat exchange for ventilation, and energy monitoring and controls. Low emissivity glass on the façade keeps the inside of the building cool and eliminates glare while maintaining transparency. Its most visible feature, the 'splash', allegedly eliminates 30 per cent of the sun's heat before it reaches the building, reduces the air conditioning load and provides shade to the main entrance on the ground floor. A 2012 case study of the project published in *CTBUH Journal*, once again authored by Jeff Schofield (who was meanwhile promoted to the rank of RMJM associate), even manages to create a compelling case for the lean making the building more sustainable: 'The building's organic shape also lends itself perfectly to savings in construction materials, despite the lean. Its rounded form presents less resistance to the wind than a rectangular building, thereby requiring less structure for lateral loads. The round perimeter encloses space more efficiently than a rectangle, so less façade surface is needed than for a conventional floor plate of identical area.' Supposedly, the result is that fewer materials are required for structure and façades. This is a reduction in concrete, steel and glass, materials which all have high carbon content and embodied energy.[7]

All true, perhaps. But a pressing question remains. What would the numbers have looked like had the building been straight? How many tons of carbon-hungry steel and concrete would have been saved in that case? The truth is that we will never know. Sustainability evaluations of buildings mostly occur in hindsight. At best, they lead to 'optimizations' during the later stages of the design process. In either case, we are well past the point of comparison to hypothetical alternatives.

Inevitably, Capital Gate's sustainability argumentation, as with many buildings, is condemned to being little more than an afterthought. Notwithstanding its brilliant engineering, it is hard to shake the feeling that the leaning of Capital Gate is merely an acrobatic act in the face of a made-up challenge—an ostentatious solution to a non-existent problem. Sheikh Sultan Bin Tahnoon Al Nahyan's rhetoric around the project speaks volumes: 'Capital Gate is a landmark development for Abu Dhabi and with this recognition the tower takes its place among the world's great buildings. It is a signature building which speaks to the foresight of the emirate.'[8]

Neighbouring emirate Dubai has already built the world's tallest skyscraper, therefore the issue for Abu Dhabi is not to go bigger or taller but to challenge the rules of architecture. Not surprisingly, the client's and the architect's motivation met in perfect sync. RMJM Dubai principal Neil van der Veen explains the motivation behind the project as follows: 'We wanted to push the boundaries and we wanted to show the world what we are capable of. And that's what it stands for and that's why it has also become an icon for the city. It's used in literature, brochures and tourist information.'[9]

Iconitis

At long last, the architect (if he is that) comes clean and the true motivation behind the project is revealed: constructing not a building but an 'icon'. One wonders. What is the difference?

When does a building *become* an icon? The Oxford English Dictionary defines an 'icon' as a person or thing regarded as a representative symbol or as worthy of veneration. But what makes a building a symbol? What about a building inspires veneration? And veneration by whom?

A Wikipedia page on architectural icons created in 2019 lists an entire collection of buildings to serve as examples, the oldest being the Parthenon (fifth century BC), the most recent Jürgen Mayer's Metropol Parasol in Seville (2011). Other buildings included are the Sydney Opera House, Gaudi's Sagrada Familia, Le Corbusier's Notre-Dame Du Haut de Ronchamps, the Guggenheim Bilbao, Herzog & de Meuron's Bird's Nest, the Berlin Philharmonic and the Burj Al Arab in Dubai, to name a few.

The world's farthest man-made leaning building, Capital Gate, is not on the list, nor is its precursor, the Tower of Pisa. Only a limited number of buildings on the list boast a (measurable) record of sorts. The Pantheon had the world's largest dome for more than 1,700 years; Joseph Paxton's Crystal Palace of 1851 was the largest modular steel and glass construction of its time; the US Pavilion at Expo 67 in Montreal was (and is) the world's largest biosphere dome and Mayer's Metropol Parasol is the world's largest wood structure.

By far the most tested route for a building to become an icon is to set a record in height. The longer the record endures, the greater the likelihood. The Eiffel Tower remained the world's tallest structure for forty-one years after its erection in 1889. The Oriental Pearl Tower, built in 1995, was the tallest structure in China until 2007, when it was surpassed by the Shanghai World Financial Center. And Burj Khalifa may one day have to concede its position as the world's currently tallest building to Kingdom Tower (Jeddah), set to contain 168 floors and measure a total of 1,008 metres in height.

It is doubtful how many of the buildings we currently refer to as icons were conceived with that word in mind. The first known use of the term in English dates back to 1572, derived from the Greek word *eikon*: a devotional painting of Christ or another holy figure, typically executed on wood and used ceremonially in the Byzantine and other Eastern Churches. Hardly a reference to buildings. According to the Google Ngram Viewer, which charts the frequency of a term in printed sources available in Google's text corpus, terms like 'iconic building' and 'iconic architecture' only really started being used in the early 1980s and accelerated rapidly after the early 2000s, with every country and every city wanting an icon in the race to compete for global recognition.

'Iconitis is a disease that's around', commented architecture critic Charles Jencks, one of the first to come up with a theory about iconic buildings. In *The Iconic Building: The Power of Enigma*, published in 2005, Jencks examines the iconic building from a semiological perspective, in the spirit of the 1960s writings of Umberto Eco and Roland Barthes, claiming that a 'successful' icon is one which has an enigmatic signifier and relies on multiple metaphors encoded into the image. Le Corbusier's Ronchamps and Gehry's Guggenheim Bilbao are two examples. Many more, however, are failed examples, such as I.M. Pei's Louvre Pyramid and the One World Trade Center—icons that have been reduced to a one-liner.

The reference to one-liners is interesting. Unwittingly, it also highlights the ambivalent relation that icons have to setting records. Records are the ultimate one-liners. Projecting Jencks's theory, one could say that 'bad' icons pursue records and 'successful' icons don't. And just as in Jencks's theory, the bad far outnumber the good. The proliferation of 'iconic records' speaks volumes: apart from the world's tallest or largest building, there are the tallest twin towers, the world's skinniest skyscraper, the largest naturally ventilated building, the building with the largest curved glass panels, the world's largest 3D printed building, the building with the most toilets, the most Instagrammed building, the tallest unoccupied building. The list is as long as it is meaningless. No longer is the notion of competition limited to vying for a record within a certain category; in the end, the records also get to compete with each other.

The Sydney Opera House, Pompidou or Guggenheim ... most of the buildings labelled by Jencks as 'successful' icons are public buildings, whereas the 'bad' ones are predominantly buildings for the private sector. The business of the private sector is competition, and economies, especially emerging ones, tend to manifest themselves in the form of skylines, the most distinguishing feature of which are tall buildings. It is hardly surprising that it is mostly the 'icons' produced by the private sector that have competed in terms of height, size, or other measurable features. It is also telling that the production of icons of this kind seems to have stalled since the financial crisis of 2008. The last two projects on the Wikipedia icon list, Burj Khalifa and Metropol Parasol, even though completed in 2010 and 2011 respectively, were both commissioned and started before 2008 (2004 and 2005, respectively). So was Capital Gate. Burj Khalifa's successor as the tallest building on earth —Kingdom Tower in Jeddah—stands unfinished to date.

The distinction between public and private sector icons notwithstanding, the ultimate, most extravagant icons seem to emerge in contexts where there is a decidedly blurry boundary between the two. Is it a coincidence that the majority of icons, and particularly the record-breaking category, are produced in the context of vaguely authoritarian regimes? Where the interests of private parties in conventional economies tend to be limited to the profit and loss accounting of their own busi-ness, such does not apply in places such as Dubai, Abu Dhabi or Saudi Arabia, where businesses tend to be part of larger holding companies under the direct control of governments, often with large sovereign wealth funds at their disposal. The developer of Burj Khalifa, Emaar, is majority owned by the Dubai royal family, while ADNEC, the developer of Capital Gate, is a subsidiary of Abu Dhabi Developmental Holding

Company PJSC (ADQ), an Abu Dhabi sovereign wealth fund. An apparent landscape of private enterprise serves as a veil for state interests, and macroeconomic considerations enter the equation. No longer is the balance sheet of a building project solely determined by construction costs and revenues from sale(s) or rent(s), the larger dividend that a building pays to its city or country starts to factor into the financials: extra visitors, wealthy new residents, the increased value of other real estate. The additional investment associated with architectural tour de forces, or challenging engineering feats to pay for themselves, is offset by the revenues for the city or the country at large. Capital Gate, Burj Khalifa—costly to build and short on revenue-generating floorspace—might make little economic sense. Then again, neither did the Eiffel Tower or the Guggenheim Bilbao.

Contrarian as it may seem, it is precisely its seemingly irra-tional features that betray the rationale behind a project like Capital Gate. Even if the building fails in terms of the con-ventional financial logic of property development, that failure merely serves as evidence of the limitations of such logic. Only when viewed in isolation is Capital Gate a folly. A very differ-ent picture presents itself, though, once we begin to notice the impact on a larger scale. Just as with the Eiffel Tower or the Guggenheim, the economy of the building is in everything *but* the building. Not the building, but all that ensues in its wake is what justifies Capital Gate. Its economic value is derived from the spectacle it creates—because it is there. The logic is simple: the presence of the 'farthest man-made leaning building' adds a premium to the adjacent convention centre, helps populate nearby malls and hotels, helps ensure Etihad Airways a steady flow of passengers. In the context of a political system where all these factors ultimately reside under the same ownership—that of the ruling family—a seemingly erratic venture like Capital Gate suddenly becomes a very real and profitable proposition. Money flows that do not register on the radar of conventional property development begin to manifest. A bigger picture starts to override partial financial stakes; 'private' parties contribute to —and benefit from—the power and profile of the state. Everyone wins. Extravagance becomes calculation.

The setting of world records is just one of the mechanisms on which this principle operates. Architecture is another. In the name of architecture, Capital Gate breaks a record which otherwise makes no functional or technical sense. Conversely, Capital Gate only registers as architecture *because* it breaks a record. The project's narrative is perfectly cyclical: a world record in the name of architecture; architecture in the name of a world record. The definitive answer to the question 'why?' is 'because we can!' Architecture serves as a demonstration of the extremes this can be taken to, an integral part of the Faustian pact between the state and its actors—the architects just one of many, despite their 'one of a kind' creation.

'We'—the supposedly respectable part of the profession— tend to view a project like Capital Gate with all the appropriate disdain, an iconic creation which should only ever be treated with the full force of irony. A lethal cocktail of eagerness and pretension is perpetuated by current and former RMJM collaborators falling over each other to pose as authors of a collectively created monster. However, the apparent nonsensicality of Capital Gate also forces us to look in the mirror. How different *is* the project ultimately from, let's say, Thomas Heatherwick's Vessel at Hudson Yards, David Adjaye's 418 11th Avenue NYC Tower, BIG's Vancouver House or even OMA's CCTV building? The 'why?' asked about Capital Gate can be asked of architecture in general. To what extent are our own preoccupations—the urge to defy gravity, our obsession with transparency, or the drift towards ever-greater abstraction —themselves acrobatic rises to self-invented challenges?

One wonders: what is the canon of modern architecture but a list of masterpieces that we as a profession have come to consider 'officially amazing'—a bag of solutions to problems which could (and might better) have been avoided? Villa

Savoye's famous ramp turns into a highly questionable feature the moment we consider the manifest inappropriateness of a complex, three-storey structure on an expansive, natural site. The Farnsworth house's elegant hovering above the flood plain of the Fox River Valley (and subsequent frequent flooding) could have been avoided had a different location been chosen. Turning the conventional logic of a building inside out, as in the case of the Pompidou, only served to compromise the very interior it was meant to salvage. And who in their sane mind would ever build a house over a waterfall? In terms of providing sensible solutions to real-world problems, modern architecture is quid pro quo at best.

And yet, for all its shortcomings, the architectural canon also upholds an important difference for projects like Capital Gate. Once architecture enters the realm of breaking records, something fundamental is lost. Records are established on the principle of reducing things to measurable properties. They constitute a challenge to be met, not one to be debated. Applying that principle to architecture represents a significant trading down. From meeting self-invented challenges, we surrender to imposed challenges. No longer is architecture driven by the creative intent of its makers—call it ideology—but by the imperative to triumph in categories it did not invent.

Record indices now exist for almost any type of architecture —the tallest, the largest, the heaviest, the costliest, the farthest leaning, the farthest underground … architecture becomes like the Olympics, hosting an ever-larger number of sports. 'The point is not to beat old records, but to think up new ones', according to Stuart Claxton, Guinness UK marketing director. The increase seems inversely proportional to the relevance.

The twentieth century made us aware of the aberrations of ideology, including perhaps those of architecture. Slowly, we are coming to terms with the opposite: the aberrations produced by an absence of ideology. In a world that has trouble establishing even the most basic level of consensus, numbers prevail. But numbers scarcely compensate for meaning. Methodically we proceed to compare one futile effort to the next, only to discover that it is ultimately the power of numbers on which the absolute rule of randomness is founded.

Flashback

After sixteen months of frantic construction, having clocked 6.5 million hours of labour by more than 1,200 workers (with no known casualties), boasting 21,500 tonnes of steel, 36,000 tonnes of concrete and 728 custom-made glass panels, Capital Gate eventually topped out in January 2010. Even though work on the interior had yet to start, the exterior was sufficiently finished for the building to appear complete in time for the World Energy Summit, held in the neighbouring Abu Dhabi National Exhibition Centre that same month. I attended that summit. I remember the rhetoric. I remember the endless professions of commitment to the cause of sustainability from delegates and I remember Richard Rogers holding the keynote speech. One thing I do not recall is a leaning tower. I need the Guinness World Records to remind me.

The **Iconic Awards: Innovative Architecture** honour the best of the best. Our internationally respected, impartial design and architecture competition honours holistic projects in the fields of architecture, interior architecture, product design and brand communication.[1] The **Arch Design Award** highlights the most interesting, well-designed, innovative solutions in the disciplines of Architectural and Interior Design. This Award honors talented designers, helps to increase their recognition and boost their visibility.[2] The **Aga Khan Award for Architecture** is given every three years to projects that set new standards of excellence in architecture, planning practices, historic preservation and landscape architecture. Through its efforts, the Award seeks to identify and encourage building concepts that successfully address the needs and aspirations of societies across the world in which Muslims have a significant presence.[3] The annual **Architecture MasterPrize (AMP)** is a global architecture award that recognizes design excellence. The AMP was created to advance the appreciation and exposure of quality architectural design worldwide. The prize celebrates creativity and innovation in architecture, interior design, landscape architecture, architectural product design and architectural photography.[4] The **2A Continental Architectural Awards (2ACAA)** has been primarily structured and designed to acknowledge and recognize the noteworthy contributions of individuals and organizations in the field of Architecture worldwide.[5] A' **Architecture Design Award** is an international, juried design accolade established to recognize and promote good architecture designs.[6] The **AIA Gold Medal** is the American Institute of Architects' highest annual honor, recognizing individuals whose work has had a lasting influence on the theory and practice of architecture.[7] The **Alvar Aalto Medal** was founded in 1967 to honour creative architecture. The medal can be awarded to living persons who have in a significant way distinguished themselves creatively within the field of architecture. Whenever possible, the medal is awarded on Alvar Aalto's birthday or other anniversary in connection with which the award ceremony for the medal can be held with the appropriate solemnity.[8] The **Curry Stone Design Prize** was borne out of the belief that while design is concerned with the built environment and people's places within it, its application is too often limited to the upper segments of society. The Foundation's hope was—and is, to support pioneering social design practitioners and to use their work to inspire others to apply design approaches to improving their own community's vitality.[9] **Dedalo Minosse International Prize for commissioning a building** would boost the quality of architecture looking at final result, analysing and focusing on project and constructive plan process and giving a special attention to people who determine the success of the work: the architect and the client, supported by the project executors (the building firms) and the public administrations.[10] Each year the **Global Award for Sustainable Architecture™** recognizes five architects who share both the principles of sustainable development and a participatory architectural approach to the needs of society, in both the northern and the southern hemispheres.[11] The **Pritzker Architecture Prize** honors a living architect or architects whose built work demonstrates a combination of those qualities of talent, vision, and commitment, which has produced consistent and significant contributions to humanity and the built environment through the art of architecture.[12] The **Newcastle Architecture Awards** celebrates design excellence in architecture in Newcastle. It is also a great way for architects to receive public and peer recognition for projects and helps the Institute to promote architects and architecture within Newcastle, NSW, across Australia and internationally.[13] The **RIBA International Prize** is awarded to the most transformative building which demonstrates visionary, innovative thinking, excellence of execution, and makes a distinct contribution to its users and physical context.[14] The **Lifetime Achievement Award** celebrates the achievements of individuals who have made significant contributions towards humanity and the advancement of architecture and the built environment in the Near East and North Africa.[15] Given in recognition of a lifetime's work, the **Royal Gold Medal** is approved personally by Her Majesty The Queen and is given to a person or group of people who have had a significant influence on the advancement of architecture.[16] The **International Architecture Awards** are dedicated to the recognition of excellence in architecture and urbanism from a global point-of-view.[17] Through the **Victorian Architecture Awards** the Australian Institute of Architects Awards program offers an opportunity for public and peer recognition of the innovative work of our Victorian architects. The **Progressive Architecture (P/A) Awards** recognize unbuilt projects demonstrating overall design excellence and innovation.[18] The **W Awards**, formerly known as the Women in Architecture awards, celebrate exemplary work by women and non-binary people, from lifetimes of achievement to the work of those with bright futures ahead, from the design of the world's most significant new buildings to contributions to wider architectural culture.[19] The **EU Prize for Contemporary Architecture—Mies van der Rohe Award** is a biennial prize highlighting outstanding architectural works built across Europe.[20] The **ABB LEAF Refurbishment Award** highlights the best new concept of an existing building.[21]

excellence

noun [U]

UK /ˈek.səl.əns/ US /ˈek.səl.əns/

the quality of being excellent:

The school is noted for its academic excellence.

3

Everyone a Winner

Each year, architecture magazine *Building Design* awards the Carbuncle Cup to honour 'the ugliest building in the UK of the last twelve months'. There is no ceremony and no prize money. There is not even a physical trophy to be given. The cup is no more than a cartoon: crimson red with two horns and a pointed tail. What the Golden Raspberries are to the Oscars, the Carbuncle Cup is to the prestigious Stirling Prize: a tongue-in-cheek response—usually granted in the same week—for 'crimes against design'.

The first-ever Carbuncle Cup was awarded in 2006 to Drake Circus Shopping Centre in Plymouth, designed by architecture firm Chapman Taylor. The reasons for the selection are probably best summed up by a review from *The Times* of that year:

> First, two parting waves of mammoth terracotta sheets, set at a jaunty, post-earthquake angle, Libeskind-style, presumably to prove that Plymouth is architecturally with it; followed, with no attempt to smooth the transition, by a huge pregnant bulge of latticed wood; then a large block of chequerboard stone (a feeble nod to local context) topped with a grid of metal panels cut into tree patterns; and then the two gigantic brick drums of the car park, which look like nothing so much as two cheeks of the monster's bum.[1]

While the Carbuncle Cup offers no possibility of an appeal—choosing a winner happens in the form of online voting—it is doubtful whether its recipients would have conducted one even if there were. The Cup is as much an insult as it is a badge of pride. Not least because of its name: an allusion to the famous 'Carbuncle Speech' by then Prince Charles at the 150th anniversary of the Royal Institute of British Architects in which he described the then-proposed extension to the National Gallery as a 'monstrous carbuncle on the face of a much-loved and elegant friend'.

Charles's speech continues to divide opinion: for some, a much-needed correction of a profession too detached from popular taste; for others, inappropriate interference from a regal chancer. The Carbuncle Cup seems to have found the ideal middle ground: an 'in your face' architecture contest with ample potential to annoy prince and architect alike. As online content, the Carbuncle Cup is perfect clickbait. 'Like celebrity bikini disasters or plastic surgery fails, who can resist clicking one more picture along?'[2] In an age so consistently marked by ugly buildings, what could be more worthy of a prize than the ugly building that gets noticed?

From student prizes to lifetime awards

The first ever architecture prize to be given was the Prix de Rome, a travel bursary awarded by Louis XIV of France to promising art and (eventually) architecture students in 1720. Contestants were subjected to a strenuous elimination contest. Isolated in closed booths, with only pencils and ink at their disposal and no reference material to draw from, each candidate had to produce detailed plan, section and elevation drawings of an assigned public building type. The winner was granted the right to stay in the Villa Mancini in Rome for a period of up to five years, with ample promise of large public commissions upon return.

During the first decades of the nineteenth century, an

expanded France (the result of Napoleon's territorial conquests) further introduced local editions of the prize in the Netherlands (1808) and in Belgium (1832). The appeal of the prize, however, well transcended French imperialism. Since 1921, the Rome Prize has also been awarded in the US. And while France itself abolished the Prix de Rome after the student riots of May 1968, Canada went on to establish its own Rome prize in 1987.

The Prix de Rome was essentially a student prize. It was not until 1848, when Queen Victoria, patron of the Royal Institute of British Architects (RIBA), instituted the Royal Gold Medal for the Promotion of Architecture that practising architects could be honoured for their achievements. The introduction of the prize followed the formation of the RIBA as a professional body in 1834. Before that, exceptional architects, such as Christopher Wren, John Vanbrugh and William Chambers, were simply knighted by the Crown or given the job of Surveyor of the King's Works. Originally struck in twenty-two-carat gold, the gold medal suffered subsequent reductions—to eighteen carats in 1932 and reduced to nine carats again in 1947 and into polished silver gilt in 1974.[3]

Other countries followed: the American Institute of Architects introduced a gold medal in 1907; the Royal Institute of Architects of Ireland launched their Triennial Gold Medal in 1934; the Australian Institute of Architects introduced a gold medal in 1960; the Royal Architectural Institute of Canada launched theirs in 1967 as did the Finnish Association of Architects in the form of the Alvar Aalto Medal. In most cases, the recipients were well beyond retirement age. Leslie Wilkinson received the Australian Gold Medal at the age of seventy-eight and Serge Chermayeff the Canadian one at the age of seventy-three. The first-ever recipient of the Alvar Aalto Medal was Alvar Aalto himself at the age of sixty-nine.

Awarding oeuvre prizes to accomplished architects was the logical next step for professional bodies like the RIBA or the AIA, the mission of which was twofold: 1) to raise the standard of professional practice in general, and 2) to strengthen the legal and societal position of the profession's members. Eternalizing the most distinguished among them through a (royally approved) high-profile award is an effective way to serve both aims.

Other oeuvre prizes have emerged over time, granted by wealthy patrons of the arts. Some of these, like the Thomas Jefferson Medal in Architecture and the Pritzker Architecture Prize have come to rival and, in the case of the latter, even surpass the prestige associated with the awards given by professional bodies. The Thomas Jefferson award, a joint initiative of the Thomas Jefferson Foundation and the University of Virginia School of Architecture, dates back to 1966 (awarded to Mies van der Rohe).

The Pritzker Prize was first awarded in 1979 (to Philip Johnson). Established by Jay A. Pritzker—the founder of Hyatt Hotel corporation—and his wife Cindy, the prize is awarded annually 'to honor a living architect or architects whose built work demonstrates a combination of those qualities of talent, vision and commitment, which has produced consistent and significant contributions to humanity and the built environment through the art of architecture'.[4] In an interview with *Forbes*, their son, Thomas J. Pritzker, explained the motivation of his parents as follows:

> As native Chicagoans, it's not surprising that our family was keenly aware of architecture. While the architecture of Chicago made us cognizant of the art of architecture, our work with designing and building hotels made us aware of the impact architecture could have on human behavior. So, in 1978, when we were approached with the idea of honoring living architects, we were responsive. Mom and Dad believed that a meaningful prize would encourage and stimulate not only a greater public awareness of buildings, but also would inspire greater creativity within the architectural profession.[5]

Awarded to an architect for career achievements, 'irrespective of nationality, race, creed, or ideology', the Pritzker Prize is considered currently the most prestigious and truly global architecture award and is generally referred to as the Nobel Prize of architecture. Even if recently subject to criticism for making former jury member Alejandro Aravena the laureate of 2016, and for a lack of stance against former winners under fire from the #MeToo movement, the Pritzker Prize counts as the leading measure of architectural excellence today. Other important oeuvre prizes, such as the Praemium Imperiale, founded in 1989 by the imperial family of Japan and the Japan Art Association, tend to feature the same laureates as the Pritzker list, roughly in the same order, generally a few years later.

Modern versus Traditional

More recent is the tendency to honour buildings instead of architects. In 1987, one year after the reconstruction of his Barcelona Pavilion, the Mies van der Rohe Award came into being. The award is a joint initiative of the European Union and the Fundació Mies van der Rohe, and since 2001, the award counts as the official prize for architecture of the European Union. Awarded biannually, it is open to all works of architecture completed in Europe within a two-year period before the granting of the prize.

The UK's prestigious Stirling Prize, in existence since 1996 as a replacement of the older RIBA Building of the Year Award (1987), operates on a similar basis, albeit annually and with a distinct national twist after the idea of a Brexit referendum was first floated in 2015. Until that year, the prize was open to all buildings completed in the EU, but since then it has been restricted to entries from the UK.

According to the rules of the Mies van der Rohe Award, works must be completed within the last two years of granting the award. While that makes its contenders contemporary by default, the origin as well as the prize's name has been seen by some to indicate a bias towards a *certain type* of architecture. As a former director of the German Bauhaus, Mies van der Rohe counts as an unequivocally modernist architect and thus the official competence of the prize—to award contemporary architecture—is sometimes considered a scarcely concealed euphemism for favouring *modernist* architecture (in the same way that the EU is sometimes presumed to be a construction of the left).

While this is less so with the Stirling Prize—where Mies's career exemplifies a singular devotion to modernity, Stirling's is more ambiguous—the Stirling Prize, too, is not free from controversy. In 2000, with five out of the seven designs shortlisted being located within the London Metropolitan Area, several architects from Scotland and Wales took the evaluation committee to court. Even if their claims were eventually thrown out by the court, the tone had been set. Where the EU's most prominent building award is deemed too modern, the UK's suffers the stigma of 'metropolitan bias'. Different words, but perhaps a similar sentiment. In the twenty-first century, the contemporary seems to have a considerable PR problem on either side of the Channel.

While the old continent indulged in modern (and metropolitan) biases, the new continent witnessed a flurry of initiatives in the opposite direction. In 2002, the Traditional Building Conference, held in the US, presented the first Palladio Award for 'the creative interpretation or adaptation of design principles developed through 2,500 years of the Western architectural tradition'. In 2003, fund manager and philanthropist Richard Driehaus started the Driehaus Architecture Prize to honour 'major contributors in the field of contemporary vernacular and classical architecture'. The prize presented itself as the reasonable alternative to the predominantly modernist Pritzker Prize. Its first edition, presented at the University of Notre

Dame, went to Leon Krier. (In 2012, the award went to then Prince Charles.) In 2005, the Henry Hope Reed Award was initiated to honour 'an individual working outside the practice of architecture who had supported the cultivation of the traditional city, its architecture and art through writing, planning or promotion'.[6] The prize was presented in conjunction with the Driehaus Prize at the University of Notre Dame. Starting the Reed Award in 2005 earned its initiator, Clem Labine, the 2020 Palladio Award.

An award for everything

Beyond award categories for different *styles* of building, there is the ever-increasing number of awards for different building *types*. After the turn of the century, high-rise buildings especially became subject to a plethora of prizes. There is the Emporis Skyscraper Award (since 2000), the CTBUH Skyscraper Award (since 2002) and the International Highrise Award (since 2003). But there are other categories, too, like the RESI Awards, given by *Property Week* magazine (since 2016), and the UK Housing Awards, 1996, bestowed by *Inside Housing* magazine and the Chartered Institute of Housing (since 1996). And in case building types are exhausted, there is always the European Prize for Urban Public Space (since 2000).

In addition to the awards for building types, there are the awards attributed to different construction materials, like the Wood Design Award (since 1984), the International Stone Architecture Award (since 1986), the Brick in Architecture Award (since 1989), the APA (Architectural Precast Association) Awards for Excellence (since 2006), the Copper in Architecture Awards (since 2008), the Metal Architecture Design Awards (since 2011) and the Innovative Design in Engineering and Architecture with Structural Steel (IDEAS[2]) Awards (since 2013).

Just as the high-rise awards are funded by their most important stakeholders—the property world and the construction industry—so are the respective material awards funded by the various suppliers and manufacturers. More recent is the tendency of architecture magazines to honour the role of the building industry. In 2007, *Architect* magazine, the journal of the American Institute of Architects, launched the first of its annual R&D awards 'to foster dialogue among architects, engineers, and manufacturers'; in 2012, with the overt support of industry sponsors, the German magazine *Detail* started its Detail Prize, and in 2018, the UK's *Architects' Journal* presented its first AJ Specification Awards.

Under the slogan 'when great products meet great design', the AJ Specification Award hopes 'to recognize the key importance of collaboration between product and material suppliers or manufacturers and architects to the success of a project'. The award has fourteen categories: 'Bathrooms', 'Brick & Stone', 'Colour & Finishes', 'Doors & Windows', 'Façades and Cladding', 'Fit-out and Interiors', 'Flooring', 'Landscaping', 'Mechanical & Electrical', 'Natural Materials', 'Offsite Fabrication', 'Roofing & Drainage', 'Stairs & Lifts', and, more broadly, 'Technology'. These categories are open to suppliers and manufacturers and architects who have collaborated on a (UK-based) project.

Shortlisted entries are published online and in print in the *Architects' Journal*, while the winners of each category are featured in a special AJ Specification issue. The construction industry badly needs the exposure, the magazine badly needs the ads, so one industry helps another. Architecture magazines thus become outlets for those involved in project execution. Architecture serves as 'product placement', as the distinction between advertisement and content becomes progressively blurred.

Trading up

The first architectural awards by magazines date back to the 1950 and '60s. The editors of *Progressive Architecture*, the in-house magazine of the American Institute of Architects, hosted the first 'Progressive Architecture (P/A) Awards' jury in 1954 to 'recognize risk-taking practitioners and seek to promote progress in the field of architecture' and in 1960, *L'Architecture française* launched its first Prix de l'Équerre d'argent (Silver Square Award) to honour groundbreaking building realizations on French soil. Such heroic missions have become rare, meanwhile. Both magazines no longer exist, and the awards have since been extended into multiple categories by other magazines.

The entry of architecture publications into the world of awards provides an important new incentive to participate. Featuring in publications is a way for architects to get noticed. From a way to reward the work of an architect, the award increasingly becomes a way for architects to *earn* work, as indicated by recent awards given by magazines such as the *Architects' Journal*, *Bauwelt* or the *Architectural Review*. Under the motto 'big ideas to small budgets', the *AJ* has launched its Small Projects Award, luring designers of 'luxury home renovations, extensions on tiny budgets, arts and cultural studios and spaces, follies and more civic and community-minded market stalls' with the promise that 'many of the winning practices have gone on to become some of the most recognized practices and architects, going on to bigger successes'.

In the same way that small projects may lead to big projects, first works may lead to more, and so in 2015 German magazine *Bauwelt* introduced an award category of 'First Work' hoping to create a springboard for starting architects. In pretty much the same way, the *Architectural Review* started its 'Emerging Architects' award category to 'support young architects and designers at a key stage in their career, promoting their best work to a worldwide audience'.

Beyond promoting architects in the 'key stages of their career', magazine awards also cater to those who might have missed out. As a belated recognition of the undervalued contribution of women to the profession, the *Architects' Journal* and *Architectural Review* jointly initiated the W Awards, formerly known as the Women in Architecture awards, to 'celebrate exemplary work by women and non-binary people, from lifetimes of achievement to the work of those with bright futures ahead, from the design of the world's most significant new buildings to contributions to wider architectural culture'.[7] There are careers to be advanced and a cause to be furthered. What better than to have the two coincide in a single prize?

Awards are by no means exclusive to architecture. In fact, architecture awards are increasingly given in conjunction with other awards, more broadly defined as 'categories of design'. Magazines like *Azure*, *Wallpaper** and *Fast Company* feature awards for 'Architecture' alongside those for 'Transportation', 'Consumer Products', '2D Design', 'Service Design', 'Interactive Design', 'Industrial Equipment', as well as (yet) more esoteric categories as 'Spaces' and 'Concepts'. In a final instance, in the context of a sheer endless tribute to creativity, even the designers of the awards themselves enter the limelight. The AZ Awards by *Azure* (an 'award-winning magazine' itself) honour seven categories each with their own 'signature trophy' credited to a promising designer (and potential future winner of the award).

Yet no trophy can rival the proximity to an all-star cast of jury members, which is the reward on offer for the winners of the *Wallpaper** Awards: not the limelight, but the sharing of it, with 'major players from the worlds of fashion, design, photography, architecture, food, and popular culture'. *Wallpaper** lists, among others, Victoria Beckham, Donatella Versace, Pharrell Williams, Kanye West, Norman Foster, Ian Schrager, Ron Arad and Pedro Almodóvar as 'judges who don't just tick boxes and send shortlists but offer astute and considered perspective on their choices and the wider design world'.[8]

One extreme triggers the other. At the opposite end of the high-profile jury is the jury with no profile, either because the judges are too large in number—the 2017 awards of the online magazine *Dezeen* have a total of seventy-five judges—or because the idea of a jury has simply been done away with in favour of online voting by readers, as is the case with the *Arch-Daily* Building of the Year Awards.

Nothing succeeds better than success. Yet, success inevitably comes at a price. And when it comes to *the* price, the presence of a high-profile jury hardly makes a difference. *Fast Company*'s Innovation by Design Award charges entry fees of up to $295, while the Dezeen Awards charges its contenders up to £300. Winners of the Dezeen Awards earn the right to be published, but only on the condition that they unreservedly grant Dezeen Limited 'a royalty-free, irrevocable, perpetual, worldwide, non-exclusive and fully sub-licensable license to use, reproduce, publish, distribute, perform, display, creative derivative works from, and otherwise exploit any such material submitted, in whole or in part, in any form, including for promotional or marketing purposes'.

Towards an awards industry

If the magazines were the first to broach awards as a business model, it is the architecture festivals who take that model to the extreme. In the context of events such as the World Architecture Festival (WAF) and the World Architecture News (WAN) Award, the granting of awards develops into its own autonomous, self-perpetuating industry, one that no longer needs the backing of the Crown, reputable professional bodies or established architecture publications.

WAF, as outlined by its media partner *ArchDaily*, describes itself as 'the biggest architectural awards program in the world'. The commercial potential proves huge, as is evident from the entry fees charged for award submissions, against which those charged by magazine awards pale in comparison. WAF, for example charges entry fees of £889 + VAT (early bird) to £1,399 + VAT (standard) per entry. Multiple entries (three or more) receive a generous discount of 10 per cent. Shortlisted entries get to present their projects at the festival, in which case they need to pay a further attendance fee of £1,399 + VAT (standard package), £1,699 + VAT (festival package) or £2,199 + VAT (accommodation package, which graciously covers the stay in a nearby hotel).

There is no prize money related to any of the awards, but the WAF website spells out ample alternative reasons to participate, such as gaining valuable insight from world-renowned juries, receiving unparalleled exposure in the global media, getting inspiration for future work, the opportunity to form partnerships with other architects, join the world's most influential architecture community and, most tempting of all, a chance to meet potential clients.

How WAF has perfected its commercial formula over the years is most clearly manifested in the number of award categories, which has escalated faster than the number of contestants: from 722 for seventeen categories in 2008 (the year the WAF first launched), to a little over 1,000 for thirty-three categories, thereby substantially increasing the chance of a win (and thus that of larger revenues from attendance fees for the festival itself).

As the number of award categories escalates, so does the length of the list of award sponsors. And WAF does little to hide the thematic link between the two: the Engineering Prize is sponsored by engineering consultants EdgeAllies; the Best Use of Certified Timber Prize is supported by the Programme for Endorsement of Forest Certification (PEFC); the Best Use of Natural Light Prize is sponsored by VELUX, a company that makes skylights and window blinds, while the Water Research Prize is sponsored by GROHE, a manufacturer of bathroom and kitchen fittings. The sponsors and their contributions are prominently displayed on the WAF website, as is the gratitude of the organizer: 'WAF is delighted that its headline partner, GROHE, once supported the Water Research Prize. GROHE is supporting research into tackling unique challenges that water presents, with the winning initiative awarded £10,000 of funding.'

WAF has no office, no permanent staff and, apart from info@ worldarchitecturefestival.com, no further email addresses registered in its name. WAF is owned by Emap, which is also the company that accounts for most of the email addresses of those quoted to be WAF's staff. Emap is a media company that, until recently, also owned the *Architectural Review* (*AR*) and the *AJ*, WAF's two main media partners.[9] The positions of WAF programme director and that of editorial director of the *AR* and the *AJ* are held by the same person. If previously the media helped sustain the awards—as in the case of RIBA's Stirling Awards— in the case of WAF *the awards* come to sustain *the media*, both in terms of providing the media with free content *and* drawing revenues from contestants hoping to be published in them. The fact that (at least part of) these media are owned by the same media company that owns WAF provides an interesting twist to the 'unparalleled attention in the media', quoted as a reason to enter the WAF awards. 'The medium is the message', and fifty years after the book, the success of WAF feels like a belated validation of Marshall McLuhan's theories.

Trumping the award that one pays to compete for is the award one pays without competing. Shortly after its formation in 2015, *BUILD*, a UK-based online magazine, launched its Architecture Awards to 'recognize and reward the incredible works conducted by the world's most innovative, imaginative and dedicated designers and architects'. The categories to enter numbered well over a hundred, from 'Most Trusted Full-service Architecture Firm' to 'Best Bespoke Kitchen Furniture Designers', from 'Most Dynamic Architecture Practice' to 'Best

Architecture Ironmongery Company', from 'Best Engineered Stones Installation Specialist' to 'Mixed Use Architect of the Year'.

The first feedback started to appear online in 2016, from unsuspecting companies, bewildered to have supposedly 'defined the world' or 'really made an impact on the industry they were in'. What followed was invariably the same: an offer to purchase expensive advertising packages in a range of other online magazines. Further browsing revealed that these magazines were all part of the same digital publishing house: AI Global Media Limited, against whom, in August 2018, the Advertising Standards Authority upheld a complaint for having misleadingly implied the recipients had been nominated and won awards when in fact AI Global Media Limited just intended to sell advertising space.[10]

Winner takes all

In 1950, there were less than ten international architecture awards. Today, that number runs well into the hundreds. The first sharp increase occurred after the mid-1970s, when private sponsors began to discover architecture awards as a vehicle to advertise their brands. Since the 1990s, the possibility of online submissions has sparked another growth spurt.

As their number escalates, so changes the nature of the awards. If in 1950, the number was evenly split between oeuvre prizes for architects and awards for individual projects, today the awards for projects constitute the overwhelming majority. The same goes for the split between prizes for which one is nominated and those which require a submission (the latter constituting the vast majority today). Furthermore, in 1950 nearly all award submissions were free, while today more than half require an entry fee. That trend is on the increase: of the awards added since 2000, as much as 80 per cent charge an entry fee.

During the last few decades, the number of awards has grown significantly faster than the number of practising architects. While in theory that would result in a more favourable award/architect ratio—and therefore a more even distribution of recognition—the real trend has been in the opposite direction. One award proves a condition to receive the next. Looking at the most prestigious architecture prizes: the Pritzker Prize, the RIBA and AIA Gold Medals, the Praemium Imperiale and the Venice Biennale's Golden Lion for lifetime achievement, one invariably finds the same list of recurring winners.

Winner takes all! The familiar trend that manifests in sports, cinema and the entertainment industry also manifests in architecture. With fifteen oeuvre prizes, a hundred national or regional AIA awards for specific buildings and fifteen honorary doctoral degrees, Frank Gehry's 'award record' is comparable to that of luminaries of the film and music business like Steven Spielberg (175 awards) and Michael Jackson (240).

In architecture, Gehry does not even rank top of the list. He is 'out-awarded' by Richard Rogers with 217 awards, Zaha Hadid with 234 and Norman Foster, whose firm holds well over 400 awards. Yet the phenomenon is by no means limited to the happy few at the top. There is hardly an architects' firm left that *doesn't* label itself as 'award-winning', and rarely does the list stop at one, two or even three. The awards themselves seem of little importance; one does not compete for any prize per se, but for the largest number.

No longer do awards qualify as gratuitous praise. They are a 'must have', a condition to earn work, triggering a rat race which one cannot afford *not* to join. To be commercially viable, one needs to keep a register of prizes. Much in the same way that ISO certificates provide a quality assurance for services and manufacturing processes, awards have become a prime indication of architectural savviness. The best firm is inevitably the most awarded firm. Having engaged, it is impossible to stop. Yet the more one does, the more one finds one's creative freedom curtailed. The award categories most easily won are also the most prescriptive: best community-engaging building of the year, most sustainable use of natural stone, best building by a woman of colour under forty, and so on. Laudable as such categories might be, it is important to realize that one never wins them on one's own terms. The more one surrenders to criteria set by others, the more one becomes oblivious of one's own. An awards record becomes a straitjacket from which it is impossible to escape.

An eerie parallel emerges with the current economic system. Global GDP, too, has exploded since the mid-1970s, only to be concentrated in the hands of an ever-smaller number of uber-rich proprietors. Just like it takes money to make money, it takes awards to win awards. Even if their number is larger than ever, and the opportunities to share in the glory seem greater than ever before, competing for awards will only have architects play catch-up.

A fine line

The Carbuncle Cup is meanwhile in its fifteenth year. Drake Circus Shopping Centre and its architects are steadily rolling along. A year after winning the Carbuncle Cup, the building went on to win *Retail Week* magazine's Shopping Location of the Year, while the website of architects Chapman Taylor lists over 250 new international design awards. In terms of 'crimes against design', too, Chapman and Taylor are in good circles. In 2006, Drake Circus Shopping Centre emerged from a shortlist which included renowned architecture firms such as Foster + Partners (Moore House, City of London), OMA (Serpentine Gallery Pavilion), CZWG (Lough Road Housing, London) and Llewelyn-Davies (University College Hospital, London). Since then, the Carbuncle Cup has been won by Grimshaw

Architects for the Cutty Sark restoration in Greenwich, London (in 2012), and by Rafael Viñoly for the Walkie Talkie building in the City of London (in 2015). Who knows what might qualify next? Twenty years into the new millennium, the line between masterpiece and carbuncle seems finer than ever.

sustainability

noun [U]

UK /sə͵steɪ.nəˈbɪl.ə.ti/ US /sə͵steɪ.nəˈbɪl.ə.t̬i/

1. the quality of being able to continue over a period of time:
   the long-term sustainability of the community

2. the quality of causing little or no damage to the environment and therefore able to continue for a long time:

   the company's commitment to environmental sustainability

4

Crisis? What Crisis?

The news broke on a Sunday, from Bloomberg's press office, twenty-four days ahead of the building's scheduled opening. 'October 1, 2017—Bloomberg's new European headquarters the world's most sustainable office building, as designed'.[1] On Monday, the architects, Foster + Partners, issued their own press release providing the evidence—a 98.5 per cent BREEAM score, the highest ever achieved by any major office development. The online architectural media instantly echoed the contents: 'Foster + Partners' Bloomberg headquarters is the "world's most sustainable office"' (*Dezeen*); 'Bloomberg's New European Headquarters Rated World's Most Sustainable Office Building' (*ArchDaily*); 'Bloomberg European HQ Named World's Most Sustainable Office Building' (*Architect* magazine); 'Foster's Bloomberg HQ is "world's most sustainable office"' (*Building Design*).

The building was the offspring of a perfect marriage, coupling Bloomberg's ambitions to reach net-zero carbon emissions by 2025 with Foster + Partners' expertise in sustainable design. Evidence of its sustainability was abundant: petal-leaf-shaped ceiling panels, combined heating, cooling and acoustic functions, as well as 500,000 LED lights; operable bronze blades on the façade allowed the building to 'breathe' naturally, reducing dependency on mechanical ventilation; special water conservation systems would save up to 25 million litres of water each year (the equivalent of ten Olympic swimming pools); smart CO_2 sensors would save 600 to 750 megawatt hours of power every year, or 300 tonnes of CO_2; and an on-site combined heat and power generation centre was expected to reduce the building's CO_2 emissions by another 500 to 750 tonnes each year.[2]

The building's opening event, three weeks later, was hosted by Michael Bloomberg himself, alongside both Mayor Sadiq Khan and Lord Foster, founder and executive chairman of Foster + Partners. It was the firm's second major office building completion, a year after Apple's Headquarters in Cupertino, California. Still, where Steve Jobs's long-awaited brainchild project had left journalists (the few who were allowed to attend, that is) in awe, the Bloomberg HQ press tour did not leave the same impression.[3] The façade's metal blades were criticized for blocking the view from within the building; the 600 tonnes of bronze used to cast them had been imported from Japan, while the exterior was clad with 10,000 tonnes of granite from India, which questioned the sustainability of the construction process.[4] The energy-saving combined heat and power genera-tion centre might have been more efficient than a conventional system, but it was still burning natural gas.[5] Was the £1.3 billion building as 'green' as BREEAM had labelled it?

The Bloomberg HQ opening was not the first time that sustainability ratings have been questioned. In 2011, *USA Today* discovered that more than 7,000 LEED-certified com-mercial buildings in the US had obtained their certification by scoring the minimum amount of points—obtained by using low-emitting paints, installing fire alarm systems that ease the stress on firefighters, providing video-game rooms for employ-ees, including a LEED expert in the design team and exhibiting educational displays about the building. Measures like these could bring up to thirty-two points out of the forty minimum points required.[6]

In 2008, The Palazzo hotel and casino in Las Vegas had relied on parking spots for fuel-efficient cars, bike racks, key cards informing guests when towels were replaced, landscaping without grass (prohibited by the State of Nevada anyway) to become rated as the largest 'green' building in the world. For the developer, the effort to get the building certified by LEED came with a US$27 million tax break. *USA Today* revealed that around 2,000 other buildings across the US had received a total of US$500 million in similar tax breaks. In the words of Michael Bloomberg: 'We believe that environmentally friendly practices are as good for business as they are for the planet.'[7]

BREEAM versus LEED

On 17 July 1987, the London Docklands Development Corporation and Canary Wharf Investment Ltd., subsidiary of Canadian property development company Olympia & York, signed an agreement to develop the largest master plan in Europe: Canary Wharf Development. Olympia & York and several other developers involved in the project, including London firms Stanhope Properties and Greycoat Real Estate, were interested in incorporating environmental features in the development as a way to gain a competitive edge. Finding it difficult to convince investors and tenants, Stanhope executive Ron German, together with architect John Doggart, partner at Energy Conscious Design (ECD), decided to pursue an alternative route and reached out to the government-funded Building Research Establishment (BRE). The BRE began in 1921, initially with the mission to conduct research into materials and construction methods for the British building industry, which was lagging behind the other European countries. Since the oil crisis of 1972, however, the centre had expanded its focus to energy efficiency. Together with developers and ECD, BRE developed a general environmental rating tool for commercial buildings. Three years later, the Building Research Establishment Environmental Assessment Method 1/90 New Offices was launched —BREEAM in short.

Something similar happened on the other side of the Atlantic a few years later. At the American Institute of Architects' 1992 annual congress, developer David Gottfried, attending the lectures of architect William McDonough (who would co-write *Cradle to Cradle: Remaking the Way We Make Things* ten years later), had the epiphany to 'change the world through sustainable buildings'.[8] Gottfried was working for his cousins' construction companies and convinced them to open a subsidiary firm to consult on sustainable building construction.

No client saw the benefit of spending more on 'greening the building' and Gottfried resigned. Seeking legal advice on environmental laws and standards, Gottfried linked up with Mike Italiano, a lawyer specializing in environmental litigation, and later that year the two opened their own environmental building consultancy. It also failed. One year later, they co-opted Rick Fedrizzi, executive at the engineering multinational company United Technologies Corporation, and founded a non-profit organization to promote sustainable building. Sixty companies and non-profit organizations joined as paying members. Fedrizzi was appointed CEO and the organization was named the US Green Building Council (USGBC).

The council soon ran into financial difficulties, leading Gottfried to resign in 1994. The USGBC then recruited Robert Watson, senior scientist at the Natural Resources Defense Council, who argued that the US needed its own sustainable building rating system. In the American context, with its large, uneven energy grid and various climate zones, adopting the British BREEAM would not have worked. In addition, BREEAM was too focused on CO_2 emissions, whereas the council prioritized energy efficiency. In 2000, LEED v.1 was released.

Today, both LEED and BREEAM equally claim to be the most used sustainability rating around the world. BREEAM accounts for 81 per cent of all sustainable certifications for commercial buildings in Europe and is recognized in eighty-six countries on all continents, among which the Netherlands, Spain, Norway, Sweden and Germany developed country-specific schemes. With Gottfried once again as founding member, the USGBC expanded internationally and formed the World Green Building Council in 2002, which now counts seventy members around the world. As of 2014, LEED's second largest market after the US is China.

Updates

Since their release, both BREEAM and LEED have gone through several updates. At first, BREEAM was developed as a 'green' label for office buildings. One year after its official release, BREEAM New Superstores and BREEAM New Homes were launched. In 1993, Industrial Buildings followed. The same year, the overall points system was introduced with labels ranging from Pass to Good, Very Good and Excellent. In 1998, BREEAM for Offices was updated, and in 2000 BREEAM New Homes was replaced with EcoHomes to minimize the CO_2 emissions from the residential sector for both new builds and refurbishments. More schemes followed: BREEAM Retail in 2004, BREEAM Schools in 2005, BREEAM Multi-Homes, BREEAM Prisons and BREEAM Bespoke in 2006. A major update came in 2008 that introduced post-construction reviews and mandatory credits and introduced the 'Outstanding' label. (Previously a developer could choose freely which credits to achieve to get the overall minimum for certification.) International versions of BREEAM's schemes were also launched that year. Another update came in 2011 when previous schemes were consolidated under BREEAM New Construction.

Today, there are five BREEAM 'standards': New Construction, for homes and commercial buildings; In-Use, for commercial buildings; Refurbishment and Fit-Out, also for homes and commercial buildings; Communities, for master-planning projects; and Infrastructure, for civil engineering and public realm works. Sustainability is measured in ten 'categories': Energy; Health and Wellbeing; Innovation; Land Use; Materials; Management; Pollution; Transport; Waste; and Water. Each category is subdivided in 'assessment issues', each with its own 'aim, target and benchmarks'. Each achieved target and benchmark brings 'credits'. The number of credits that results, combined with the category's weighting, gives the category score. The sum of all weighted category scores is the building's final performance rating. The available ratings are: Acceptable (In-Use schemes only), Pass, Good, Very Good, Excellent and Outstanding.

Assessment and certification can take place at any moment in a building's life cycle, from design and construction to operation and refurbishment. The process starts with the client appointing a certified assessor to sign the project to the correct BREEAM standard. The assessor then registers the project, conducts a pre-assessment, collects the relevant information from the client and designer, reviews it, checks its compliance to the standard and submits it to the assessment body for a decision.[9]

LEED started as a green building rating tool for any new construction. Its pilot version had sixteen credits, of which a minimum of twelve were required to obtain the certification. Four credits were mandatory—wastewater, waste disposal, lead in drinking water and smoking ban. There were no weightings; for each criterium, one credit was available. In the version launched publicly, the number of credits was expanded to forty. The weighting system came with LEED v.2, in which the criteria were organized in five categories: Land; Water; Energy; Materials; and Indoor Environmental Quality. The number of credits was further increased to sixty-nine. New schemes followed: LEED Core & Shell in 2004, LEED New Construction, LEED Existing Buildings, LEED Homes and LEED Commercial Interiors in 2005. LEED v.3, in 2009, consolidated LEED's schemes into Green Building Design and Construction, Green Interior

Design and Construction, and Green Building Operation and Maintenance.

The current version, LEED v.4.1, launched in 2018, is available for buildings, communities and cities. There are five schemes available: LEED for Building Design and Construction (BD+C), which is divided into New Construction, Core and Shell, Data Centres, Health Care, Hospitality, Retail, Schools, and Warehouses and Distribution Centres; LEED for Operations and Maintenance (O+M), for Existing Buildings, Data Centres, Hospitality, Retail, Schools, and Warehouses and Distribution Centres; LEED for Interior Design and Construction (ID+C), for Commercial Interiors, Hospitality and Retail; LEED for Residential, for Single Family Homes, Multifamily Homes, and Multifamily Homes Core and Shell; and LEED for Cities and Communities, the latter divided into Plan and Built Project.

A maximum of one hundred credits can be achieved, divided into nine categories: Sustainable Sites; Water Efficiency; Indoor Environmental Quality; Materials and Resources; Energy and Atmosphere; Location and Transportation; Innovation; Regional Priority; and Education and Awareness. Based on the overall score, the project can be labelled as Certified (40–49 points earned), Silver (50–59 points earned), Gold (60–79 points earned) or Platinum (80+ points earned). The process is carried out together with a LEED-certified assessor and takes between twenty and twenty-five business days. Clients must pay a flat certification fee as well as a registration fee ranging from US$1,200 to US$10,000, depending on project size and LEED certification goal. Once the project is certified, an additional fee of US$0.009 to US$0.0057 per square foot is required depending on whether the certification is for design, construction or both.

Applying for and obtaining BREEAM and LEED certifications increases the cost of the investment but also comes with financial benefits. The 'Why Choose BREEAM' section on BRE's website highlights what developers have to gain: 'BREEAM helps clients manage and mitigate risk through demonstrating sustainability performance during planning, design, construction, operation or refurbishment, helping to lower running costs, maximize returns through market value and attract and retain tenants with desirable places to live and work.'[10]

A similar reasoning is mentioned on USGBC's 'Why LEED' page: '61% of corporate leaders believe that sustainability leads to market differentiation and improved financial performance.' The site adds that: 'LEED-certified buildings command the highest rents, while lease-up rates typically range from average to 20% above average; vacancy rates for green buildings are an estimated 4% lower than non-green properties.'[11]

Three hundred years of sustainability

The manifest financial benefit of sustainability certifications might seem somewhat at odds with environmental concerns, but it is not entirely surprising considering the context in which the notion of sustainability appeared. Its origins can be traced to early eighteenth-century Germany. In his treatise *Sylvicultura oeconomica, oder haußwirthliche Nachricht und Naturmäßige Anweisung zur wilden Baum-Zucht* published in 1713, Hans Carl von Carlowitz, the administrator of a mining area around Freiberg, Saxony, warned about a looming economic crisis in Europe as a result of centuries of extensive deforestation. The scarcity of wood and its rising prices were threatening the timber-dependent mining industry with bankruptcy. To avoid the crisis, Carlowitz proposed that timber be harvested with care so that there is a 'continuous, permanent, and sustained use' [*continuierliche beständige und nachhaltende Nutzung*].[12] A balance was necessary between cutting and replanting. Man could no longer rely on nature's abundance, Carlowitz pointed out. In taking care of present needs, he had the responsibility to make sure that future generations enjoyed the same resources.

Carlowitz died one year after the publication of *Sylvicultura oeconomica*, but the book became a mandatory reading among cameralists—the public administrative servants in Germany. The concept of *Nachhaltigkeit* was developed further in books like *Grundsätze der Forst-Oeconomie* [*Basic Principles of Forest Economy*] (1757) by forest scientist Wilhelm Gottfried Moser, and *Über den Zustand des Bergbaus und Hüttenwesens in den Fürstentümern Bayreuth und Ansbach im Jahre 1792* [*On the State of Mining and Metallurgy in the Principalities of Bayreuth and Ansbach in 1792*] by Alexander von Humboldt. The theory was put into practice in Saxony and Thüringen, where forests started to be surveyed and planned. Academies were established to teach the art and science of forestry and soon Carlowitz's *Nachhaltigkeit* spread beyond the German-speaking world. In French the term was translated as *produit soutenu* and in English as 'sustained yield'.[13]

The concept of sustainability reached the US at the beginning of the twentieth century, where it became known as 'wise use', a term coined by Gifford Pinchot, the country's first professionally trained forester. For Pinchot, who learned about the European practice of managing forests in France, 'wise use' meant the conservation of resources for future generations— 'the wise use of the earth and its resources for the lasting good of men', as he wrote in his memoirs.[14] That being said, Pinchot's conservation had little to do with preservation, advocated by naturalists like John Muir—the Scottish-born father of the national parks movement in his adopted home of the US—who valued nature for its spiritual qualities. Rather, Pinchot believed that conservation served economic benefits: 'The forests which are most profitably used are the forests which are best preserved.'[15] Pinchot based his philosophy on Jeremy Bentham's utilitarianism, to which he added one more element: time. 'Conservation is the foresighted utilization, preservation and/ or renewal of forests, waters, lands and minerals for the greatest good of the greatest number for the longest time.'[16]

It was not until half a century later that sustainability moved beyond such enumerations and became a topic for the entire planet. In 1968, for the first time, the world saw the Earth from space, photographed on Christmas Eve by Apollo 8 astronaut Bill Anders. A small blue Earth rising behind the lunar surface against the backdrop of space raised consciousness about the finite nature of the planet. 'To see the earth as it truly is, small and blue and beautiful in that eternal silence where it floats, is to see ourselves as riders on the earth together, brothers on that bright loveliness in the eternal cold—brothers who know that they are truly brothers', wrote poet Archibald MacLeish in the *New York Times*.[17]

The economic system based on perpetual growth, which gave the West worldwide hegemony, was beginning to be questioned and two books voiced these concerns most eloquently, both published in the spring of 1972. *A Blueprint for Survival,* signed by some thirty British scientists and written by Edward Goldsmith and Robert Prescott-Allen of *The Ecologist* magazine, warned that industrialization was the path towards the destruction of humanity. 'The principal defect of the industrial way of life with its ethos of expansion is that it is not sustainable', the report began.[18] Intensive agriculture and the use of pesticides threatened to disrupt the predictability of ecosystems, on which humans' survival depended. Failure of food supplies and exhaustion of resources were going to break up communities, cause unemployment and encourage crime, ultimately leading to the total collapse of society. The way to avoid this doomsday scenario, the report concluded, was 'to create a society which is sustainable, and which will give the fullest possible satisfaction to its members'.[19] That could be achieved by converting to an economy of stock, stopping population growth and creating a new social system of decentralized small communities. *A Blueprint for Survival* inspired the *Manifesto for a Sustainable Society*, adopted by the Ecology Party of the United Kingdom, later renamed the Green Party.

The other publication—*The Limits to Growth*—had by and large the same message as the *Blueprint for Survival*; the difference lay in its method. The research, commissioned by the Club of Rome and conducted by a group of seventeen researchers, used a mathematical model of the world developed by systems scientist Jay Wright Forrester of MIT, which analysed the growth of five components—population, capital, food, non-renewable resources and pollution. Different scenarios were tested—'unlimited' resources are available through nuclear energy, pollution is capped by reducing CO_2 emissions and recycling, food increased by high-yield crops, and population controlled through voluntary birth control. The result was inevitably the same—the end of growth by 2100. 'The basic behavior mode of the world system is exponential growth of population and capital, followed by collapse.'[20]

If some believed that the solution to these problems was technology, for the authors that was only a distraction from the fundamental problem of growth in a finite world. What they proposed instead was a new model defined by a state of equilibrium in which population and capital would remain stable. 'We are searching for a model output that represents a world system that is: 1. sustainable without sudden and uncontrollable collapse; and 2. capable of satisfying the basic material requirements of all of its people.'[21]

By the 1970s, the word 'sustainable' had come to define more than a way to manage resources; it implied a way of living. The future was no longer relegated to the foresight of a few visionaries; it was in the hands of everyone. To expect that subsequent generations would enjoy at least the same prosperity as the postwar generation, a lifestyle based on unrestrained consumption and growth needed to be subjected to a radical revision.

The evidence presented by scientists, however, was not sufficient for politicians, nor for society. The *New York Times'* review of *The Limits to Growth* firmly dismissed the idea that stopping growth was the solution: 'To insist that pollution control is pointless without a halt to growth is not simply wrong; it is noxious.'[22] The journalists claimed that an earlier world model developed by Forrester, which did not lead to collapse, was purposely avoided in the book. Prices did indeed rise shortly after, when the members of the Organization of the Petroleum Exporting Countries instated an oil embargo against the countries that supported Israel during the 1973 Arab–Israeli War. The crisis that followed prompted the West to reduce its dependency on 'Arab' oil and explore alternative sources of energy. The discussion on sustainability gained momentum; curtailing growth, on the other hand, no longer seemed to be a priority.

In 1983, UN secretary-general Javier Pérez de Cuéllar invited former Norwegian prime minister Gro Harlem Brundtland to establish and chair an independent commission tasked with defining a global agenda for achieving sustainable development by the year 2000 and beyond. The UN was seeking greater cooperation in dealing with environmental concerns from all counties irrespective of their economic and social development. The World Commission on Environment and Development, or the Brundtland Commission as it became known, included politicians, civil servants and environmental experts from twenty-one countries, more than half of which were in the Global South. In its inaugural meeting in Geneva in 1984, the commission agreed to hold open public hearings throughout the world in which scientific institutes, non-governmental organizations, governments and individuals would be invited to express their views and advise on how to implement the environmental agenda. More than 10,000 pages of written submissions were reviewed.

In 1987, 900 days after its inaugural meeting, the commission published its report, *Our Common Future*, also known as the Brundtland Report. In the introduction, Gro Brundtland stated: 'What is needed now is a new era of economic growth —growth that is forceful and at the same time socially and environmentally sustainable.'[23] Unlike the authors of *The Limits to Growth* and *A Blueprint for Survival*, the report found the idea of economic growth essential for sustainable development. Gro Brundtland's team dismissed the doomsday predictions of the 1970s and put its faith in humanity's capacity to overcome limits through technology. Just as in the *New York Times'* critical review of *The Limits to Growth*, the commission believed that the market economy would discourage the exploitation of scarce resources before they would be fully exhausted. The major challenge in achieving a sustainable future, according to the commission, was poverty. 'Poverty reduces people's capacity to use resources in a sustainable manner; it intensifies pressure on the environment.'[24] Achieving a sustainable future therefore required the eradication of poverty and for that economic growth—which, during the 1980s, was declining for the first time since the end of World War II—was imperative. The discussion about sustainability was shifting its focus from the West to the Global South, and industrialized nations had a responsibility to help poor countries implement sustainable measures through international financial institutions. The global economy became the means to tackle planetary environmental problems. Sustainability entailed more than environmental concerns; it also involved economic and social issues.

Sustainability consolidated its place on the global political agenda in 1992 at the United Nations Conference on Environment and Development held in Rio de Janeiro, otherwise known as the Rio Earth Summit, where 175 countries signed a five-page declaration consisting of twenty-seven principles that would guide countries to a sustainable future. The declaration was accompanied by a non-binding action plan named Agenda 21. The Rio Summit put sustainability on national agendas for the years to come, but it did so on the terms of the private sector. Facing the prospect of environmental regulation for being the largest global polluters, transnational corporations took it upon themselves to make their businesses seem more sustainable and lobbied to play a role in defining Agenda 21. From potential subjects of critical evaluation, transnational corporations became partners in dialogue. Instead of being considered a problem, they were allowed to present themselves as the solution. The discourse on sustainability descended into a discussion about production efficiency, in which technology and innovation acquired the leading role.

Measuring sustainability

Agenda 21 acknowledged that the implementation of sustainable measures relied on data collection. Existing indicators such as the gross national product, measurements of resources and pollution were not considered adequate and new methods were deemed necessary: 'Indicators of sustainable development need to be developed to provide solid bases for decision-making at all levels and to contribute to a self-regulating sustainability of integrated environment and development systems.'[25]

In 1995, the Commission on Sustainable Development, tasked with implementing Agenda 21, approved the Programme of Work on Indicators of Sustainable Development. Under the coordination of its secretariat, various UN departments together with the World Bank, the World Resources Institute and Eurostat, among others, identified around 134 indicators and methodological descriptions related to each chapter of Agenda 21, published in *Indicators of Sustainable Development: Framework and Methodologies*. The indicators were divided into four categories—social, environmental, economic and institutional—and ranged from life expectancy at birth, emission of greenhouse gases and gross domestic product per capita to contraceptive prevalence rate, concentration of fecal coliform in freshwater and number of internet subscribers per 1,000 inhabitants. The guidelines were revised in 2001 and once again 2007, reducing the number of indicators to 96 and 50, respectively. At the 2015 United Nations General Assembly, the goals of Agenda 21 were reiterated and expanded to form the Sustainable Development Goals, colloquially known as Agenda 2030. As of 2017, the global indicator framework includes 231 unique indicators organized around 169 targets and seventeen goals, defined in Agenda 2030.

Since the UN's call to develop sustainable development indicators in 1992, many more indices have been proposed, including the Genuine Progress Indicator (1992), the Ecological Footprint (1996), Barometer of Sustainability (1997), the Living Planet Index (1998), environmental pressure indicators (1999), the Environmental Sustainability Index (1999), the Eco-Index methodology (2000), the Dashboard of Sustainability (2001), the G Score method (2001), the Environmental Performance Index (2002), the ITT Flygt Sustainability Index (2002), the Compass Index of Sustainability (2005), Baumgartner's Composite Sustainability Development Index (2005) and Singh et al.'s Composite Sustainability Performance Index (2007).

For the World Business Council on Sustainable Development (WBCSD), such methodologies paid too little consideration to the relation between the environment and the economy, and in 2000 the council created its own measurement tool, the eco-efficiency indicators. Introduced by Schmidheiny in *Changing Course*, the concept of eco-efficiency was defined by the WBCSD as 'the delivery of competitively priced goods and services that satisfy human needs and bring quality of life, while progressively reducing ecological impacts and resource intensity throughout the life cycle to a level at least in line with the earth's estimated carrying capacity'.[26] Calculating eco-efficiency was therefore the ratio between product or service value and environmental influence. The WBCSD's framework distinguished between 'generally applicable' and 'business specific' indicators based on eight principles 'which ensure they are scientifically supportable, environmentally relevant, accurate and useful for all kinds of businesses around the globe'.[27] The eco-efficiency indicators have been adopted by the United Nations Economic and Social Commission for Asia and the Pacific in line with its 'green growth' policy.

Since cities and buildings have been identified as major contributors to global CO_2 emissions and resource depletion, various indices have been advanced to measure urban sustainability: the Urban Sustainability Index, the City Blueprint approach, the EEA Urban Metabolism Framework, the European Green Capital Award, the European Commission's Green City Tool, the European Green City Tool, the European Green Leaf Award, the Global City Indicators Program, the Reference Framework for Sustainable Cities, the STAR Community Rating System, the Urban Audit, the Urban Ecosystems Europe–Informed Cities, among others. Some cities developed their own indices, such as the Sustainability Index for Taipei, Sustainable Seattle: Developing Indicators of Sustainable Community, and the Compass Index of Sustainability, developed for Orlando, Florida.

Besides BREEAM and LEED, a building's sustainability can be measured with, for example, HK-Beam (1995), Haute Qualité Environnementale (1996), Minergie (1996), CASBEE (2000), Green Globes (2000), the Tokyo Green Building Program (2002), CasaClima (2002), Green Star (Australia 2003, New Zealand 2006), the BCA Green Mark Scheme (2005), the Living Building Challenge (2006), DGNB (2007), QSAS (2007), Homestar (2009), Miljöbyggnad (2010), Fitwell (2016).

LEED is now complemented by additional rating systems administered by Green Building Certification Inc.: SITES, for sustainable landscapes (acquired in 2015); TRUE (Total Resource Use and Efficiency), for solid waste diversion performance (acquired in 2016); PEER (Performance Excellence in Electricity Renewal), for power system performance (launched in 2015); IREE (Investor Ready Energy Efficiency), for projects and investors to reduce transaction costs and engineering overhead (acquired in 2018), RELi, a resilience-focused rating system (launched in 2019), EDGE (Excellence in Design for Greater Efficiencies), for more resource-efficient buildings (launched in 2015), and WELL, a performance-based rating system for measuring features that impact human health and wellbeing (launched in 2014).[28]

Back to Earth

We are, meanwhile, forty-three years behind schedule in fulfilling the sustainable development goals of Agenda 2030.[29] Only Norway is on track to reach these targets. Most other countries have hardly surpassed the level they were at in 2015, with some countries, like Brazil and the US, even going backwards. Climate change remains a perpetually renewed promise. If all the targets submitted so far to the UN were fulfilled, carbon emissions should be reduced by less than one per cent by 2030.[30] As goals become more elusive, an ever-larger number of methodologies is being developed. On 22 September 2021, the World Meteorological Organization published a report on *Climate Indicators and Sustainable Development: Demonstrating the Interconnections*, which aimed to demonstrate that climate change affects sustainable development goals in a far greater way than Agenda 2030's Goal 13 for climate action did.[31]

Meanwhile, the value of the global sustainability market is only increasing. Green, social, sustainable and sustainability-linked bonds passed the half-a-trillion-dollar mark in 2021, while green stocks are in such demand that economists fear a green bubble.[32] Carbon emissions are a new commodity, traded in dedicated markets. Industrial companies finance reforestation projects in the Amazon in exchange for carbon credits that help them comply with carbon emission caps, or simply buy them from specialized retailers or companies that overachieve their sustainability goals. Sustainability consultancy has risen from the exclusive domain of boutique firms to a worldwide lucrative business led by Deloitte and McKinsey. A chief sustainability officer is the new must-have board member for a company to gain its competitive edge. Sustainability equals corporate responsibility.

Architecture's embrace of sustainability has moved beyond the circles of William McDonough and the like and is now well established in the mainstream. The design community is firmly in tune with the world's most urgent concerns and practices, and around the world companies take every opportunity to advertise their expertise in the field and commitment to the cause. The sustainability consultant is an indispensable piece of the design team puzzle for any serious project. The practice is breeding new concepts: green buildings, eco-friendly buildings, ecocentric design, environmentally friendly construction, ecotecture, passive houses, zero-heating buildings, zero-energy buildings, energy-plus buildings, carbon-neutral buildings, carbon sink buildings, circular construction, urban metabolism, metabolic vitalities. David Gottfried's dream to change the world through sustainable buildings is unfolding in front of our very eyes.

If there was ever the suspicion that adhering to a sustainable design ethic implies abstinence from the pleasures of life, Danish architect Bjarke Ingels reassures us that the two do not need to stand in opposition: 'Sustainability can't be some kind of a moral sacrifice or political dilemma, or even a philanthropical cause. It has to be a design challenge.'[33] Architecture can be not only good for the environment but also great for people to live in—an ethos that Ingels calls 'hedonistic sustainability': sustainability as a more enjoyable way of life, organized fun for the ecologically aware. If only.

wellbeing
noun [U]
UK /ˌwelˈbiː.ɪŋ/ US /ˌwelˈbiː.ɪŋ/
the state of feeling healthy and happy:

> *People doing yoga benefit from an increased feeling of well-being.*

5

All WELL

In July 1976, some 2,000 members of the American Legion, a non-profit US war veteran association, attended a three-day annual convention, held that year at the Bellevue-Stratford Hotel in Philadelphia. Built in the early 1900s in a high-rise version of French Renaissance, the hotel was one of the largest in the US, with 1,090 guest rooms. Some days after the convention, legionnaire Ray Brennan, a sixty-one-year-old retired Air Force captain, complaining of feeling tired, died suddenly of an apparent heart attack at home. Within a fortnight, a dozen more members died, each after having complained of tiredness, chest pains, and fever. One hundred and eighty-six legionnaires had fallen ill with pneumonia-like symptoms, in addition to several other people who had been near the Bellevue-Stratford Hotel—passers-by on the street, as well as the air conditioner technician.

As epidemiologists struggled to determine the cause, the outbreak entered the spotlight of the media. Bob Dylan wrote a song about it, "Legionnaire's Disease".

It took one more year and another outbreak for the source of the mysterious illness to be identified. A bacterium—named *Legionella* after the outbreak—was discovered thriving in the hot waters of building cooling towers. *Legionella* easily aerosolized and spread through air-conditioning ducts (even billowing outwards along the façade of the building), especially when sudden summer spikes in temperature caused the system to promptly swing into action. The Bellevue-Stratford itself did not survive the ordeal. In November 1976, some four months after the Legion convention outbreak, faced with abysmal occupancy rates due to the negative publicity, it closed its doors.

The consequences, however, went well beyond the Bellevue-Stratford. In 1983, the World Health Organization released a report suggesting that up to 30 per cent of new and renovated office buildings were subject to complaints about poor indoor air quality. This report coined the expression 'Sick Building Syndrome' (SBS), described as 'a collection of nonspecific symptoms including eye, nose and throat irritation, mental fatigue, headaches, nausea, dizziness and skin irritations, which seem to be linked with occupancy of certain workplaces'.[1] The WHO set a minimum 'density' of complaints for a building to be considered 'sick': 20 per cent of the building occupants must present symptoms.

Among further 'signs and symptoms' mentioned by an article in the NCBI/*Indian Journal of Occupational and Environmental Medicine* are 'sensitivity to odours', 'personality changes', but also 'palpitations, nosebleeds, cancers, pregnancy problems and miscarriages'. The authors added that 'the cause of the symptoms is not known. It reduces work efficiency and increases absenteeism. Most of the complainants report relief soon after leaving the building, although lingering effects of neurotoxins can occur.'[2]

While some registered grave concerns such as these, others expressed a rather flat befuddlement. The Transport Salaried Staffs' Association UK described SBS as 'a generic term used to describe common symptoms which, for no obvious reason, are associated with particular buildings'.[3] Swedish researcher and doctor Ake Thörn at the Karolinska Institutet noted a wide array of causes that have been linked with SBS: mechanical ventilation, particularly air conditioning, steam and evaporative humidification, volatile organic compounds, illumination, formaldehyde, dust, wall-to-wall carpets and textiles, noise, indoor temperature, work with photocopying, subordinate position in the work hierarchy, gender, tobacco smoking, atopic disease history and psychosocial discontent.[4]

Sick building syndrome was part of a constellation of complaints registered by white-collar workers—'office illness', 'humidifier fever', 'building-related illness', 'Monday Fever', 'occupational asthma', 'problem buildings', 'building-related occupant complaint syndrome', or 'abused building syndrome'. The American National Institute for Occupational Safety and Health received 150 complaints regarding workplace environmental quality in 1980—8 per cent of total complaints. By 1990, a staggering 52 per cent of complaints stemmed from concerns with 'sick' working environments.

Architecture for health

Vitruvius recommended that cities be created in places neither misty nor frosty. Le Corbusier was convinced of the importance of light in treating tuberculosis. In designing the Paimio Sanatorium, Alvar Aalto considered his architecture as a 'medical instrument'. The history of architecture betrays a long preoccupation with disease. It can even be argued that its sister discipline, urbanism, largely emerged as a measure of public health. Haussmann's transformation of Paris was effectively a public sanitation project, introducing the city to contemporary drainage and piping. Central Park was devised as necessary lungs to the city of New York. And works such as the Thames Embankment drained the marshy, purportedly cholera-ridden banks to introduce a modern sewage system. By 1884, a popular event such as the International Health Exhibition in London, popularly known as the Healtheries, featured a recreated seventeenth-century Old London street, where visitors could marvel at the cramped, insalubrious conditions of the unhealthy medieval city strolling along inns and taverns with 'darksome little upper rooms'.[5]

'When we learn to build our bodies with the same careful precision and the same scientific accuracy with which the modern builder constructs his houses, it will be possible to become healthy', wrote naturopathic doctor and *Los Angeles Times* health columnist Dr Philip Lovell.[6] The choice of Austrian-American architect Richard Neutra to design his family's Health House in Los Angeles in the late 1920s seems an evident one. Neutra saw architecture as a 'branch of preventive medicine' and argued that the survival of the human species depended on designers focusing on 'physiological space'. He established a regime of air, sun, movement and diet, which became the script for the Lovells' residence, whose swathes of glass façades melted the distinction between inside and outside, with nude sunbathing terraces extending from living spaces. Neutra vigorously resisted the 'corpulent excesses of ornament and curvature', adopting clinical white walls as a salutary measure.[7]

In a descriptive image, a picture of the steel frame of the in-construction Lovell House overlays a medical drawing of the human circulatory system.

Spanish flu: an end to the role of architecture

After World War I and the Spanish flu, vaccine development took off. In conjunction with the emergence of national health programmes, diseases which until then could not be properly treated soon were significantly reduced—yellow fever (1932), the flu (1937), polio (1952), measles (1963). Under the aegis of entities such as the Pan American Health Organization, the World Health Assembly and the World Health Organization, founded in 1948, came sweeping organizational efforts to snuff out diseases. Smallpox, a major contagion present throughout human history, was finally eradicated, the last naturally occurring case documented in Somalia in 1977. Sir Frank Macfarlane Burnet, the Nobel Prize–winning virologist, stated in 1962 that 'to write about infectious disease is almost to write of something that has passed into history'.[8]

With the success of medicine and public health initiatives, architecture seemingly no longer had a role to play, and its separation from health was consummated. In the sunset of the age of communicable disease, new agents began to enter the limelight: lifestyle-related chronic diseases such as diabetes, lung diseases related to smoking, cardiovascular disease related to sedentarism and overeating. These were conditions which buildings could not influence. Or could they?

Evidence-based design

By the mid-1980s an empirical methodology which gathered information on recorded psychological and performative reactions in human subjects opened a new way of looking at the impact of buildings on people: the field of evidence-based design (EBD). 'View through a Window May Influence Surgery Recovery Time', a 1984 study by Roger Ulrich, was foundational to EBD. Ulrich's study, carried out using recorded observations at a Pennsylvania hospital between 1972 and 1981, concluded that patients who had a view of nature suffered less complications, used less pain medication and were discharged sooner than those who had a view of a brick wall.

A plethora of research followed. Researchers observed the effects of concrete modifications on test subjects—artificial and natural lighting, noise, materiality of interior surfaces, presence or visibility of nature and vegetation. Aside from externally evident factors such as patient recovery time, they also noted things such as heart rate, muscle tension, skin conductance and pulse transit time—a technique which reveals systolic blood pressure.[9]

Evidence-based design is the half-sibling of the elder evidence-based medicine (EBM), which has been around, by some counts, since 1662, with the first controlled clinical trial on the effectiveness of bloodletting, described by Jan Baptist van Helmont: 'Let us take out of the Hospitals, out of the Camps, or from elsewhere, 200, or 500 poor People, that have fevers or Pleuritis. Let us divide them in halves, let us cast lots, that one half of them may fall to my share, and the others to yours; I will cure them without blood-letting and sensible evacuation; but you do as ye know ... we shall see how many Funerals both of us shall have.'[10]

EBM prescribes a 'conscientious, explicit and judicious use of current best evidence in making decisions about the care of individual patients'.[11] On the other hand, 'an evidence-based designer makes decisions—with an informed client—based on the best available information from credible research and evaluations of projects. Critical thinking is required to draw rational inferences from information that seldom fits a unique situation precisely.'[12] Whereas clinical EBM demands 'best evidence', EBD requests 'credible research'; EBM prescribes a 'conscientious, explicit, and judicious' method; EBD contents itself with drawing 'rational inferences'.[13] Unlike EBM, EBD typically operates on *existing* recorded information rather than carrying out its own experiments; the data it compiles does not necessarily correlate, especially as definitions such as 'open plan' or descriptors of a space such as 'large' are often not explicitly defined—or, as one advocate of EBD puts it: 'this calls for an exceptionally creative and ever-changing interpretation of new data.'[14]

Central to the worldview of evidence-based design was the seductive notion that the patient was being centred. No longer were the interests of the doctor, the technical staff or vast, faceless hospital bureaucracy allowed to govern; at long last, it was the *human*. If EBD was initially used in the context of hospital architecture, the notion that a building could impact its inhabitants' health meant that the technique soon found its way to a broader application.

If a technique like EBD could reveal which factors caused patients' recovery to speed up, it also, by implication, signalled the factors that caused patients—or, more generally, people in a variety of contexts—to remain sick for longer. It wasn't long before the methodology of EBD was transplanted from an exclusively medical context to a wider purview, expanding the notion of health from strictly physical factors, such as 'physiological stress indicators', 'cardio-metabolic risk factors', 'musculo-skeletal issues', 'skin/eye/nose/throat irritation', 'tiredness' and 'headache' to wider concerns, such as 'visual comfort', 'thermal comfort', 'unpleasant odour', 'overall comfort', 'sleep quality', 'mood', 'general annoyance', 'interpersonal relations' and 'perceived organisational support'.[15]

> The findings of the relationship between interior office space and health are threefold. First ... open-plan offices, shared rooms and higher background noise are the only features found to negatively affect health. Second, the other features analysed in the papers more often improve health than do nothing for health. Third, positive relationships with health are reported for all features of interior space. Features that encourage physical activity, including sit–stand and bike desks, and increased distances to communal facilities, are found to have a positive relationship with physical well-being. Similarly, the increase of (day)light and individual control and the presence of plants and outdoor views show positive results for both physical and psychological well-being. Small, shared rooms support social well-being.[16]

The same report concludes that an open workspace of six or more people tends to have a negative impact on health. More recent studies, such as the Danish 'Sickness Absence Associated with Shared and Open-plan Offices' have also suggested that certain building typologies can lead to absenteeism. Through a national survey of the Danish workforce, the study concluded that open-plan office workers reported the highest amount of sick days, followed by those sharing an office with two to six people. The most present—and therefore supposedly healthy—workers were those working in their own cellular offices.

Search inside yourself

Whereas EBD limited its findings to the health effects of the predominant work environment of the time—the office—multiple concepts have since emerged to take this causality further. As the notion of 'work' becomes more blurred, so does that of the work environment. The increasing elimination of temporal or spatial limitations on the concept of labour, either in the form of remote working, the elimination of fixed working hours or both, has come to imply that we work everywhere all the time. No longer is it just the modern office affecting our condition for a fixed eight hours a day, it is our environment as a whole that affects us, unrelentingly without intermission, built and beyond. When it comes to optimizing labour productivity, no external factor can be ruled out—including and particularly those factors previously considered unrelated to work.

An interesting situation presents itself. The greater the number of factors identified as impacting our health, the smaller, inevitably, the ability to fully control these. While, in theory, the impact of an individual office environment on the health of its users can still be subject to top-down design processes or guaranteed through implementing a defined number of (measurable) standards, such guarantees are not possible in the face of a theoretically infinite number of causes.

As the circumstances impacting our health (and productivity) become more ubiquitous and general, so does the language that is being applied to them. What used to be 'the office' has become 'the workplace'; what used to be our 'health' has evolved into our 'wellbeing'. Negligible as the shift in semantics might appear, an important change nevertheless is underway.

While understandings of being 'healthy' or 'well' might not significantly differ, the implied responsibility for either differs radically. Health, up to a point, can be attributed to external factors that individuals can expect to have taken care off *for* them; wellbeing, however, is largely a matter of individual choices *by* them.

Once rebranded as 'wellbeing', the notion of health moves from being a right to being an obligation—a non-negotiable condition in terms of labour participation, all the seemingly benevolent language notwithstanding. Mantras such as 'work hard, play hard' are little if not euphemisms to promote the unconditional, never-ending nature of work. The design of the modern office is an integral part of this. The more indistinguishable the conditions of work and leisure, the more surreptitiously working hours can be extended. To work best, we should never actually feel like we are working. Still, who's kidding who? Bootcamp or playground, despite the prevailing metaphors, the workplace is exactly what it claims to be: a place to work.

Not surprisingly, the sectors which have been at the forefront of the trend have also been the ones to take things further, beyond the immediate physical environment of work, into the incorporation of established health practices such as meditation and yoga. Spurred not infrequently by Silicon Valley wunderkinds, numerous movements-cum-businesses to this effect have emerged, either as corporate programmes or for individual consumption. At Google, Buddhist monk-cum-Google employee number 107, Chade-Meng Tan, launched *Search Inside Yourself*, a programme to help Google employees handle stress and defuse tense workplace emotions through techniques with names such as 'Stop, Breathe, Notice, Reflect and Respond'. Ariana Huffington developed GPS for the Soul and a slew of other apps such as Calm, Headspace, Breathe, 10% Happier, or BetterMe. The fitness industry has seen conventional sport and exercise spill over into a ubiquitous lifestyle concern, spawning a market of attendant apparel, *athleisure,* to stake its place in daily life.

In body, mind and spirit

The ultimate sector to benefit, however, has been the so-called 'wellness industry', which has made the notion of health as personal responsibility its founding principle. 'Wellness requires the proactive, voluntary engagement of individuals to adopt activities and lifestyles that move us toward an optimal state of wellbeing in body, mind, and spirit', states the Global Wellness Institute (GWI), a non-profit organization 'with a mission to empower wellness worldwide by educating public and private sectors about preventive health and wellness'.[17]

GWI defines wellness as the opposite end of an imaginary spectrum that starts with traditional health. While health remains the duty of doctors and clinicians, wellness is driven by self-responsibility. What that entails precisely, however, remains fuzzy. Definitions include anything from being in a good mood to a focus on the community, stress resilience, restfulness and joy. If healthcare cures, wellness is all that prevents us from becoming sick, and, like healthcare, it is subject to perpetual progressive insight.

Wellness is, meanwhile, big business. According to the GWI, the wellness market represents 5.3 per cent of global economic output; the world spends US$7 trillion on healthcare alone and spends an *additional* US$4.2 trillion on feeling well. This considerable piece of the economic pie is comprised of anti-aging products, healthy eating, fitness, preventive medicine, wellness tourism, complementary medicines, and the so-called 'spa economy'.

In declaring real estate its next frontier, wellness is also the domain where the notion of health and building are reconnected. At the time of writing, wellness real estate—for the most part, resorts and health 'villages' or housing—comprises 740 projects in thirty-four countries and is valued at US$134 billion. The two countries that by far lead wellness real estate are the US at US$52.4 billion and China at US$19.9 billion.

'The way our homes have been built in the last century is reinforcing lifestyles that make us sick, stressed, alienated, and unhappy', says the GWI. The institute cites a WHO report, whereby 23 per cent of global deaths (12.6 million deaths) in 2012 were due to 'modifiable environmental factors'. It goes on to cite a World Economic Forum study, according to which 'the cumulative global economic impact of chronic disease could reach $47 trillion by 2030'.[18]

The GWI is not alone in attributing disease to the built environment. Today, the list of illnesses caused by buildings and 'unhealthy' urban environments is matched by a slew of definitions and organizations for fixing them. The Healthy Building Index (HBI), Sustainable and Healthy Environments (SHE); Arc, Fitwel and WELL building standards for offices; Building Healthy Places for cities. When not fervently allying themselves with these entities, architecture offices have sometimes developed their own in-house programmes, such as Atkins's Putting People First.

What might some of these organizations recommend? The Building Healthy Places standard encourages urban designers to 'incorporate a mix of land uses', 'host a farmers market' and, just in case anyone was still ignorant of the matter, to 'select building materials that are not known to emit harmful toxins'.[19]

Yet the latest generation of healthy architecture seeks to go beyond the traditional tools of placemaking into a domain of quantified high-tech. The Villa Valencia by Location Ventures, which was set to open in 2021 but is, at the time of writing, still under construction in Coral Gables, South Florida—not too far from Seaside, the mecca of New Urbanism—intends to employ new technologies to guarantee that residents feel healthier. The sales pitch highlights 'hospital-grade air, energizing light and pollutant-free water to protect from contaminants, free radicals and aging'.[20] Residents can set alerts for certain allergens and be notified when these reach a critical level indoors, automatically turning on the HVAC to circulate fresh air. Together with landscaped rooftops and a hammam-style spa, the makers of Villa Valencia aim to create a home that makes you live longer.

'We're catering for a clientele, an affluent clientele, and what we want to provide—and I'm careful to say this, it's important —we want to create the healthiest home environment possible', says Rishi Kapoor, head of Location Ventures. 'What is wealth without health?'[21]

Wealth from health

Since 2014, Paul Scialla, former Goldman Sachs partner, has been focusing on the inverse: generating wealth from health. 'If you believe in the wellness trend, why not apply it to the largest asset class there is?' Scialla is the founder and CEO of Delos, the company that certifies the air quality at Villa Valencia.[22] Under the mantra of 'Innovate Well', Delos manages a number of real estate health labels and systems, the largest of which, the WELL standard, is now the most widely implemented certification for office buildings in the world. According to the Delos website, the beneficiaries of WELL and its sibling programmes number 3.4 million people and counting—a figure based on the cumulative surface of WELL-certified projects, 45 million square feet, at an occupancy of 150 square feet per person (200 projects, twenty-one countries). Who are the people behind WELL? The website mentions a team made up of triathletes, chemists, urban cycling enthusiasts, backyard gardeners, non-toxic product aficionadas and globetrotters, 'who problem solve, innovate and challenge the status quo to build a healthier world'.[23] In its report *Investing in Human Health*, Delos explains how the company aims to 'introduce preventative medical intentions into buildings' by merging medical science and building science:

> We spend around 90% of our lives indoors ... Modern living has had a massive, increasingly negative impact on our overall well-being, with sedentary lifestyles, unhealthy diets, pollution and nature-deprivation leading to increased health concerns, stress, social isolation and loneliness. Our efforts to maintain healthier lifestyles can be significantly undermined by seemingly subtle forces such as the quality of indoor air and water, thermal comfort and the quality of lighting. Indoor environments can influence almost every aspect of our lives—from our moods and energy levels to how well we sleep and how productive we are throughout the day.[24]

While the subjective quality of wellbeing cannot be pinned down, both the GWI and Delos seem to converge on one thing: being 'well' means performing better. The merely healthy 'feel better', whereas the truly well 'thrive'. The driven, self-responsible worker is the building block of a more profitable company. 'An investment in employee health and well-being is an investment in the health of the business', writes Rachel Hodgdon, CEO of Delos's WELL arm.[25] Or, more simply: 'Health is material to the bottom line.'[26] It's easy to see how wellbeing correlates with financial ramifications for employers —research cited by WELL indicates that workplace stress costs American companies US$300 billion annually from lost productivity, higher absenteeism, and medical and insurance expenses for stress-related illnesses.[27]

Together with the Mayo Clinic, Delos launched the Well Living Lab (WLL) in 2014, a test space where numerous environmental conditions can be simulated, along with evaluating their impact on humans. At 5,500 square feet, the lab features movable partitions that allow researchers to re-create several different interiors.

The lab has been fitted with sensors that monitor key environmental elements such as air quality, lighting, temperature, and humidity. The human data we collect includes cognitive performance metrics via a WLL designed application and subjective responses via surveys. Additionally, we collect physiological information via wearables devices and sensors including heart rate, skin conductance, sleep metrics (sleep stages, sleep interruptions, movement), skin temperature, etc. The lab currently has over 500 sensors in the inventory.[28]

A pilot study by the lab generated nine gigabytes of data per week, but it has yet to publish unique findings that incorporate data from its array of sensors. Delos has nonetheless advanced, in parallel with the lab, the WELL certification programme. WELL breaks a building down into a neo-Galenic collection of elements that must be kept at optimum levels to enhance indoor environmental quality. 'Air', 'Water', 'Nourishment', 'Light', 'Movement', 'Thermal Comfort', 'Sound', 'Materials', 'Mind' and 'Community' are the categories that must be addressed in order to ensure that a building can be considered healthy. For each element, Delos prescribes a set of 'Preconditions', which need to be met willy-nilly, and 'Optimizations', which are weighted in a point system and can be picked/combined by the building owner as they see fit.

Let's look at the fundamental prerequisites under the category 'Air'. 'This WELL feature requires projects to bring in fresh air from the outside through mechanical and/or natural means in order to dilute human- and product-generated air pollutants.'[29] Adequate ventilation is ensured by following existing standards such as ASHRAE (the American Society of Heating, Refrigerating and Air-Conditioning Engineers) or CEN (the European Committee for Standardization). Almost all the requirements are par for the course for any building constructed today; under the category 'Materials' it is required, for instance, to avoid the use of asbestos.

What about the WELL Optimizations? They could be 'something as simple as the intelligent placement of hydrating stations—where there's a visible sightline to water', explains Scialla.[30] Candidate projects can garner more points from a palette of improvements such as 'enhanced ventilation' by increasing outdoor air supply (maximum of three points); implementing 'demand-controlled ventilation' (maximum of three points) and 'advanced' air distribution where air diffusers are located no more than eighty centimetres from an individual user's head (maximum of three points). Other optimizations include 'circadian' lighting design to 'provide users with appropriate exposure to light for maintaining circadian health and aligning the circadian rhythm with the day-night cycle'. Or including visible stairs to encourage exercise or promoting mental health courses for employees.[31]

'Altruism' is also a WELL optimization. 'Research demonstrates beneficial health and wellness outcomes associated with acts of generosity and charity.'[32] Paid time off for charity work —sixteen hours a year—earns a project one optimization point. For further explanation of the varied vocabulary of WELL, there is a *Wellopedia*.

The final 'wellness score' of a building is calculated by dividing the achieved preconditions and optimizations over the total possible quantity. The minimum passing score is 5—which bags the Silver category (5–6 points). A score of 7 or 8 earns Gold, and 9 or 10 attains the vaunted Platinum status. The wellness score is calculated using the following equations.

FAIL: *if* $(PA/TP) < 1$ *then* $WS = (PA/TP) \times 5$

PASS: *if* $(PA/TP) = 1$ *then* $WS = 5 + (PA/TP) \times 5$

All Preconditions need to be met for a project to pass, but no Optimization requirements need to be met. Put differently, *any* building that follows existing American or European codes and

standards automatically qualifies as a WELL Silver building—
automatically, that is, once the fees are paid to Delos.

Interestingly, the requirements for daylight are remarkably
low: 30 per cent of all workstations should be within six metres
of transparent envelope glazing. The optimizations request, for
example, transparent envelope glazing giving access to views for
a minimum of 50 per cent of regular building occupants. Indeed,
WELL also suggests cost-saving methods that allegedly repro-
duce the positive aspects of a view outside; the guide offers tips
for bringing nature inside in the form of plants or water features,
listening to nature recordings on headsets or streaming videos
showing woods, lakes, flowers or other elements of nature.

In 2016, CBRE's Madrid office was the first project in Spain
to be awarded WELL certification. They addressed several of
WELL's concepts in varying levels of complexity—earning them
a Gold accreditation.

> In addressing the concepts of **air, comfort, light,** and **mind,** a
> biophilic theme of 'forest cabin' was introduced to the office.
> This scheme focused on providing dynamic and diverse spaces
> for different user needs. The office incorporates high levels of
> planting and a range of lighting options to address the need
> for task lighting as well as comfortable, ambient electric and
> natural light. The company now also provides a wide range
> of healthy food for its staff with all nutritional information
> available. This—alongside fitness classes such as Pilates, yoga,
> and a running club—address the concepts of **nourishment,** and
> **fitness.**[33]

CBRE saw a return on their investment in their Madrid offices-
slash-forest cabins within a year. They found that 80 per cent of
employees subsequently felt more productive, and 90 per cent
felt the WELL scheme had a positive impact on them.

In addition to the touted productivity benefits of a WELL
office, the standard also lends its aura to the hospitality sector,

enabling operators to charge a premium on minor adaptations to existing rooms. '*Choose* a Stay Well room', New Age guru Deepak Chopra instructs in a video ad on the website. 'Stay Well brings a holistic approach to your hotel experience, where medical science and technology meet to have a positive impact on you and your environment.'[34] This includes a branded shower infuser that lowers chlorine content in the water, aromatherapy that creates a 'relaxing, mood-enhancing environment', or branded StayWell air purifiers that reduce allergens, toxins, smoke and microbes in the air. (Do normal rooms in the same hotel, by implication, not filter any toxins from the air?) According to *Forbes*, the MGM Grand in Las Vegas manages to charge an extra 20 per cent on Stay Well rooms.[35]

Wellbeing seems to be doing well. A LEED evaluation of a 100,000 square-foot property costs US$13,000; WELL charges US$20,000 for the same property. The WELL standard is certified by the US Green Building Council, the same group that administers LEED certification. Unlike the GBC, which is a nonprofit organization, Delos is a for-profit company. Since 2014, Delos has raised US$237 million and was valued at US$800 million in early 2019, according to *Forbes*.[36]

Deepak Chopra is among the celebrities on Delos' advisory board. So are golfer Greg Norman and Leonardo DiCaprio, who describes himself as 'Sustainability Advocate, Actor'. Chopra, co-founder of the Chopra Center for Wellbeing, pitches self-styled 'quantum healing' and claims to be able to treat chronic disease, believing that a person may attain a state of 'perfect health', 'free from disease, that never feels pain, that cannot age or die'. Chopra is also an adjunct professor of marketing at Columbia Business School. The remainder of the Delos board is a mix of investment managers, hospital directors, politicians, real estate consultants, architects and sustainability advisors. Delos balances its American interests with significant overseas board members, whether a manager from Abu Dhabi–based Ventura Capital, which has invested in companies such as

Uber and Lyft, or the CEO of major Chinese real estate player Sino Ocean Group. Perhaps tellingly, WELL Living Lab is set to open a second space in Beijing.

Chopra and DiCaprio are not only board members at Delos, they have also been inhabitants of the foundation's own residences in Manhattan. These feature antimicrobial coatings on surfaces, vitamin C filtered showerheads, 'posture supportive' oak flooring, aromatherapy incorporated into the ductwork and, once again, circadian-adjusted lighting systems. These solutions are part of Delos' curiously named residential system, DARWIN. What better name for a system intended to make one the *fittest*?

(In)conclusion

Forty years after the term 'sick building syndrome' was coined, concrete pathological evidence has yet to be found. The prevailing stipulation—'building-related symptoms'—has meanwhile become the subject of some scepticism among scientists.[37] Perhaps it is worth noting that at the time of the WHO report in 1983, buildings were heavily affected by energy conservation measures in response to the oil crisis of a decade earlier. In the US, the previous standard ventilation rate had been rationed down to one third the recommended amount. A less medical, more architectural approach—operable windows?—might have sufficed. Will Covid-19 serve as a wake-up call?

Singapore's greatest virtue is in how it reinvents itself. But the city state should be careful about the need to balance urban renewal with the conservation of built heritage. **Oslo** has made it easy for young technology businesses to set up. These future technology businesses are sorely needed to plug the gap as Norway's fossil fuel industry gradually fades away. **Brisbane's** new under-river rail link and airport extension are finally taking shape. Combined with sunny climes and the low cost of living, more and more people are calling this city home. **Fukuoka** has given a helping hand to families and is now working on making life easier for start-ups and trying to relax restrictions on visas for entrepreneurs from overseas. We will be watching closely. **Auckland** has restricted foreign ownership of property in a bid to solve the city's affordable housing conundrum. Meanwhile the much-needed airport overhaul gives a warmer welcome to visitors. **Dusseldorf** has plenty of pluck if you are looking for fine dining, a vibrant nightlife, and world-class architecture. Alas, the city should rethink its opening times to serve an increasingly international populace. Despite 'gilets jaunes' and the Notre Dame blaze, life goes on in **Paris**, and it's not bad. In preparation for the 2024 Olympic games, the Grand Paris Express will add 200 kilometres of new metro lines. In **Barcelona** emotional and ideological fissures connected to Catalan secessionism have hampered progress. One cause for celebration though, is the green redevelopment of Glòries Tower. For all **Kyoto's** stunning temples, the city has a modern side, with ambition, plans and subsidies to nurture start-ups and small manufacturing ventures into world-class businesses. Although **Hong Kong** may be known for its spectacular cityscape, locals zealously guard public parks, the green lungs of the densely populated metropolis. Property prices are rising exponentially, though. **Vancouver's** housing market has cooled down and new sectors are reinvigorating its economy, from its nascent technology hub to a growing number of independent firms. **Amsterdam's** transformation from an international village to thriving metropolis continues apace. The opening of the North–South metro line has finally linked up the rest of the city with the north. Ever since the revoking of the city's strict lockout laws, endlessly sunny **Sydney** is the city to come to for an outdoor lifestyle. Global talent continues to arrive to **Stockholm**, attracted by abundant nature, charming neighbourhoods and enviable work–life balance encouraged by various government measures. **Melbourne** is on track to become Australia's largest city by 2030. Despite its booming population, it has shunned some of the less charming hallmarks of global cities—namely chain stores and uninspiring mega malls. **Lisbon** has seen an economic boost in recent years, along with a dropping unemployment rate, the city itself is imbued with a new energy. Its enviable cultural agenda spans everything from art to music festivals. **Berlin's** economy is flourishing, but if the city is to retain its identity in the long term, its leaders will need to find creative solutions that balance the need for growth with the preservation of open spaces. Wider pavements, communal benches and complementary phone charging points in the metro are signalling **Madrid's** efforts to make Spain's busiest city more accommodating. Why not add a city beach on Madrid's Rio? **Hamburg** offers much more than the architectural beauty that it's praised for. With the deepening of the Elbe river to boost traffic to the port, it looks like the future is bright for this transport hub. Over the past year, **Helsinki** unveiled its impressive central library and long anticipated contemporary art museum. New low-cost housing units are popping up in the suburbs, too. In **Vienna** major urban planning and transport projects are ticking along, yet tradition is writ large here: Centuries-old green parks and vineyards offer respite within city limits, and higher education is nearly free—reflecting a long-standing focus on intellectual pursuits. As ever, **Copenhagen** boasts a young and vibrant population attracted by the capital's influential design industries, first-rate education facilities and a mouth-watering culinary scene. More affordable homes are needed to meet the demand. There are many reasons why **Munich** is a great place to live—incomes are high, prices are reasonable and things work as they should. However, opportunities and spaces for artists, designers and creative entrepreneurs have been somewhat stifled due to the housing bubble. Eat a bowl of Ramen, or try some dazzling multi-course kaiseki, shop at Uniclo or buy a bespoke suit—**Tokyo** has always been a city of high and low, and the mix is still intoxicating. What continues to impress most of all, though, is that for its size and pace, this is a megapolis for the heart, where small courtesies still matter. **Zurich** gives you the feeling that all is right with the world, from its clean-swept streets to punctual transport. On a bright summer's day, you'd be forgiven for thinking you've landed in the med, thanks to lively pavement cafés serving aperitifs, and people hopping into the lake for a midday swim between meetings. Restaurants and bars should stay open later, though. So many seem to call it a night far too early.[1]

liveability

noun [U] mainly UK (also mainly US livability)

UK /ˌlɪv.əˈbɪl.ə.ti/ US /ˌlɪv.əˈbɪl.ə.t̬i/

the degree to which a place is suitable or good for living in:

Fixing the walkways will enhance the liveability of the area.

We are going to find scary things happening in terms of the liveability of the planet.

6

Vancouver™

Since 1998, global human resources consulting firm Mercer has
been publishing an annual list of the most liveable cities in the
world. It does so by assessing the living conditions of more than
450 cities worldwide, 231 of which make it to the actual list.
The list aims to provide internationally operating companies
with a basis upon which to establish hardship allowances for
employees sent on assignments abroad.

The evaluation happens along a fixed set of criteria—thirty-
nine to be precise, grouped in ten categories: 1) the political and
social environment, assessing factors such as political stability,
crime and law enforcement; 2) medical and health considerations, looking at medical supplies and services, the prevalence of
infectious diseases, potable water, air pollution and the presence
of dangerous animals or insects; 3) public services and transportation, listing electricity, water, public transportation and traffic
congestion; 4) consumer goods, considering the availability of
food and daily consumption items; 5) recreation, looking at the
availability of restaurants, theatres, cinemas, sports and leisure
facilities; 6) the sociocultural environment, weighing (media)
censorship and limitations on personal freedom; 7) the natural
environment, focusing on the city's record of natural disasters;
8) housing, assessing the standard and cost of (rental) accommodation, household appliances, furniture, and maintenance
and repair services; 9) the economic environment, considering
currency exchange regulations and banking services; 10) education, focusing on the availability of international schools.

Each of the thirty-nine criteria receive marks on a scale of o to 10. The average of the marks within each group of criteria determines the eventual mark for each of the ten categories. Marks per category are then weighted according to perceived importance. Not all categories weigh equally. The further a category is down the list, the lower its share in the weighted average between categories. The top four: the political environment, health considerations, public services and the availability of consumer goods account for respectively 23.5, 19, 13 and 10.7 per cent—two thirds of the overall scoring—while the remaining categories each contribute less than 10 per cent.

Depending on their overall score, cities emerge as 'ideal' (80–100 per cent), 'acceptable' (70–80 per cent), 'tolerable' (60–70 per cent), 'uncomfortable' (50–60 per cent), 'undesirable' (less than 50 per cent) or 'intolerable' (no percentage given), which is further explained as there being 'few', 'some', 'certain', 'substantial', 'extensive' or 'insurmountable' challenges to liveability.

In 2019, Vienna emerged as the winner for the tenth year in a row, on account of its security, good public transport and diversity of cultural and recreational facilities, while war-torn Baghdad emerged as the world's least liveable city—even if the city had shown 'considerable improvements compared to the year before'.[1]

Mercer's Quality of Living Survey is one of three major city liveability rankings. The others are the annual Global Liveability Index by the Economist Intelligence Unit (EIU), *The Economist*'s research and analysis division, published since 1999, and the 'most liveable cities index' by lifestyle magazine and media brand *Monocle*, published since 2008.

Both indices use comparable methods to Mercer's. The EIU's Global Liveability Index is based on thirty criteria grouped in five (weighted) categories: 1) Stability (25 per cent), 2) Culture and Environment (25 per cent), 3) Infrastructure (20 per cent), 4) Healthcare (20 per cent), 5) Education (10 per cent). Recently, the percentages have been adjusted upon the insertion of a sixth category: Spatial Characteristics, which includes a city's green space, sprawl, natural and cultural assets, as well as its connectivity and level of pollution. As of 2012, spatial characteristics account for 25 per cent of the overall score, reducing the relative weight of the original five categories.[2]

The method underlying *Monocle*'s list is somewhat more frivolous. It does not group criteria under a limited number of categories but relies on a fixed number of indicators, such as policy developments, international connectivity, religious and sexual tolerance, healthcare, public transport, levels of violent crime, business conditions, the cost of living (from the rent of a three-bedroom house to the price of a cup of coffee), urban design, quality of architecture, environmental awareness, access to nature and the number of sunny days. With each new addition, fresh indicators are added to the list, including 'nocturnal metrics' such as closing times of clubs and the number of restaurants which still serve a good meal after 22:00.

Despite the differences in measuring methods, the lists tend to feature the same cities. In 2019, Vienna topped not only Mercer's rankings but also the EIU's index, while it occupied a comfortable fourth place on *Monocle*'s top ten; Zurich, the number two on Mercer's list, featured first on *Monocle*'s; Copenhagen featured on all three lists; Munich featured on two out of three, as did Vancouver and Melbourne. Such homogeneity may have a lot to do with the sources upon which they relied: 'in-house experts' in the case of the EIU, 'correspondents' in the case of *Monocle* and expatriates already living in the reviewed cities in the case of Mercer.[3] In all three cases the 'objective' data concern the subjective opinions of individuals. Mercer even relies on the opinions of those who chose their city based on Mercer's prior lists. The mechanism which ensues is predictable: Favourable reviews attract more expats; more expats generate more favourable reviews, and each list becomes input for the next. Last year's liveability rankings barely differed from those of the previous year, or the year before that.

Liveable, livable, vital

The term 'live-able' was first recorded around 1610, in England, where towns suffered severe outbreaks of the bubonic plague. It was used in the now-obsolete sense of 'likely to survive' and generally had to be accompanied by the prefix 'un'. The first time the word 'liveable' occurred in modern literature was in Jane Austen's *Mansfield Park*, used in relation to the proposed modification of a country estate: 'There will be work for five summers at least before the place is liveable.'[4] No longer does the term relate to the possibility of life itself; it is now applied to the habitat *in which* we live and the possibility of its constant improvement.

The term entered discourse on the city with Lewis Mumford's essay 'Restored Circulation, Renewed Life', published in 1956: 'If the city is to become *livable again*, and if its traffic is to be reduced to dimensions that can be handled, the city will have to bring all of its powers to bear upon the problem of creating a new metropolitan pattern.'[5]

Like Austen, Mumford applies the term to the human habitat. The word 'again', however, signifies an important difference. With Mumford, 'livable' is a condition presumed to have once existed but is now lost—the cause of which, he leaves little doubt, is attributable to rampant modernization and mass ownership of the automobile which has deformed cities beyond recognition. No longer is the term 'liveable' weighed against the forces of nature and decay; it is the technologies unleashed by humanity itself which must be mitigated.

The same polemic also underlies Jane Jacobs's *The Death and Life of Great American Cities*, which appeared five years later. Where Mumford used the term 'livable', Jacobs speaks of 'urban vitality', defined as 'something that the plans of planners alone, and the designs of designers alone, can never achieve'.[6]

Jacobs's mistrust of the powers of planning owes much to her own personal history as a resident of Greenwich Village—a neighbourhood subject to plans for a large overhaul by then-New York City planning commissioner Robert Moses. The potential uprooting of the area in which she lived, which would have undoubtedly followed Moses's plans, inspired the early activism upon which much of Jacobs's later life and work are founded. She (successfully) campaigned against plans for a lower Manhattan expressway, which would have passed directly through Soho and Little Italy and, after being arrested in 1968 for inciting a crowd at a public hearing on the project, she continued her efforts to protect existing neighbourhoods in her adopted home of Canada, where she joined the opposition to the Spadina expressway along with the associated network of expressways planned in and around Toronto.

Maoists, Communists, pinkos, left-wingers and hamburgers

Such controversies prevailed in many North American cities at the time. But it was not New York City or Toronto but Vancouver in which Jacobs's views—which until then had taken the form of protesting pending developments—first resulted in a propositional alternative.

By the early 1960s, Vancouver had grown into Canada's third largest city. In the decade before, it had witnessed a sprawl of suburban development and massive increase in car use. To cope with the city's increasing transportation problems, the ruling Non-Partisan Association (NPA), which had been governing the city since 1932, had created the Technical Committee for Metropolitan Planning in 1954, which, together with several neighbouring municipalities and the provincial government, had submitted the so-called *Freeways with Rapid Transit* report in 1959: a US$450 million master plan for freeway construction across the Vancouver region.

However, with no central authority responsible for working

on the city's freeways—decision making was divided between the federal, provincial and civic governments—the city council was left on its own to raise funds for the freeways. Hoping to secure funding from the federal government, which was charged with building the Trans-Canada Highway, the city prioritized the construction of a freeway that would connect the downtown with the highway. Incidentally, the freeway would cross Chinatown and Gastown, two neighbourhoods that qualified for urban renewal funding from the provincial and federal governments.

Rather than solving traffic problems, the approach caused political turmoil. Leading figures in the city began to speak out against the proposal. At the University of British Columbia, an array of guest lecturers highlighted the negative impact of freeways on cities, essentially turning Jane Jacobs's *The Death and Life of Great American Cities* into a manifesto of popular resistance against the plan. The idea of a freeway across Vancouver's Chinatown also met with opposition from the business community—Chinese businessmen pointed out that the freeway would suffocate their businesses while the Chinese Property Owners Association emphasized that Vancouver's most important tourist attractions would be lost.

In the spring of 1967, in a meeting at the headquarters of the Chinese Benevolent Association, a broad coalition against the city council was formed. When, despite promises to re-evaluate the freeway's planned route, the city decided to press ahead regardless, protests broke out. A march took place through the neighbourhood, participants dressed in black for the occasion. The protests were supported by the city's upper-income groups, too. A stinging article in the *Vancouver Sun* protested vehemently against the city council's plans, raising the argument of lost liveability: 'The democratic process has been thwarted … by people who are planning a city the majority of citizens don't want to *live* in.'[7]

In the North America of the late 1960s, protests to new freeway plans were by no means a rarity. In the US alone, at least twenty-six cities experienced such protests, including New York, Boston, Chicago and San Francisco. Activists in the last city saw some success—the proposed Embarcadero Freeway was stopped.

Encouraged perhaps by the success of those protests, opposition against Vancouver's freeway plan persisted and the first results seemed to manifest in the fall of 1967, as the federal government announced that it would no longer contribute to Vancouver's freeway through Chinatown. Following the announcement, support within city council for the plans began to wane. Other organizations in the city, too, such as the Board of Trade, the Building Owners and Managers Association and the Downtown Business Improvement Association, took a stance against the municipality. Later that year, the Great Freeway Debate ended with Vancouver's City Planning Commission chairman resigning, leaving the plan to be scrapped in January of the next year.

A freeway construction programme remained on the political agenda, however. But with city hall unable to muster either the cash or a political majority to execute such a programme, responsibility was transferred to the federal and provincial governments, with most of the money coming from Ottawa. Initially hesitant to adopt the new plans given the previous experience, the city council accepted the proposal in 1969. New protests erupted and the city was eventually forced to suspend its decision. Asked for a reaction, then-mayor Tom Campbell blamed 'Maoists, Communists, pinkos, left-wingers and hamburgers' for having sabotaged the plans.[8] Notwithstanding his feisty rhetoric, the federal government formally struck down provincial commitment to the project in 1972.

The Electors' Action Movement

The success of the protests put an end to forty years of uninterrupted rule of the NPA. In 1967, on the heels of the Great Freeway Debate, a new local political party formed: The Electors' Action Movement, operating under the acronym TEAM. TEAM had been the initiative of two key players in the freeway protests: University of British Columbia geography professor Walter Hardwick and Art Phillips, head of a successful Vancouver investment firm. Their liaison—a joining of academic and business forces—produced a centre-left political party which aimed to appeal to persons of all political ideologies. NPA's handling of the freeway crisis had helped profile TEAM as the progressive, more community-oriented alternative. Having successfully contested the outcome of earlier municipal elections, both Hardwick and Phillips had occupied seats on the council since 1968. Their position as aldermen proved a perfect platform to promote their political programme. In the municipal elections of 1972, TEAM won a majority on the city council and Phillips was elected mayor of Vancouver.

Once in power, TEAM made some radical changes. No longer was city-owned property sold off to private parties, using the proceeds to keep taxes low. Instead, Phillips created the property endowment fund, where all revenue from the city's extensive holdings was deposited, invested and used for the benefit of the city. This paved the way for a much greater role of the city in its physical planning. For the inner city, a new planning policy was introduced with a focus on mixed land use, social diversity, environmental awareness and public housing. Freeways and high-rise buildings were out; neighbourhood planning was in.

A first opportunity to implement those policies presented itself in the form of the redevelopment of the industrial lands on the south shore of the False Creek inlet, directly adjacent to

Vancouver's downtown. With a freeway crossing no longer on the cards, the TEAM-dominated council saw the opportunity to transform the area, previously assigned for industrial use, into a showcase of their new urban planning policies. Under federal funding a master plan was developed for a mix of one third each of non-market rental housing, co-ops and condominiums. Social interaction between residents was promoted via the introduction of ample outdoor public space (including the public use of the waterfront) and indoor public facilities such as the False Creek Community Centre. Several renowned local architecture firms were involved in the design of the individual buildings, which, through a gradual increase in height of the buildings—from three- or four-storey townhouses near the water to eight-to-twelve-storey buildings further away—maintained mountain views for all residents, irrespective of tenure. To add further credibility to the new development, Mayor Phillips and his family moved to a condo in the fledgling neighbourhood themselves.

After Phillips left office in 1976, False Creek South became the calling card of Vancouver's new urban planning policies. Until Phillips's tenure, the default growth model for North American cities had been the creation of suburbs, connected to a monofunctional downtown area via an ever-expanding freeway network. False Creek proved that cities could also grow inward. As a mixed-use, mixed-income neighbourhood designed by multiple architects, geared towards pedestrians and achieving a high density without a single high-rise building, False Creek was the place where the ideas of Jane Jacobs, the woman who had inspired the protests, acquired physical form: a built critique of the failed urban renewal policies of the 1950s or, in the words of Art Phillips: 'A place which brought people in, not threw them out, making the city a place to enjoy, where people wanted to *live*.'[9]

The liveable region 1976/1986

The political shift which had taken place in Vancouver in the early 1970s was mirrored by a similar shift on a provincial level. In 1972, British Columbia had taken a significant step to the left with the election of its New Democrat provincial government. The presence of likeminded governments at the municipal and provincial levels created significant momentum for the revision of planning policies, not just in the city of Vancouver, but across the entire region.

From just over half a million inhabitants in the mid-1950s, the Vancouver region was expected to grow to about 1.5 million by the mid-1980s. Sandwiched between the mountains and the water, the region's natural setting, the land available for new developments was limited—a situation which was exacerbated by British Columbia's policy of protecting agricultural lands. Since 1968, local governments had been informally collaborating under the umbrella of a new regional authority: the Greater Vancouver Regional District (GVRD). In 1969, the GVRD further integrated its approach by appointing its first regional director of planning, Harry Lash.

Having averted the doom of a yet further expanded freeway network, Vancouver's new political ideology spelled 'liveability' and was embraced equally by the municipal and provincial governments. It is not unequivocally clear where precisely the term originated or who first used it. In his book *Planning in a Human Way*, from 1976, Harry Lash attributes the first use of 'liveability' as a planning term to Alan Kelly, the regional board's chairman from 1972 to 1975. Kelly allegedly launched the word at a weekend seminar of the GVRD Planning Committee in 1970 as the new goal for Greater Vancouver: 'The Livable Region Plan would be a map showing where housing, commerce and industry would go; where the roads, transit links and parks should be located; and it should show where those things should be built.' In that meeting, Kelly said that 'the expert's job was to produce the map, maybe with some explanation; then, since no one in his right mind would expect everyone to agree that what the planner had produced was good, the planner had better produce the map in jig time so that the arguments could start and the board decide who was right'.[10]

Despite the bravura with which it was launched and the unquestionable status it was beginning to acquire, nobody at the time seemed to know precisely what liveability entailed, let alone how to implement it in the form of planning policies. In Lash's words: 'Perhaps if we could decide what we needed to measure this would suggest the kind of proposals that we needed ... But we passed it by, because we found that indicators by themselves were a dead end; they did not lead to the formulation of a Program Plan.'[11]

In the end, the conclusion was predictable. 'Quite suddenly, early in 1972, we did discover the signpost: find out from the public what *livability* means; abandon the idea that planners must know the goals first and define the problem; ask the people what *they* see as the issues, problems and opportunities of the region. We decided to go to the public and simply raise the question of *livability*, with as little "inspiration" from ourselves as possible and see how they responded.'[12]

In short: liveability is what *the people* say that liveability is. Following that conclusion, Lash led an extensive public consultation process which would last until the end of his tenure in 1975. The findings of this process are laid down in the report which would serve as his main legacy: *The Livable Region 1976/1986: Proposals to Manage the Growth of Greater Vancouver*. The report made five recommendations on how to achieve a liveable region: residential growth targets in each part of the region; a balance of jobs to population; regional town centres; a transit-oriented transportation system; and regional open space. It painted an optimistic picture of the cumulative result of these measures in its description of the region in ten years: 'Greater Vancouver is an enjoyable place to *live*. No other

Canadian metropolitan region is so close to mountains and water, farmlands and forests, yet so cosmopolitan in its variety of culture, educational opportunities, and business activities ... During the past decade we have seen great changes in this beautiful area. There has been a burst of new restaurants, shops, and theatre and music groups. The Vancouver Region is a *livelier* place than it was ten years ago.' It also nonetheless included a note of caution: 'However, the region's fortunes may not last for much longer'.[13]

The report's horizon qualifies as uncanny foresight. In 1986, to celebrate its centenary, Vancouver hosted the World Expo on Transportation and Communication. What should have been (or perhaps was) a defining moment in the recognition of Vancouver as a global city also revealed the first cracks in the city's policies of considered urban growth and carefully guarded social diversity. In the run-up to Expo '86, pressures on the housing market resulted in the eviction of 500 to 850 residents from the Downtown Eastside and surrounding areas. That same year, the old Non-Partisan Association regained control of the city council for the first time since 1972.

Living first

The next ten years marked a period of strong growth for Vancouver, both economically and demographically. From a population of just under 1.5 million in 1986, the GVRD crossed the 2 million mark shortly before the turn of the millennium. An important driver of the district's accelerated growth was immigration from overseas—particularly from Hong Kong, uncertain about its future after its reversion to China. Like Hong Kong, Canada was part of the former British Empire and Canada's relaxed immigration policies, coupled with a large existing Chinese community in the city, made Vancouver an obvious choice for relocation.

Anxieties about the consequences of such growth manifested as early as September 1990, in *Steps to a More Livable Region*, the sequel to *The Livable Region 1976/1986* and the preparatory report for *The Livable Region Strategic Plan* from 1996. The report describes Vancouver's liveability as a composite of its natural setting, its unique and envied lifestyle, and a thriving economic and cultural life—all under a perceived threat of an imminent 'degradation which plagues so many large cities in the world'.[14]

No longer was liveability something that needed to be discovered, it was something that needed to be protected from unfettered population growth. The answer was sought in the development of 'a compact metropolitan region', one that preserved the area's natural setting and farmlands at all costs.

The scarcity of land that inevitably followed, coupled to a steady decrease in the number of persons per household, created considerable pressure on the housing market. Despite the enhanced regional cooperation, most of these pressures landed on the city of Vancouver itself, which, through its 'living first' policy, had opened the gates for extensive residential developments in its downtown area and waterfront land following the dismantling of the Expo '86 fairgrounds.

Under the subsequent pressure of the 1990s property boom in Vancouver, it became common practice among developers to go after plots they suspected the city might be open to allowing a higher quantum of residential development than strictly prescribed by the zoning plan. This so-called 'rezoning' of plots proved highly profitable—both for developers and for the city itself, the latter claiming its fair share of the upturn in land values (sometimes taking as much as 75 per cent). Moreover, the city could insist that new developments created certain 'planning gains' in the form of public facilities like libraries or museums or that developers contribute to the financing of public spaces and public parks.

Although arguably a conflict of interest, the 'joint property venture' between the public and private sectors benefited both sides. In the 1990s, Vancouver's downtown successfully absorbed a population increase from 40,000 to 80,000—all of which occurred in the context of a total city population, which, even after the increase, didn't equal more than 600,000. In fact, the approach worked so well that a new set of problems was created in its wake. The 'planning gains' did not cover the provision of affordable housing or commercial uses. As a result, Vancouver's city centre came to suffer a desperate lack of both, with many of its wealthy residents having to commute to the suburbs for work while the downtown area increasingly needed to be serviced by less wealthy residents travelling in from their affordable homes in the suburbs. Twenty years after its introduction, Vancouver's 'living first' policy had turned it into a strange, inverse echo of the scenario it had so desperately tried to avert in the 1970s and against which the whole idea of liveability had been predicated.

Liveable, sustainable, affordable

In 2005, a moratorium was announced against further high-end residential development in Vancouver's downtown. To spread development more evenly across the city, then-mayor Sam Sullivan launched the concept of 'EcoDensity', in which future residential growth was to be accommodated via a series of dense urban developments around transport nodes across the city.

According to the *EcoDensity Initiative Document*, the approach would 'reduce housing costs, increase housing choice, reduce urban sprawl, alleviate traffic congestion and reduce fossil fuel emissions, preserve industrial and agricultural land as well as green space, make transit and community amenities more viable, keep taxes low and the local economy vibrant and healthy, reduce Vancouver's ecological footprint and keep Vancouver's high rank in the quality-of-life surveys'. EcoDensity was to make Vancouver 'more livable, sustainable and affordable' and ostentatiously ticked all the boxes required for doing so.[15]

To its critics, however, it was more of the same: a mere veil to yet more luxury high-rises encroaching on the city. Many of the proposed high-rise clusters replaced existing single-family homes, with many local communities complaining they had not been properly consulted. Once again, planning had become a top-down affair, dictated by infrastructure and the demolition of existing neighbourhoods. Forty years after the Great Freeway Debate, Vancouver was back to square one. Jane Jacobs died in 2006, the same year the initiative was launched.

Top of the list

That year, for the fourth time, Vancouver earned the top position on *The Economist*'s Global Liveability Index. It would retain that position for another five years, until 2010. However, in the 2000s the notion of what constitutes liveability had come to differ significantly from the early seventies. No longer was the term associated with the counterculture that had flourished in the context of protecting local communities. Liveability had become mainstream.

And with that came a distinct twist on the post-materialist values that had once underlaid the term. Inevitably, these values were rediscovered as a source of material value, ready to be marketed and consumed. Liveability inevitably comes at a price. In the time that Vancouver held the top spot on the EIU liveability index house prices in the city increased by more than 300 per cent, more than they had in all the previous century. The cost of living proved directly proportional to the city's increased liveability.

The fact that the term 'liveability' had never been defined properly in its own right—initially it was oppositional to prevailing powers, but once these had been overturned, it was left for 'the people' to define—made it a welcome hobby horse for almost any political course. (After the NPA reclaimed power in 1986, use of the word only intensified, despite the massive increase in house prices.) In retrospect, the meaning of the term evolved neatly in line with the political leanings of Vancouver itself—at first activist, then participatory and finally consumerist. Liveability was whatever Vancouver said it was. The term and the city had become synonyms, making any further search for meaning redundant. When it comes to Vancouver occupying the number one spot on *The Economist*'s list, one wonders: was Vancouver a reflection of the properties on the list, or was the list a reflection of the properties of Vancouver?

All three former directors of Vancouver's planning department—Ray Spaxman, Ann McAfee and Larry Beasley—enjoy active retirements in the private sector, selling 'Vancouverism' to municipalities globally as a formula to emulate. With their city consistently occupying a high position on liveability rankings, the facts speak loudly. What the Guggenheim was to Bilbao, *The Economist*'s Global Liveability Index is to Vancouver: the validation for a city, seemingly emerging out of nowhere, to suddenly qualify as a global model. The home of a world-class museum ... the world's most liveable city—captured in objectively verifiable data, be it visitor numbers or expatriate feedback, the success is beyond question.

Conclusion

Given the astounding popularity of liveability rankings over the last two decades, no longer do Mercer, *The Economist* or *Monocle* hold a monopoly over the idea. Their number now runs into the dozens: the EU Urban Audit, the OECD Better Life Index, the Livability Index by the American Association of Retired Persons, the Property Council of Australia's Australian City Liveability Index, the Healthy Livable Communities

Urban Liveability Checklist, and so on. Singapore has started its own Centre for Liveable Cities to convince the world that it is not Vancouver but Singapore that exemplifies liveability. The Urban Living Index does the same for Sydney and in 2019, the LivCom Award for the most liveable city in the world went to the German city of Münster.

The more such rankings proliferate, the more their core purpose—to relate the idea of liveability to measurable properties—becomes questionable. Their sheer number invalidates their aura of objectivity. Pending the criteria invoked, any city can top any list at any time. Increasingly, the lists feel like the self-portraits of cities looking to make their mark. Take the properties of a (any) city, package those as key factors for liveability and the same city emerges as the fair winner.

Once again, the idea of liveability becomes elusive. The dismissal of material, and therefore *measurable*, facts of life in the 1970s led society to project the idea of measurement on immaterial values in the decades after, only to find out that the value of these was, indeed, immeasurable. Somewhere in the early nineties—nobody knows exactly when—the term 'standard of living' gave way to 'quality of life'. More recently, though, the EIU renamed its quality-of-life index to the where-to-be-born index. Whereas people's standard of living was something that could be raised, the latter notion has an almost fatalist connotation. It seems that the more things we can measure, the fewer we can change.

Postscript

In 2017, the City of Vancouver introduced the Empty Homes Tax on properties that stand vacant more than six months. Ever since the city ranked top of the Liveability Index, property speculation and condo ownership by absentee landlords have become major problems. In 2018 the Downtown and West End districts reached record-high vacancy rates—5 and 6 per cent, respectively—safeguarded for residential uses as part of the city's mid-eighties 'living first' policies. The net revenues of this tax are to be invested in the construction of affordable homes.

The spirit of Jane Jacobs is still out there, if only because of her seventy-year-old son Ned, who acts as a tour guide through what is left of Mount Pleasant—once a bustling working-class neighbourhood, it is presently one of Vancouver's most sought-after places for real estate investment and unaffordable for anybody on a median salary. Twenty years into the new millennium, living and liveability are two very different things.

As both an overarching idea and a hands-on approach for improving a neighbourhood, city or region, **placemaking** inspires people to collectively reimagine and reinvent public spaces as the heart of every community. Strengthening the connection between people and the places they share, **placemaking** refers to a collaborative process by which we can shape our public realm in order to maximize shared value.[1] **Placemaking** is a core value of sustainability. Maintaining liveable urban environments is essential to protecting natural resources and the landscape from further destruction.[2] **Placemaking** is both a process and a philosophy. It is centred on observing, listening to, and asking questions of the people who live, work and play in a particular space in order to understand their needs and aspirations for that space and for their community as a whole.[3] **Placemaking** is the way all of us as human beings transform the places in which we find ourselves into places in which we live. It includes building and tearing buildings down, cultivating the land and planting gardens, cleaning the kitchen and rearranging the office, making neighborhoods and mowing lawns, taking over buildings and understanding cities. It is a fundamental human activity that is sometimes almost invisible and sometimes dramatic. **Placemaking** consists both of daily acts of renovating, maintaining and representing the places that sustain us and of special, celebratory one-time events such as designing a new church building or moving into a new facility.[4] **Placemaking** always begins with the community and the users. **Placemaking** capitalises on a local community's assets, inspiration and potential, with the intention of creating public spaces that promote people's health, happiness and wellbeing. **Placemaking** is extremely context specific, presents itself in many different forms and may be implemented at various stages of an urban development process.[5] **Placemaking** does not have a determined final image; it begins by doing small interventions (quick wins). Users begin to organize and provoke new interventions. You're just never done.[6] **Placemaking** comes in more than one variety. In most instances, **placemaking**—what I would call '**standard placemaking**' —is an incremental method of improving a location over a long period of time through many separate small projects or activities ... However, **placemaking** can also be called upon to create and implement larger-scale transformative projects and activities—converting a location in a short period of time into one that exudes a strong sense of place and serves as a magnet for people and new development. Complete streets, form-based coding, and New Urbanism foster this kind of **placemaking**.[7] **Creative placemaking** is a differentiator that can produce distinctive and successful real estate projects and can turn developments into destinations.[8] The notion behind **creative placemaking** is not simply about undertaking **placemaking** in a creative way, but rather it is about leveraging art and culture as a catalyst for urban and community development.[9] Applying **creative placemaking**, design principles and community engagement can be used to uncover unique ways to create a new node in real estate redevelopment projects. When properly applied, **creative placemaking** strategies can help differentiate a real estate development project while simultaneously addressing social, economic, environmental and other challenges.[10] **Digital placemaking** is the integration and appropriate and strategic use of technology to support, enhance or accelerate **traditional placemaking** practice, the strengthening of community connection through collaborative group process to shape the public.[11] **Tactical placemaking** is an increasingly popular approach to planning that emphasizes testing projects through a series of phases rather than constructing projects straight from the drawing board. Common examples include crosswalks, pedestrian plazas and bicycle lanes.[12] Architecture is about turning spatial challenges into **placemaking**.[13] Successful master planning is rooted in **placemaking**, community and an understanding of the daily journeys, interactions and opportunities for connection. When you're building a community, everything matters, especially the natural.[14] Designing to strengthen and support communities is all about creating places that bring people together. A key approach to achieve this is through **placemaking**, which is to create quality places that spark an emotional attachment for people and that thrive when users have a range of reasons to be there.[15] **Placemaking** is about understanding the complex layers of the city, linking them in unexpected ways and creating new narratives to allow curiosity and desire to interlace with the physical space, both existing and new. In this experiential design process, the role of the placemaker is that of a creator, bringing new ideas, as well as a mediator, linking existing processes and people.[16] There's so much more to **placemaking** than creating seating or painting murals. There is huge financial gain.[17] In terms of area development, **placemaking** is important not only in the planning and the development phase, but during the management phase as well. Measuring impact is a crucial part of this 'place management' or 'place keeping'.[18] At the simplest level, it shows that spending an extra 50 per cent on **placemaking**, in markets where this leads to a higher sales value and faster sales rate, can boost the land value by around 25 per cent, depending on required rates of return.[19]

placemaking
no entry found

7

Here nor There

People tend to sit where there are places to sit.
William H. Whyte, *The Social Life of Small Urban Spaces*

They thought he was onto something—and he was.
Fred Kent on William H. Whyte

'Not space but place...' The words mark a distinct turn in the conversation, which, until they were uttered, had progressed broadly along rational lines. I'm tempted to frown, raise an eyebrow, but I'm mindful not to. This is the client speaking, and clients' directives make sense by definition—even, or particularly, when they don't.

A short lull in our exchange allows me to take stock of the surroundings: a former industrial yard cleared of most of its buildings, about to be redeveloped. I see space, lots of it, but no place. Given the bland development formula about to be applied: a mix of commercial and residential uses, 60 per cent at market rate, 40 per cent affordable—if it's up to the client team, a lot less of the latter—it is difficult to imagine any sense of place materializing here. I try to think of a way to voice my hesitations, dissuade my client from entertaining unrealistic ambitions, make him see the charm of other qualities—celebrating the vastness of the space perhaps, the uninterrupted horizon or relying on the few remaining artifacts to give character to the area...

'It's all about placemaking!' he decidedly interrupts my thoughts. 'If we want to make this a successful development, placemaking must be at the heart of our strategy!'

Another silence ensues—a potentially more embarrassing one this time. The client has spoken, even if only in the form of a single word. Inevitably, it is this word that will determine our joint undertaking from here—his vision, my brief. A comprehensive briefing package is not to be released until the week after, but I already know that nothing in the official documents is likely to shape the objective of our work more decisively than the magic, one-word formula that has just been shared. There is only one problem: I have no idea what he means.

What *is* placemaking? It is the first time I hear the term, yet something in my client's confident manner tells me that it won't be the last. I'm at a loss on how to respond. In the end, I opt for a knowing look, followed by an approving nod.

A nod is all he needs: 'What, am I rambling? I'm sure you're more than familiar with this stuff, you must have pulled this off a thousand times before. Placemaking must be second nature to you.'

Look it up

I have a confession to make. More than ten years after that conversation with my client, I am no clearer. I must have heard the word more than a zillion times, meanwhile, but I still have no idea what placemaking is. Its prolific use has done little to undo my lack of understanding. Then again, I'm not sure if anyone does. The term, for one, does not feature in any English dictionary and, until recently, was underlined by Microsoft Word as a spelling mistake. Entering the term 'placemaking' into the Oxford English Dictionary delivers no match. Instead, the OED comes back with a question. 'Did you mean: policymaking; lovemaking; placating; placeman; plateauing?' I did not. The

Cambridge English Dictionary gives a similar result, albeit that it generates a slightly wider range of alternative search suggestions: policymaking; clockmaking; placating; caretaking; deal-making; lacking and leaking. www.thesaurus.com politely offers to set me straight: 'Please make sure that you spelled the word correctly…' The site even offers a recommendation for a grammar coach to improve my writing.

I opt for a Google search. The first two results literally echo my question: 'What is Placemaking?' A promising beginning. Still, the sources (the architectural media) make me sceptical of the type of information I might receive. I click on Wikipedia instead, which comes with a warning: 'the content of this article has multiple issues; it reflects a personal view or argument and needs additional citations or verification.' I continue, undeterred. 'Placemaking', I learn, is

> a multi-faceted approach to the planning, design and management of public spaces. Placemaking capitalizes on a local community's assets, inspiration, and potential, with the intention of creating public spaces that promote people's health, happiness, and well-being. It is political due to the nature of place identity. Placemaking is both a process and a philosophy that makes use of urban design principles. It can be either official and government led, or community driven grass roots tactical urbanism, such as extending sidewalks with chalk, paint, and planters, or open streets events such as Bogotá, Colombia's Ciclovía. Good placemaking makes use of underutilized space to enhance the urban experience at the pedestrian scale to build habits of locals.[1]

The definition is accompanied by an image of someone playing a public piano, 'effectively adding to the sense of place of Washington Square Park, Manhattan, New York'.

I have my definition at last, even if it comes with a lot of words (145) and includes a somewhat clumsily inserted (evidently necessary) example of a bike path in Bogotá. 'Placemaking',

according to Wikipedia, operates on the basis of clearly established principles: 'the community always knows best (1);
placemaking is not about design but about places (2); it should
make and act on observations (3); it is a group effort (4), an
ongoing process (5) which requires vision (6) and patience (7).
It should ignore naysayers (8); form should support function
(9) and money should not be an issue (10).'

I am secretly beginning to grow fond of a world in which
placemaking rules. Yet there is one principle on the list that
I struggle with—that of 'triangulation', defined as 'the strategic placement of amenities, such that they encourage social
interaction, and are used more frequently'. For example, if a
children's reading room in a new library is located next to a
children's playground in a park and a food kiosk is added, it is
presumed that more activity will occur than if these facilities
were located separately. The principle seems strangely at odds
with the others. As one of the underlying principles of an activity that emphatically claims not to be about design (principle 2),
triangulation does seem to assume a remarkable level of control.

The explanation of the principle is curiously operational.
What it has in common with the other principles—and with the
article as a whole—is that rather than tell us *about* placemaking,
it mostly seems to argue *for* placemaking but without properly
revealing why. The object of worship (place) finds proof in
the worshipping (placemaking). There are eleven principles in
total. Without triangulation, that number would have been ten,
which, given placemaking's near-biblical ambitions, would seem
more appropriate.

www.pps.org

The list of placemaking principles comes with a link to another
Wikipedia page, which, in turn, redirects me to www.pps.org,
the official website of *Project for Public Spaces*, which refers

to itself as a 'Project for Sunday afternoons, walking your dog, running into friends, people watching, and losing track of time; Project for observation, experimentation, collaboration and common sense, as well as Project for making places for and by everybody'. The site gives information about conferences (International Placemaking Week), grants (for community placemaking), courses (Making Placemaking Happen) and projects (for a centre for transformative placemaking). The website even features a placemaking handbook, titled 'How to turn a Place around'.

The placemaking handbook starts by telling us 'what makes a place great'. It does so in the form of a diagram. 'Place' occurs at the intersection of four main sectors of influence: uses and activities (illustrated with a pictogram of musical notes), access and linkages (a tram carriage), comfort and image (a bench) and sociability (a speech bubble). There are two further concentric bands, one with adjectives indicating the qualities which make a great place. A great place must be 'fun, active, vital, special, real useful, indigenous, celebratory, sustainable, safe, clean, green, walkable, sittable, spiritual, charming, attractive, historic, diverse, cooperative, neighborly, proud, interactive, welcoming, connected, readable, convenient and accessible'. More intriguing is the second, wider concentric ring, which indicates the larger societal factors upon which these depend, such as rent levels, traffic conditions, demographics and general condition of the built surroundings, among other elements.

The diagram is notably ambiguous. Should we read it inside out or outside in? Do the adjectives arise as a result of placemaking (at the heart of the diagram) or are they the product of external factors (the outer, largest circle of the diagram)? Are the adjectives an effect *of* or a condition *for* placemaking? Placemaking, it seems, is an effort that is at once modest and megalomaniacal—a curious case of both omnipotence and impotence. Cause and effect seem engaged in a never-ending dance that intentionally defies resolution. To 'make a place' supposedly requires but small interventions—a piano, a bench, a small artwork—yet its ultimate success depends on a level of control over long-term, large-scale conditions beyond the powers of even the most top-down planning apparatus. The piano or society at large?—that is the question.

Pps.org helpfully includes a page titled 'What is Placemaking?' The answer is broadly in line with the definition I found on Wikipedia, listing the same eleven principles with verbatim the same explanation. Wikipedia has included its disclaimer for good reason: the page on placemaking, it turns out, was created in 2006 by Nick Grossman, one of PPS's staff, who also wrote a number of articles on PPS's website. The fact all my information so far is from the horse's mouth serves as a slight consolation.

Who are the people of PPS? Pps.org reveals a young, predominantly female (9/2) staff. (Nick Grossman, I discover, is no longer working there.) This balance is gradually inverted as we go up the ranks—to affiliates (2/2), board members (2/4) and ultimately to the founders (1/2): geographer Fred Kent, his then-partner, environmental designer Kathy Madden and Steve Davies, 'an advocate for livable communities'.

Fred Kent

Notwithstanding the courteous alphabetical listing on the organization's website, it does not take much browsing to discover that by far the most eminent of PPS's founders is Fred Kent, abundantly present on the internet in the form of written articles (by and about) and YouTube videos. According to his résumé, Fred Kent has taken over half a million photographs of public spaces and their users, either published in scientific magazines or posted via his Twitter and Instagram accounts.

Fred Kent seems like a really nice guy. Travelling over 150,000 miles each year, Fred offers technical assistance to communities and gives major talks across North America and internationally. Fred is also intimately involved with the expansion of placemaking into a global agenda, helping to achieve a level of international engagement that rivals other major international development efforts.[2] According to a 1978 *Washington Post* article covering the emerging portfolio of PPS, he and his group spent hours in the street carefully counting pedestrians and people in vehicles to get a feeling for what can't be quantified—to get the 'sense' of a place.[3] A story in the Professional Convention Management Association's magazine *Convene* relays the story of PPS's first project. PPS had been founded in 1975 and was operating rent-free in the Rockefeller Center, which had given PPS the space in exchange for advice on how to improve the public space in front of the centre. Rockefeller's staff was looking for a way to discourage people from sitting on the ledges of the planters and asked Fred what kind of spikes would do the job. To their surprise, Fred proposed making seating even more comfortable by adding benches and luring even more people, who might also be tempted to shop at the centre's stores. That is exactly what happened and the Rockefeller Center 'has probably become the best square in the world—almost by coincidence and a little bit of luck', Kent concluded.[4]

PPS did not start using the term 'placemaking' itself until somewhere in the 1990s, but much of the underlying thinking can be traced to earlier days. Fred Kent studied geography at Columbia University, taking anthropology classes with Margaret Mead and lessons in economic development from Barbara Ward. Mead and Ward, each in their own way, held critical views of the relation of the West to the rest of the world, Mead in the field of human relationships, Ward in terms of wealth distribution, viewing a more equal sharing of prosperity as a way towards collective economic progress. Ward's argument soon came to include the conservation of planetary resources. Her book *Only One Earth: The Care and Maintenance of a Small Planet* is generally seen as a precursor to the Club of

Rome's later *Limits to Growth*. In the winter of 1969–1970, Fred Kent was among a group of Columbia University students to coordinate the New York edition of Earth Day—triggered by a massive oil spill in Santa Barbara the year prior, the day aimed to raise public awareness of the world's environmental problems. In New York alone, more than 100,000 people took part, forming the largest gathering in the nationwide celebration. The event relied strongly on the support of then-mayor John Lindsay—the organizers were allowed to use the mayor's offices and staff—and received a big boost from his decision to close off Fifth Avenue for cars, enabling marches and picnics in the blocked-off streets.[5] In Fred Kent's own words: 'Earth Day transformed New York—literally. We turned Fifth Avenue into a "place" by eliminating traffic from 59th Street to Union Square. People poured out of offices and apartments to walk down the middle of the most important street in New York on a beautiful spring day to draw attention to protecting the environment in cities.'[6]

Between 1970 and 1972, Kent worked as programme director for Mayor Lindsay's Council on Environment. Lindsay's time in office (1966–1973) marked a shift away from Robert Moses's highway projects towards a focus on urban life. Lindsay started to preserve the city's scarce green spaces and orchestrated the creation of lot-sized neighbourhood parks—the so-called vest pocket parks, scattered throughout the five boroughs.[7] It was during his days as a civil servant that Fred Kent met William Whyte, his later mentor. William H. Whyte, described on his Wikipedia page as a people watcher, claimed to have developed a method to analyse the substance of urban public life in an objective and measurable way; this was implemented in the Street Life Project, which put a cadre of researchers onto New York City's streets to observe pedestrian flow and record patterns of interaction. In 1972 Kent became a researcher for Whyte's Street Life Project, tasked to study a two-and-a-half block-long stretch along Lexington Avenue with a camera. Kent spent a summer photographing the streets, becoming an expert at what he came to call the 'ergonomics of place'.[8] As part of the experiment, he studied the different ways men and women use public spaces (men cluster around entrances; women are more particular about the places they frequent), the strange rites of girl-watching and the spots where couples are likeliest to kiss (in locations more prominent than private). They also outlined the 'three-phase goodbye', and they discovered that pedestrians give wider berth to a woman in makeup and a dress than to the same woman in a ponytail and sweats.[9]

Since his inauguration into the Street Life Project in 1972, Fred Kent has come a long way. His CV boasts a milestone achievement in New York City practically every year: from helping to turn around Exxon's Mini Plaza with the addition of movable chairs and tables (1978) to widening the sidewalk on Sixth Avenue by three feet (1990); from developing the Allen Street Mall vision with Asian Americans for Equality (2004) to a Kellogg Food and Fitness Initiative for work around food access and walkability in the city's most underserved neighbour-hoods (2007–2009), and from launching the By the City/For The City digital Placemaking app to working for the September 11 Memorial to analyse and develop recommendations for visitor experience. In 2015, after opposing the Brooklyn Bridge Park Pier 6 redevelopment plan, Kent was evicted from the proceedings of a Brooklyn Bridge Park community meeting. Crowds chanted 'let him speak!' but the residential tower that so irritated the local community was eventually built in 2019.

Fred Kent does *not* like architects. And his disputes with them have a long history: a 1993 *New York Times* Week In Review profiled Fred Kent as 'One Who Would Like To See Most Architects Hit The Road'.[10] In indicating all the things that place-making is not—top-down, reactionary, design driven, a blanket solution or quick fix, exclusionary, car-centric, one-size-fits-all, static, discipline driven, one-dimensional, dependent on regu-latory controls, a cost/benefit analysis, project focused—PPS's website is pretty clear who has created the very problems place-making is fixing. Most memorable is his exchange with Frank Gehry during the Aspen Ideas Festival of 2009. Kent introduces his group as 'the department of corrections' which needs to go into cities all over the world to fix public buildings and spaces after the work of iconic architects has run its course. 'I think I travel as much as you do', he concludes, prompting Gehry to respond: 'Not my places you ain't fixing…'[11]

Professional placemakers

Kent versus Gehry … it seems an odd paradox. Yet the same theme dominates the next stop on my exploration: a book titled *Placemaking: The Art and Practice of Building Communities*. I've decided to break out of the closed internet loop and resort to Amazon to order some literature on placemaking in print. Neither of the book's two authors are known to me, but it is the only title that comes up without an adjective. Before familiarizing myself with healthy, creative, or Latino placemaking, it seems sensible to focus on its art and practice.

According to the publisher, the book 'addresses the current need for design professionals (placemakers) to work with constituents in creating space, and provides excellent advice to help designers understand the human requirements which are at the core of their profession'. The book's mission as identified by the publisher—to educate designers/placemakers—seems strangely at odds with the definition the authors themselves give of placemaking: 'Placemaking is the way all of us as human beings transform the places in which we find ourselves into places in which we live. It includes building and tearing buildings down, cultivating the land and planting gardens, cleaning the kitchen and rearranging the office, making neighborhoods and mowing lawns, taking over buildings and understanding cities.'[12] According to the authors, placemaking is an activity engrained in every human being; it is what each of us does on a daily basis and therefore hardly the result of education or professional training. It is thus almost by definition a *non-professional* activity.

Quoting Heidegger, they continue: 'As long as humans have dwelled on earth, we have found ways to make our places meaningful.' However, 'Over the course of the last century we have been losing our ability to make our places locations for dwelling.'[13] The book seems to argue for participation en masse, viewing work on the built environment as a kind of permanent DIY. All the more bizarre, therefore, is the solution offered: Turn the practice concerned with making places into the full-time vocation of architects, planners, building tradespeople, facility managers, interior designers, engineers and landscape architects. To rescue the world from the hands of professionals, you need professionals. The authors resolve the contradiction by stating that the most important task for professional place-makers is the creation of 'dialogic space'—spaces that 'enable and facilitate others who also wish to work on places'.

I have lost the plot. I am only on page six.

Bryant Park

I decide to shift focus to the implications—to understand the concept not through miscellaneous attempts at definition, but through what has actually been created in its name.

PPS's first major feat in terms of a physical legacy dates back to the early 1980s, well before the term 'placemaking' had been introduced, in the form of its work on Bryant Park. This is a small public park in midtown Manhattan, on the corner of Sixth Avenue and 42nd Street, across from the New York Public Library. At the time, the park was mainly a hangout for drug addicts and dealers and therefore pretty much a place to avoid. In 1980, with the support of the Rockefeller Brothers Fund, the

Bryant Park Corporation (BPC) was founded—a not-for-profit, private management company expressly created to improve the image of the park and change its use. At the request of BPC, PPS provided recommendations on how to give physical shape to the transformation.

Their proposed interventions included installing two food kiosks at the main entrance, opening up the other entrances, removing shrubbery that prevented people from seeing into the park, and the placement of a large number of movable bistro chairs. In tandem, the BPC put forward several new activities, such as chess, pétanque, ping-pong, an outdoor reading room, and a small carousel. BPC also launched a number of events, such as daily lunchtime performances and an outdoor movie series to attract users to the park at night. An elaborate planting strategy—several perennial beds, a large number of planter containers and a signature two-acre lawn—was rolled out to complete the park's makeover, in combination with the installment of new lighting both in the park and from a nearby rooftop to improve the sense of nighttime security. A restaurant and outdoor café were built on an empty area at the rear of the New York Public Library.

Interesting is the spin PPS itself puts on the transformation of Bryant Park: 'Additional revenue-generating activity includes a sponsored free skating rink and a holiday market, both of which attract activity at night and in winter—a time when, in the past, *no one* would be found in the park.'[14] A choice of words that is strangely at odds with the statement of Adrian Benepe, the city's parks commissioner, that the park 'was overrun with drug dealers and other frightening activity'.[15] The brave new world that ensues after placemaking evidently does not count junkies and drug dealers as people.

Still, in terms of the mission the BPC and PPS had outlined for themselves, Bryant Park is undoubtedly a success story. Architecture critic Paul Goldberger describes the mood of the upgraded park as 'easy, relaxed, chatty, like the square of a small town, with security guards who smile and say, "Good morning" and maintenance workers pick up papers as soon as they fall to the ground'.[16] The park's renovation was lauded as the Best Example of Urban Renewal by *New York Magazine* and described by *Time* as a 'small miracle'. It also received the Design Merit Award from *Landscape Architecture Magazine* in 1994.

According to a 2008 *New York Times* article, the park, which at one point was considered a symbol of the fall of New York City, meanwhile has '4.2 million yearly visitors that spend anywhere from a few minutes to three hours in the park; the median stay is 35 minutes'. In fact, the success of Bryant Park is such that it is at risk of being the victim of that same success. The same *NYT* article quotes Daniel Biederman, one of BPC's founders, as saying: 'We are making plans to remove some ivy beds to accommodate more tables and chairs. Five hundred new green chairs and 100 more tables have been ordered, and there are plans to order several hundred more chairs … Sometimes people are standing and waiting for chairs now.'[17]

Biederman's words betray an undeniable mercantile instinct. And his instinct is increasingly recognized as time goes by. In 1996, Bryant Park received an Award for Excellence from the Urban Land Institute. In its award citation, ULI wrote: 'The success of the park feeds the success of the neighborhood.'[18] By 2003, Bryant Park's office rents had come to outperform the rest of Midtown Manhattan, only to receive another boost from the construction of One Bryant Park, a fifty-one-storey, 2.1 million-square-foot office tower on the northwest corner of the park, anchored by the Bank of America. In the words of Mary Ann Tighe, a chief executive of the New York tristate region at CBRE: 'Bryant Park is now established as a hub of top-priced office space, and the park itself is the nucleus of this submarket.' In 2012, Bryant Park office rents were the highest in all of Midtown.[19]

Campus Martius

While PPS had been able to maintain a certain discretion about the private interests served by its interventions in its work for Bryant Park, such discretion became significantly harder in the context of the job they took on almost two decades later. In 1999, PPS was approached by Detroit 300 Conservancy, a private non-profit organization (apparently owing its name to the film *300*), to work on Campus Martius, a run-down space in the middle of an intersection in downtown Detroit. PPS was asked to put forward ideas for how the park might function, as well as a schematic plan with suggestions for park design. Its efforts helped trigger a significant raising of the area's profile, with Detroit mayor Dennis Archer announcing that Campus Martius was going to be 'the best park in the world' and businesses such as Compuware and Quicken Loans moving their headquarters to Campus Martius shortly after. In 2010, Campus Martius received national recognition as the first-ever winner of the Urban Land Institute's Amanda Burden Urban Open Space Award.

However, this was not solely to PPS's credit, as the company's involvement in Campus Martius ended in 2000 with the selection of landscape architecture firm Rundell Ernstberger Associates (REA) to design the new park space. However, the group renewed its affiliation in 2013, when they were asked to propose a placemaking vision for all of downtown Detroit's public spaces by the Downtown Detroit Partnership (DDP), a miscellaneous group of businesspeople, philanthropists and government officials, which since 2009 had also included Detroit 300 Conservancy. The DDP's mission was 'to advance Detroit by driving engagement, development and programs that benefit businesses, residents and visitors throughout the Downtown's urban core'.[20]

On the DDP's executive committee were Quicken Loans CEO Dan Gilbert and Christopher Ilitch, youngest son of billionaire businessman Mike Ilitch, CEO of Ilitch Holdings Inc.

In 2013, the latter unveiled plans to revive the area between Detroit's now-thriving mid- and downtowns under the name District Detroit: a fifty-block sports and entertainment neighbourhood, anchored by the 20,000-seat Little Caesars Arena. The Ilitches promised US$200 million for the development of the neighbourhood while the city contributed US$324 million in public tax money for the construction of the arena (money that, as highlighted by an HBO documentary, would have otherwise gone towards Detroit schools).[21] To fund the regeneration, the Ilitches were handed an additional tax break from local leaders in early 2014, the same year that Detroit slid into the nation's largest-ever municipal bankruptcy. Mike Ilitch's estimated net worth at the time was US$5.1 billion.

When the 20,000-seat arena opened in 2017, the US$200 million promised by the Ilitches had been consumed by the development of two parking decks, a Google office building and a headquarters building for the Little Caesars Pizza fast food chain (a company owned by the Ilitches). On blocks where historic buildings once stood lay surface parking lots that charged up to US$50 per spot. At the same time, the additional public funds required to allow the developer to meet his contractual obligations were estimated at US$74 million.

The Ilitches admittedly played a cunning trick: neighbourhood development had served as a pretext for the acquisition of public money, which was then mostly spent on giving the arena its much-needed parking facility. As a business proposition, the arena had come to replace the District. According to an article in *metrotimes*: 'It's walkable, livable, mixed-use, and world-class. The only thing is that it doesn't really exist.'[22]

The Ilitches were likely forgiven their trick because of the benefits it brought to multiple parties. The arena project had come to play a pivotal role in the further gentrification of Detroit's central districts. One party that certainly benefited was Ilitch's fellow DDP board member Dan Gilbert, owner of multiple properties in the neighbouring downtown district and CEO of Quicken Loans, which had been one of the first companies to relocate its headquarters to Campus Martius.

Three years after the launch of PPS's public space vision in 2013, the scarcity of housing—strategically exacerbated by the district's lack of real development—had caused median home sale prices in the downtown district to double.[23] Gilbert had been acquiring property there from 2011, paying as little as US$8 a square foot. By 2017, he owned five buildings surrounding Capitol Park as well as the site of the old Hudson's department store. The location of Gilbert's properties broadly coincided with the area covered by PPS's placemaking vision. And indeed, from 2013, Gilbert's real estate company, Rock Ventures, closely collaborated with Kent's team on an extensive effort to fill the public spaces and areas around Quicken-owned buildings with people and events. In Gilbert's own words: 'Fred specializes in something called "placemaking" ... The goal here is to make downtown Detroit nothing less than an attraction and destination for both residents and visitors alike.'[24] The love was reciprocated by Kent himself: 'Dan has a vision of a city that is more like Paris than anywhere, because historically Detroit was defined by Paris. Now, if you can reach to Paris, you're reaching to the best of the best.'[25]

'The Post-Apocalyptic Detroit', a *New York Times* article from 2014, captured the ambiance created by the men's combined placemaking effort:

> Jaunty music plays in parks and outside office towers. On sidewalks, there are lounge chairs and giant 'Alice in Wonderland' chess pieces. In front of the Qube, in Campus Martius Park, nearby companies have set up a café; there is ice skating in the winter, and in warmer months there are Motown Music Fridays, table tennis and a beach. All of this is an attempt to recreate at least a bit of the energy and confidence that pervaded the area back when Detroit was a city of two million and produced most of the world's cars.[26]

The journalist shared his first-person account of being confronted with a phenomenon he viewed with apparent bewilderment, including a relay of his encounter with his source, Dan Gilbert. 'He told me: "Here, man, oh, man, it's a dream. Anything can be created in Detroit. Down here, like in basketball, you can create your own shot." Investing in Detroit, he said, wasn't like sitting at a roulette table and hoping it landed on seven. He was affecting the outcome—in a positive way, he hoped. He held to a maxim that you could "do well by doing good". He could enrich a city and himself at the same time.'[27]

Doing well by doing good—self-interest equated with the interests of the city in general. What is good for Dan Gilbert is good for Detroit. For Gilbert and Kent, placemaking is ultimately a political concept: one not driven by the idealism of Earth Day and the 1960s, but rather a physical manifestation of 'the third way', in which all opposition between private and public interests have supposedly dissolved.

Since the completion of Campus Martius in 2004, multiple other US cities have followed Detroit's example and placed the future of their downtown areas in the hands of private, non-profit management vehicles. In Houston, Texas, the Discovery Green Conservancy sponsored the regeneration of Discovery Green (2008): 'An uncommonly beautiful, urban green space in the heart of Houston that serves as a village green for our city, a source of health and happiness for our citizens, and a window into the incredible diversity of arts and traditions that enrich life in Houston.'[28] In Pittsburg, Pennsylvania, the Pittsburgh Downtown Partnership led the makeover of Market Square (2009): 'Market Square Farmers Market inspires, celebrates, educates and entertains the entire Pittsburgh community!'[29] In Boston, Massachusetts, the Greenway Conservancy ran the upgrade of the Rose Kennedy Greenway (2008): 'Make today an adventure.'[30] And in Seattle, Washington, the Downtown Seattle Association occupied itself with Occidental Park (2015): 'Giant Valentine's Day ice sculptures melting hearts in Seattle.'[31]

Such development was not always for the better: Seattle currently counts as the third most gentrified city in the US, where rising property values and rents increasingly push original residents out of their neighbourhoods and a movement for rent control is enjoying increasing support. More and more often, the third way simply proves a front for the old ways.

Places for people

'Neighborhoods, cities, and regions are awakening to the importance of "place" in economic development ... A community without place amenities will have a difficult time attracting and retaining talented workers and entrepreneurs, or being attractive to business.'[32] Thus spoke Michigan governor and former venture capitalist Rick Snyder in 2011, in a special message to the Michigan legislature about community development and local government reforms.

An increasing number of cities seem to be taking his advice. San Francisco has adopted a placemaking ordinance entitled 'Places for People': 'a comprehensive, interagency permitting framework that streamlines the community-based development of public space demonstration projects'.[33] In Edinburgh, Scotland, members of the public were asked to participate in a placemaking consultation about how they want the heart of Scotland's capital to look, feel and function. In Bloomington, Minnesota, the Creative Placemaking Commission advises the city council on using arts, design, culture and creativity to help accomplish the city's goals for change, growth and transformation. Hamilton, Ontario, has announced a Placemaking Grant Pilot Program. Kitchener, Ontario, has developed a Neighbourhood Placemaking Guide and Toolkit. Auckland, New Zealand, links placemaking to Indigenous culture, borrowing from the Mauri word 'Aroha'—love for all things, living and otherwise.

Slowly but surely, placemaking is becoming an official part of urban governance, with an ever-larger number of city officials acquiring new job titles: Head of Placemaking, Director of Place, Placemaking Officer, Chief Placemaking Officer, Place Consultant, Placemaker, Principal Placemaker...

The public sector's preoccupation with placemaking is mirrored in the private sector: in the UK, real estate agents like Savills highlight the 'importance of placemaking' as the prime feature valued by homeowners. Savills is joined by Jones Lang Lasalle: 'Regeneration and placemaking: shape meaningful places we all value.'[34] From real estate agents it is a small step to real estate developers, for whom placemaking is the perfect business formula—a suitably cost-effective mode to maximize the return of new developments. *Creative Placemaking: Sparking Development with Arts and Culture*, a 2020 paper by the Urban Land Institute, identifies placemaking as 'a differentiator that can produce distinctive and successful real estate projects and can turn developments into destinations. Development that demonstrates best practices in creative placemaking provides models for public/private partnerships, creative financing, and return on investment for a wide range of projects, from low-cost pop-ups that create a buzz for future development, to larger mixed-use projects ranging from US\$250 million to US\$1 billion in value.'[35]

Jacobs's revenge

The times that placemaking was an exclusively Anglo-Saxon phenomenon are well behind us.

Placemaking, a term which never made its way into the English dictionary, is now an integral part of global speech—one that doesn't need to be translated and subsequently also isn't. Placemakingplus, Placemakers, We Are Placemaking, Village Well ... specialists in placemaking are taking hold all over the world, including architects (like Place-Make) as well as property developers (the Placemaker Group). Placemaking is everywhere. In 2016, Vancouver was the first to organize a Placemaking Week, followed by Amsterdam in 2017, Stockholm in 2018 and Valencia in 2019. There is global porch placemaking week; Bangalore, India, has a placemaking weekend. Placemaking is like a pandemic, including the ability to develop mutational strands over time: healthy placemaking, creative placemaking, strategic placemaking, tactical placemaking, digital placemaking, Afrocentric placemaking … all is placemaking, and placemaking is all.

Placemaking has become a universal approach to urban revival, viewed favourably by the public sector and the market alike, replacing the exorbitant 'starchitect'-designed museum projects of the pre-2008 financial crisis—quicker, lighter and above all cheaper. While it is easy to make fun of today's unrelenting faith in placemaking, the same could be said of the prolific museums of the 1990s and 2000s. But perhaps it is precisely in relation to each other that the two acquire their real meaning. What if the museum boom and the current obsession with placemaking are flipsides of the same coin? What if the seeming alternation between one extreme and the next is simply an ongoing dialectic—call it class struggle—between two fundamentally different disciplines: architects and engineers, on the one hand, and writers and sociologists on the other, each contesting the same field of urbanism—more plainly, the city.

Fred Kent owes many of his ideas to William H. Whyte and Jane Jacobs, crucial voices in opposition to the demise of American inner-city neighbourhoods during the 1950s, which they blamed on the reductionist practices of modern planning. In 'Downtown Is for People', a 1958 article in *Fortune* magazine written by Jacobs at the request of Whyte, she comments on the ongoing downtown redevelopment projects throughout the US as being 'clean, impressive, and monumental: the attributes of a well-kept, dignified cemetery'.[36]

No secret is made as to the culprits. 'This is a vicarious way to deal with reality, and it is, unhappily, symptomatic of a design philosophy now dominant: buildings come first, for the goal is to remake the city to fit an abstract concept of what, logically, it should be. But whose logic? The logic of the projects is the logic of egocentric children, playing with pretty blocks and shouting, "See what I made!"—a viewpoint much cultivated in our schools of architecture and design.' Suggesting an alternative approach, she adds: 'A sense of place is built up, in the end, from many little things too, some so small people take them for granted, and yet the lack of them takes the flavor out of the city: irregularities in level, so often bulldozed away; different kinds of paving, signs and fireplugs and streetlights, white marble stoops.'

Perhaps it is no coincidence that Bryant Park—Fred Kent's first major accomplishment—was created in 1934, just after Robert Moses became New York's parks commissioner. Perhaps Fred Kent's reinvention of Bryant Park as a 'place' counts as revenge on Jacobs's behalf.

Still, that revenge is doubly edged. Negligeable as it may seem, the step from 'place' to 'placemaking' is an important one. Different than 'place', 'placemaking' elevates an acci-dental condition to the status of a planning paradigm. The ensuing conundrum is predictable: once the accidental outcome becomes the target of planning—a product of intentions—it stops being accidental. Creation and experience enter a con-voluted relationship, condemning city planners to be like cats chasing their own tails, trying to control the uncontrollable, script the unpredictable, invariably insisting on 'making place' where they should leave it be. Coupled with an increase in sur-veillance masquerading in the form of public art and design, placemaking is likely to transform spaces of spontaneity into preprogrammed, overdetermined areas. A dead end.

In placemaking we trust

Our project was completed eighteen months later and successfully acquired planning permission a year after that. Most of the objectors' arguments concentrated on placemaking; similarly, much of the rebuttal focused on placemaking. Placemaking was a term that could be levelled *for* and *against* the project—both a form of criticism and support.

I wonder if that perhaps is the whole point—a lack of definition to enable a consensus between opposing interests, one that inhibits people from seeing eye to eye and continues business as usual. We can read into the term whatever we want. Its meaning is a matter of private conviction. Like the existence of God, placemaking cannot be verified, nor should it be. I still do not know what placemaking is; I doubt if anyone does. I wonder if anyone wants to.

creativity
noun [U]
UK /ˌkriː.eɪˈtɪv.ə.ti/ US /ˌkriː.eɪˈt̬ɪv.ə.t̬i/
the ability to produce or use original and unusual ideas:

Too many rules might deaden creativity.

Creativity, ingenuity and flair are the songwriter's real talents.

8

Rule Bohemia!

He was the only person in the office who wore a suit and the only one never to be spotted after 5:30. He failed to tick two important boxes of the industry he was meant to represent: casual dress code and flexible working hours. I still don't know why or how it happened, but that winter our managing director had been asked to act as the figurehead for the creative industries of the Netherlands. The request had come from the Dutch Ministry of Economic Affairs as part of an outreach programme to various sectors to help formulate government policy on how to strengthen the competitive position of the Dutch economy. One-and-a-half million euros of pending investment were up for grabs, to be shared among the energy, water, agriculture, food, life sciences, high-tech, logistics, chemical and creative sectors—sectors in which the Netherlands considered itself 'top of the world'. It made the title of the programme—To the Top —seem strangely incongruous. Evidently, no top position endures without effort. To reach the top, one needs to excel; to remain at the top, one needs to excel yet further.

Each of the industries had its so-called 'Top Team', the composition of which was invariably the same: a mixed group of entrepreneurs, academics and civil servants, headed by an eminent personality who had earned his (all Top Teams were headed by men) stripes in the field. It was hard to picture our MD as the face of the creative industries. White, male, early generation X (or late baby boomer) and unmistakably straight, he possessed none of the associated traits. He had been headhunted

not long before and had little to no prior experience in any creative field. None of that mattered. In the context of our office,
his express mandate was *not* to be creative. A good MD was
primarily there to keep a level head, remain blissfully insensitive
to the misguided preoccupations of architects, isolate himself
from the madness that drove much of the floor and serve as
a guardrail against the organization's permanently pending
derailment. All of which he managed with a certain detached
flair and—as far as we were qualified to judge—a fair amount
of competence. The role suited both his personality and his
résumé. Our MD was basically doing fine.

But then things changed. Once he had to act as the figurehead
of the industry whose excesses he initially had been hired to
combat, the productive dialectic between presumed opposite
ends of the spectrum—between spontaneity and calculation,
involvement and detachment, responsibility and frivolity,
passion and calm—was no longer tenable in the same way.
Nor was it opportune to recognize that any such dialectic even
existed. To enable proper and holistic representation of the
sector, the entrepreneur and the architect needed to morph into
a single, integrated persona.

He all too happily volunteered, getting rid of his tie and
jacket, starting to wear colourful shirts and adhere to more
flexible working hours (further reducing his presence in the
office). He stopped referring to the architects as 'architects'.
Instead, he referred to them as 'creatives'—a description that
soon came to include the public relations, human resources,
business development, finance and legal departments. Our office
was to evolve into 'the most creative company in the world'.
Subsequent PowerPoint presentations outlined the implications:
when it came to being creative, nobody should be allowed a
monopoly—'please note how the mission doesn't mention
architecture'. Everybody had to do their part. Creativity was
all, and all was creativity.

From culture to creative industries

> This cultural policy is also an economic policy. Culture creates
> wealth ... Culture adds value, it makes an essential contribution
> to innovation, marketing and design. It is a badge of our industry.
> The level of our creativity substantially determines our ability
> to adapt to new economic imperatives. It is a valuable export
> in itself and an essential accompaniment to the export of other
> commodities. It attracts tourists and students. It is essential to
> our economic success.[1]

Thus spoke Australian prime minister Paul Keating in 1994, introducing the *Creative Nation*, a cultural policy offering US$250 million to cultural institutions to boost the Australian economy. It was the first time the relation between culture and the economy was formulated this overtly by a government and turned into national policy.

It can be safely assumed that, at the time of launching its own policy, the Dutch government was aware of the Australian precedent. Yet the more likely source of inspiration may have been closer to home. In 1997, Tony Blair's newly installed Labour government had set up a Creative Industries Task Force, whose activities were part of a newly created Department of Culture, Media and Sport. Each of the department's competences represented prospective sources of economic wealth: fresh industries to compensate for Britain's waning old. Culture was an obvious first in terms of the alphabetical order, but there may have been more. Whereas the economic impact of media and sports were well documented and well known, the economy of culture was a lesser-known quantity. To be on a par with media and sports, culture needed a degree of political prioritization.

The aim of the Creative Industries Task Force was 'to achieve recognition within government that there was something called "the creative industries", that they could be measured, and that they were a significant part of the economy'.[2] To this effect, a so-called mapping document was produced the following year, concluding that the UK's creative industries were large and growing. The document qualified as creative 'those activities which have their origin in individual creativity, skill and talent and which have a potential for wealth and job creation through the generation and exploitation of intellectual property'.[3] As examples, it listed advertising, architecture, the art and antiques market, crafts, design, designer fashion, film, interactive leisure software, music, the performing arts, publishing, software, television and radio.

Considerable time and effort had been spent for this definition to crystalize. Within the Labour Party, 'the creative industries' had been a topic of discussion since the early 1980s, well before the term itself existed. In fact, much of the party's initial deliberations had revolved around finding the words to frame what was actually being discussed. When the term 'creative industries' finally surfaced, it was mostly a matter of luck. Reminiscing about those earlier days, later-secretary of state for culture, media and sport, and the driving force behind the creation of the Creative Industries Task Force, Chris Smith stated: 'I sort of dreamed it up. What I was trying to do was to establish, in a fairly precise form of words, what it was that made these activities different. And I was also wanting, I remember distinctively, to record in that definition the crucial importance of protecting intellectual property value.'[4]

To get the term accepted involved broaching considerable resistance, both from traditional cultural industries and the political establishment. Prior to 'the creative industries', the arts had been referred to as 'the cultural industries'. It had proven a lethal linguistic cocktail, dismissed by those active in the cultural field as an oxymoron: the inappropriate commodification of culture. The arts were oblivious to money, and therefore they should not be associated with money. Ironically, it was the same argument that turned off the world of politics, to whom the idea that culture could ever contribute to the economy was simply too good to be true—no more than wishful thinking.

The semantic shift from 'cultural' to 'creative' industries amounted to a sea change, not least because of its carefully considered open-endedness. 'Somebody writes a book, somebody writes a song, somebody creates a video game, somebody creates a new fashion concept. These are individual acts of creativity that have some kind of root in the arts and culture rather than in science; their real value is in the fact that they're generating intellectual property', confessed John Newbigin, special advisor to Chris Smith.[5] In defining the creative industries largely in the negative—they were *not* science—much of the cultural sector's earlier resistance became moot. At the same time, the repackaging of seemingly light-hearted activities as 'intellectual property' also changed the attitude of the political sphere.

More so than cultural activities, creative practices should be read as part of an economic cycle. This allowed the task force to track their growth over time, generating the much-needed figures and statistics upon which a political case could be built. In the words of British filmmaker and Labour Party insider David Puttnam: 'We actually got them to see the arts, or what we then termed the creative industries—because that was the big shift, moving the words from the arts to the creative industries —we got them to see it as a potential economic driver, not simply as a "nice to have".'[6]

The *Creative Industries Mapping Document* was made public on 11 November 1998. Its findings paved the way for a government-wide endorsement of the creative industries as integral to the mainstream UK economy. In 2005, the creative industries minister, James Purnell, launched the Creative Economy Programme. In 2008, the Department for Culture, Media and Sport, the Department for Business, Enterprise and Regulatory Reform, and the Department for Innovation, Universities and Skills (DIUS), jointly produced *Creative Britain*

2008, the first interdepartmental paper on the importance of the creative industries to the UK economy. In 2013, a manifesto from the National Endowment for Science, Technology and the Arts concluded that 'the UK's creative economy had become one of its great national strengths, historically deeply rooted and accounting for around one–tenth of the whole economy, providing jobs for 2.5 million people (more than in financial services, advanced manufacturing or construction) and that, in the years leading up to the manifesto, the creative workforce had grown four times faster than the workforce as a whole'.[7]

In 2020, a King's College report looked back on the evolution as follows: 'We have travelled some distance since 1998: from the creative industries to the creativity economy and soon, perhaps, to a stage at which creativity becomes so embedded within understandings of what the economy is, and how contemporary economies function, that the adjective becomes redundant. This is simply "the economy".'[8]

A class of their own

The UK was not the only country to obsess over the idea of the creative industries at the turn of the millennium; the phenomenon had also been gaining traction in the US, where the concept was seen to offer a welcome second lease of life for the decaying industrial cities of the Rust Belt—not only in economic but also in sociological terms.

If the industrial revolution bore the concept of the working classes, the creative industries gave rise to a class of their own, immortalized in Richard Florida's best-selling novel of 2002, *The Rise of the Creative Class*. In the book, Florida charts a shift away from traditional manufacturing economies to post-industrial economies in which 'creative professionals' are the drivers of new economic wealth. His argument is simple: the creative class chooses to locate themselves in cities with cultural amenities, favourable environments and diverse populations. Once cities invest in these, the creative industries and the related economic growth will follow more or less automatically.

Focusing his research on North America, Florida used the US Standard Occupational Classification System to break down the creative class into two groups of professions. The first group is the 'super-creative core'—people working in engineering, education, computer programming and research, with arts, design and media workers forming a small subset. The primary function of this group is to be creative and innovative. 'Along with problem solving, their work may entail "problem finding".'[9] The second group are the 'creative professionals', the classic knowledge-based workers employed in healthcare, education, the legal profession and the world of business and finance. This second group 'draws on complex bodies of knowledge to solve specific problems'.[10] At the time of his research in 2002, Florida's 'super-creative core' made up roughly 12 per cent of all US jobs. He predicted that the creative class would become the leading force of growth in the US economy, growing by over 10 million jobs in the next decade and equalling 40 per cent of the population.

Intriguing is the somewhat mysterious third group of the Bohemians, identified by Florida as an underexplored economic class, with a significant yet undervalued impact on urban prosperity. As 'Bohemian', he qualifies the occupations of authors, designers, musicians and composers, actors and directors, craft-artists, painters, sculptors, and artist printmakers, photographers, dancers, artists, performers and related workers.

In a 2002 paper, 'Bohemia and Urban Geography', Florida claims that the presence of these professions, in the form of so-called Bohemian enclaves, acts as a key trigger in attracting other talented—or, as Florida labels them, 'high human capital' —individuals. Akin to Marxism—to which Florida claims to be deeply indebted—the creative class is subject to reproduction. Class breeds class. In Florida's own words: 'The presence of high human capital, in turn, attracts innovative, technology-based industries.'[11] Thus, the presence of Bohemians becomes the defining measure for the 'creative success' of cities.

In the same paper, Florida launches the so-called Bohemian Index, which ranks places according to the relative presence of bohemians. More precisely, the index is a quotient that compares the percentage of bohemians in a given region to the percentage of bohemians nationwide and divides it by the population of that region compared to the national population. According to Florida, 'the Bohemian index is an improvement over previous measures of cultural and lifestyle amenities in that it represents a direct measure of the producers of cultural and creative assets.' It makes the results no less predictable: applied to large cities, the Bohemian Index shows New York City, Seattle and Los Angeles at the top, with nine bohemians per thousand inhabitants, while San Antonio, Oklahoma City, Buffalo, Cleveland, Pittsburgh, Albany and Baltimore rank at the bottom.

Talent, technology, tolerance

When it comes to measuring intricate factors of urban life, the Bohemian Index is in good company. Initially it lost its primary position in 2003 to the Composite Diversity Index—an aggregation of the Gay Index (developed by Carnegie Mellon graduate student, Gary Gates), the Melting Pot Index and the Bohemian Index, which in 2004 he again replaced with the Tolerance Index. The Bohemian Index was removed from the Tolerance Index in 2010. The sheer amount of indices, however, defeats their purpose—there are enough of them for each city to consider itself successful at least according to one.

While *The Rise of the Creative Class* had an exclusively North American focus, its international success inevitably resulted in some of its methodology going global. The escalation of territory is mirrored by an escalation of focus. Since 2004, Florida, through the Martin Prosperity Institute, part of the University of Toronto's Rotman School of Management, has published the Global Creativity Index (GCI), a creativity ranking of nations worldwide. Global presence requires a simple message—no longer is the ranking based on a complicated melee of intertwined indexes, but on the simple causal relation between three Ts, believed to be the basis for all economic growth and lasting prosperity: *talent, technology* and *tolerance*. Tolerance attracts talent; talent, in turn, is the crucial basis for the emergence of new creative technologies. In 2015, following a global survey of 139 countries, the Global Creativity Index was topped by Australia, followed by the United States, with New Zealand third. In the intellectual universe of Richard Florida, globalization remains a predominantly Anglo-Saxon affair.

Bicycles, bars and bistros

Meanwhile, Florida's work has become well known, internalized by all too many an aspiring mayor and local politician as a quick-fix formula to success. Admittedly, Richard Florida can be persuasive. His impressive fifty-six-page CV features multiple books, academic papers, working papers, presentations, appearances, and a long list of articles and op eds. He holds three honorary doctorates, along with several professorships at the University of Toronto; he is director of cities at the Martin Prosperity Institute at the Rotman School of Management, a Walton Family Foundation fellow at Heartland Forward, a distinguished fellow of New York University's Schack Institute of Real Estate, the co-founder and editor-at-large of *CityLab* and a board member of Art Basel Cities. The distinctions he has received include the following: world's most influential thought leader; world's most influential management thinker; among the

140 best Twitter feeds; and European ambassador for creativity and innovation. Since publication of *The Rise of the Creative Class*, multiple cities have sought Florida's advice. In 2002, he was next in line to be hired by the city of Pittsburgh, which has a long history of trying to reinvent itself (more about that later). Pittsburgh was followed by Providence, Syracuse and Wilmington, then Austin, Cincinnati, Dayton, Denver, Madison, Memphis, Phoenix and Richmond. Internationally, there was Winnipeg, Barcelona, Brisbane, Dublin and Pamplona. Meanwhile, entire US states like Michigan and Ohio, and even the United Nations, have put their faith in Florida for a brighter future. In 2015, as a case of full-circle irony, even the eternal city of Jerusalem brought in Florida to aid a revival.

Florida's advice is invariably the same: the road to a brighter future begins with the accommodation of a particular lifestyle. Members of the creative class enjoy travelling, antique shopping, bike riding and running. The lifestyle of the creative class calls for active participation in a variety of experiential activities. Florida uses the term "street-level culture", which may include a 'teeming blend of cafes, sidewalk musicians, and small galleries and bistros, where it is hard to draw the line between participant and observer, or between creativity and its creators'.[12] Florida's advice to his patrons involves few facts or data. Most of his argument relies on impressionistic accounts of hip cafés, buzzing robotics laboratories and thriving neighbourhoods, occasionally supplemented with a flattering personal anecdote about a talented new individual who relocated to the city in question from San Francisco or New York in search of a more balanced life.

Florida has headed multiple lucrative consultancies, like Catalytix, the Creative Class Leadership Program and the Creative Class Group, charging as much as US$250,000 for their reports. There are few notable differences between the reports produced by these consultancies, consistently recycling the same abstract terminology for each case: 'focused impact areas', 'success factors' or 'tactics and action plans'. It is estimated that during the five years following the release of *The Rise of the Creative Class*, Florida gave presentations in several hundred cities, while in that same period he reaped well above the usual US$35,000 or US$40,000 for overseas visits. His fees were typically paid by local foundations or by ticket prices of more than US$100 for crowds well into the hundreds. So frequent were the speeches that in 2004 Florida allegedly quit his job in Pittsburgh for one at George Mason University just to be nearer to a major airport.[13]

After Florida, creative consulting became a highly popular business model, with prolific organizations modelling themselves on his approach, not seldom with his direct involvement. To name a few: Cincinnati Tomorrow is a group that supports efforts to make the city appealing to creative workers, such as artists, scientists, writers and computer programmers. 'Fun lures them to cities—and jobs keep them there.'[14] The Austin Independent Business Alliance has launched Keep Austin Weird. The trademarked slogan features on T-shirts, hats and mugs. Other cities have since mimicked the nickname. There is Keep Portland Weird (2003), Keep Louisville Weird (2005), as well as Keep Indianapolis Weird (2013). Community empowerment organization DaytonCREATE established the Young Creatives Summit, aiming to make the city of Dayton more creative, vibrant and liveable. 'Revitalizing a city that has suffered major setbacks isn't an easy task and the young creatives deal with plenty of naysayers. Still, members of the group remain positive.'[15] In Michigan, the Cool Cities Initiative aims to spur growth and investment in Midwestern cities by reducing the brain drain of Michigan students seeking employment out of state.[16] CREATE: Detroit is responsible for Detroit's inaugural Ideas Fest on City Building: 'All throughout history, cities have risen and fallen. But what makes some cities more resilient than others? What is the catalyst for renewal and change? It's the creative soul of the city.'[17]

The post about the Detroit event is from Richard Florida's wife and business partner, Rana Florida, CEO of the Creative Class Group, one of Richard Florida's consulting businesses. Rana, too, is a bestselling author. She is CEO of multiple consultancy businesses and features on Richard Florida's Wikipedia page as his spouse, but a separate Wikipedia page on Rana Florida does not exist. There is, however, a LinkedIn page which speaks of her involvement with the Canadian Freestyle Ski Association. Further browsing returns multiple photographs of the power couple, mostly from glossies, showing off their lavish house. Lifestyle evidently matters to the Floridas, more than just a theoretical construct guiding the future of cities. The *Toronto Star* features an article about the pair's long struggle to have a baby (involving sixteen rounds of IVF). At fifty-eight, America's 'premier celebrity urbanologist' is 'a spring chicken compared to some other aging celebrity dads like Paul McCartney and Clint Eastwood'.[18]

Richard Florida, too, wears a suit, perhaps as a token of the conceptual distance he likes to maintain to his subject, as with some of the other outward manifestations of his existence. Until *The Rise of the Creative Class*, Florida appears to have had a distinctly underwhelming career, spending much of his earlier life in the dusty corridors of academia. He has more than made up for that in the remainder of his career. Still, it is important not to forget. Remembering one's humble beginnings can be a powerful source of business. Often the new is little more than the well-forgotten old. Reminiscing on his first major job as a creative consultant in a 2020 interview, Florida states: 'So much of America has become embroiled in becoming rich and becoming a celebrity culture … The fact that Pittsburgh is a set of neighborhoods with neighbors who know one another makes it this Mister Rogers kind of place. Do everything in your power to protect that.'[19]

All too common

There is startlingly little data to suggest that Florida's involvement had an impact on Pittsburgh's revival—or that there was
one at all. When it comes to revival, in fact, Pittsburgh has a
long history. In the early 1950s, the slum-riddled city, with its
smoky air and supposed lack of cultural refinement, had been
subject to an ambitious redevelopment plan at the hands of the
city's elite; this included damming rivers, passing smoke-control
laws, clearing large swaths of the downtown and surrounding
neighbourhoods, and erecting office towers, luxury condominiums, parks, an arena and a mall. The plan's wholesale neglect of
the city's manufacturing base, and the subsequent bias towards
the interests of its wealthy over its working class, lead to predictable social and economic fallout.

A new opportunity came during the early days of the Cold
War. In 1956, in an effort to attract federal funding, electric
company Westinghouse renamed the former Steel City the
research capital of the world. Brute labour and coal drove
old Pittsburgh; brainpower would become its new primary
resource. In the former Pittsburgh, a handful of industrial
monopolies had exploited workers to the benefit of the happy
few; Pittsburgh's new industries would develop reactors, robots
and immunotherapy that would benefit all.

From industrial city to tech town and again ... Pittsburg
has gone through the transformation multiple times, only to
end up where it started. In 2009, the Obama administration
toured Pittsburgh with the G20: 'A model for turning the page
to a twenty-first century economy.' That was in the midst of the
financial crisis. A new future for Pittsburgh is being announced
almost every decade; the sheer repetition throws in doubt the
validity of the claim. Florida's involvement with Pittsburg is
one in a long series of 'expert' involvements, all with a similar
outcome for each: a remaking of the city in the interest of business and wealthy homeowners. Doctors, bankers and engineers

find prosperity, while the working poor continue to suffer the same, or worse, poverty as they do elsewhere in the United States.

Pittsburgh's story is all too common, and it is comparable to that of other cities that have sought Florida's advice. There is something sad about the fate of each of these cities. While it is tempting to put Florida at the centre, it is doubtful if such straightforward blame would stick. It is the task of the consultant to observe, and often that is all he does. There is a fine line between being an observer and becoming a spectator. One can question where Florida actually sits: is he advising on a course of action, or is he simply providing an elaborate description of a process that unfolds regardless—with or without him?

Paradoxically, the prevailing criticism of his work—legitimizing processes, not acting upon them—also absolves him from blame. If he can't be credited for triggering the process, he can hardly be blamed for the consequences. In his own words: 'I've given them [the cities he served] the facts ... about what they were up against. I never tried to give them false hope. I encouraged them to work on their assets, but I tried to be honest and objective in helping them engage their problems. I hope they don't feel let down.'

The new urban crisis

Critiques of Florida's creative class theory have abounded— from questioning if the correlation between wealth growth and the presence of creatives exists at all to accusations of the theory paving the way for gentrification and legitimizing prevailing inequalities, to more personal attacks questioning Florida's own motives—admonishments that have become as well known as the theory itself.[20] Still, perhaps the most apt of critiques has come from Florida himself, during a talk at the London School of Economics in 2017: 'They said I gentrified anti-gentrification.'[21]

Public mea culpas, as at the LSE, are hardly an exception anymore. When it comes to his former convictions, Richard Florida has apologized profusely, even if mainly by stating that the only thing he can really be faulted for is underestimating the virulence of the phenomenon he once identified. He has done well in reinventing himself in the process.

His latest book, *The New Urban Crisis*, can be read as an intellectual U-turn, an attempt to roll back some of the malignant forces his earlier work may have helped to unleash some twenty-odd years ago. *The New Urban Crisis* paints a gloomy picture of 'winner-take-all urbanism'. Charting the rise of New York, London, Tokyo and other 'superstar cities', the book shows how 40 per cent of the world's economic growth is created in metropolitan areas which, combined, hold no more than 7 per cent of its population. Supported by an arsenal of data, it shows how the most creative cities are now also the most unequal, how urban segregation persists, and how the next big crisis will be the suburbs. Going back to his intellectual roots—a fusion of Karl Marx, Joseph Schumpeter and Jane Jacobs—Florida focuses on those on the receiving end of our great rush back to the city, who he labels 'the service class': an army of low-wage workers providing the cheap labour to support the creative class yet who cannot afford to live in the city themselves: the new urban proletariat—in, but not of, the city.

The book concludes with 'seven pillars' for a new inclusive 'urbanism for all': better jobs, more affordable housing, improved public transport and 'a global effort to build stronger, more prosperous cities in rapidly urbanizing parts of the emerging world'. Florida's list of commonplaces is hard to disagree with. Still, the book provides little detail as to how any may come about. There is a brief mention of the benign potential of a land value tax, but when quizzed about the specifics in an interview in *The Guardian*, he merely replies: 'It's time for new thinking. Many of the solutions may not work, but we need to try things and talk about new solutions. We need incentives for greater development, not only of housing in general, but of affordable housing ... I don't have all the answers; I always say: "Here's a menu of things that seem interesting, but you guys are gonna have to figure out what works best for you".'[22]

Richard Florida is like a cat with nine lives, incorporating and appropriating criticism where he sees fit. My thoughts go back to a line I read from one of his early criticasters who described him as 'a relentlessly genial fellow who tries to disarm skeptics by accepting their points in good cheer, as if to suggest there is really no difference of opinion at all'.[23]

Loose ends

What are the creative industries? Who is the creative class? The apparent appeal of the concepts is as widespread as the concepts themselves are vague. The occupations included seem the result of an arbitrary selection, based on a level of education more than on their inherent creativity. Florida's creative class includes claim adjusters, funeral directors, tax collectors; there is no mention of airplane pilots, ship engineers, millwrights, and tailors, which somewhat unfairly seems to suggest that the latter occupations are inherently uncreative.

Where does this leave my own profession, I wonder. In the UK, the birthplace of 'the creative industries', architecture was included from the moment the term became policy. In 1998, in order for the sector to grow, the *Creative Industries Mapping Document* identified the challenges facing architecture professionals as follows:

> responding to the emphasis clients increasingly place on value for money, indicated by the rise of the project manager and of design and build; promoting the importance of design quality in building, alteration and conservation; promoting the cultural, social and environmental benefits of well-designed buildings; exploiting overseas markets and ensuring that unreasonable

barriers are not placed in front of UK architects wishing to work abroad, and private sector initiatives to educate clients and the general public in the importance of excellent architecture.[24]

More than twenty years later, the same challenges are fully intact, making it an open question whether, by aligning itself with the creative industries, the architecture profession has traded up or traded down—whether, as a creative class, architects are better or worse off. As with any alignment or association, there is inevitably the question of who ultimately benefits. Regardless of what may be in it *for* architects, there is certainly something that the creative industry gets *from* architects. What applies to cities equally applies to buildings: to make the creative economy thrive, creative professionals must be made to feel at home. The environment in which they work is crucial to the success of their enterprise. The interior design of a creative office is a key factor, both in terms of branding and in harnessing the (creative) energy of its members. Movable desks, pods, nooks, sofas, bean bags, swings, ping-pong, pool and foosball tables, carpets (preferably green), indoor plants (preferably tropical), indoor running tracks, slides, climbing walls, blackboards, whiteboards, post-it boards, espresso bars, music rooms, gyms and pet-friendly furniture are indispensable ingredients in harnessing creativity. Add a 'smart'—read bright—palette of colors and as much natural light as possible, complemented by an assortment of LED, halogen incandescent and compact fluorescent lamps and the recipe is complete—a formula embraced by ever more companies around the world, from start-ups to insurance companies and banks. Popularized by Silicon Valley tech giants Google, Facebook and Microsoft in the early 2000s, the creative office space finds its protohistory in the vision of a man otherwise known for his taste for minimalism—Steve Jobs. As CEO of Pixar, Jobs envisioned its new headquarters as a place that 'promoted encounters and unplanned collaborations'. In his biography, he is quoted saying: 'If a building doesn't encourage that, you'll lose a lot of innovation and the magic that's sparked by serendipity.'[25] The design by Bohlin Cywinski Jackson—the architects of Bill Gates's 6,000-square-metre mansion near Lake Washington—broke with the conventions of the cubicle-filled open floor of the 1990s and introduced a large central atrium where employees could mingle, freely chilling on sofas, sitting at the café or playing foosball. The office space was left to be personalized by each user as they pleased and it has everything from a jungle pod, tiki cabin, rock'n'roll stage and love corner. 'I've never seen a building that promoted collaboration and creativity as well as this one', commented John Lasseter, Pixar's chief creative officer.[26] In 2006, Disney bought Pixar for US$7.4 billion. After meeting with Jobs to discuss the acquisition, Walt Disney Company CEO Bob Iger exclaimed: 'I felt breathless as I described to Tom [Staggs, Walt Disney Company CFO] the level of talent and creative ambition, the commitment to quality, the storytelling ingenuity, the technology, the leadership structure, and the air of enthusiastic collaboration—even the building, the architecture itself. It was a culture that anyone in a creative business, in any business, would aspire to.'[27]

And yet again … confronted with the paraphernalia of so-called creative spaces, and all the other evidence of the symbiotic pact between creatives and the creative industry, I cannot help but wonder: who benefits? Who comes out on top when work is home, labour playtime and production pleasure? Who wins in the context of win–win?

Obituary

Our MD left in 2013. He relinquished his position as figurehead of the Dutch creative industries not long after. Clearly, the creative industries benefited more from him representing an architect firm than the architect firm could hope to benefit from him representing the creative industries. I guess that answers my question.

Beauty includes everything that promotes a healthy and happy life, everything that makes a collection of buildings into a place, everything that turns anywhere into somewhere, and nowhere into home. It is not merely a visual characteristic, but is revealed in the deep harmony between a place and those who settle there. So understood, beauty should be an essential condition for planning permission ... Ugly buildings present a social cost that everyone is forced to bear. They destroy the sense of place, undermine the spirit of community, and ensure that we are not at home in our world. Ugliness means buildings that are unadaptable, unhealthy and unsightly and which violate the context in which they are placed. Preventing ugliness should be a primary purpose of the planning system ... Our built environment and our natural environment belong together. Both should be protected and enhanced for the long-term benefit of the communities that depend on them. Settlements should be renewed, regenerated and cared for, and we should end the scandal of abandoned places, where derelict buildings and vandalised public spaces drive people away. New developments should enhance the environment in which they occur, adding to the health, sustainability and biodiversity of their context. Those three aims must be embedded in the planning system and in the culture of development, in such a way as to incentivise beauty and deter ugliness at every point where the choice arises. To do this we make policy proposals in the following areas ... Beautiful placemaking should be a legally enshrined aim of the planning system. Great weight should be placed on securing these qualities in the urban and natural environments. This should be embedded prominently as a part of sustainable development in the National Planning Policy Framework (NPPF) and associated guidance, as well as being encouraged via ministerial statement. Local Plans should give local force to this national requirement, defining it through empirical research, including surveying local views on objective criteria. Schemes should be turned down for being too ugly and such rejections should be publicised ... Local councils need radically and profoundly to re-invent the ambition, depth and breadth with which they engage with neighbourhoods as they consult on their local plans. More democracy should take place at the local plan phase, expanding from the current focus on consultation in the development control process to one of co-design ... Our proposals aim to change the nature of development in our country. In the place of quick profit at the cost of beauty and community, we aim for long-term investment in which the values that matter to people—beauty, community, history, landscape—are safeguarded. Hence places, not units, high streets not glass bottles, local design codes, not faceless architecture that could be anywhere ... Too many places in this country are losing their identity or falling into dereliction. They are noisy, dilapidated, polluted or ugly, hard to get about in or unpleasant to spend time in. Such places create fewer jobs, attract fewer new businesses and have less good schools. They do not flourish. Government should commit to ending the scandal of 'left-behind' places. We need to ask 'what will help make these good places to live?' It is never enough to invest in roads or shiny 'big box' infrastructure. Development should be regenerative not parasitic ... Too much of what we build is the wrong development in the wrong place, either drive-to cul-de-sacs (on greenfield sites) or overly dense 'small flats in big blocks' (on brownfield sites). We need to develop more homes within mixed-use real places at 'gentle density', thereby creating streets, squares and blocks with clear backs and fronts. In many ways this is the most challenging of our tasks, which is to change the model of development from 'building units' to 'making places' ... Urban development should be part of the wider ecology. Green spaces, waterways and wildlife habitats should be seen as integral to the urban fabric. The government should commit to a radical plan to plant two million street trees within five years, create new community orchards, plant a fruit tree for every home and open and restore canals and waterways. This is both right and aligned with the government's aim to eradicate the UK's net carbon contribution by 2050. It should do this using the evidence of the best ways to improve well-being and air quality. Green spaces should be enclosed and either safely private or clearly public ... Our evidence gathering and discussion have discovered widespread agreement on the need to invest in and improve the understanding and confidence of professionals and local councillors. Crucial areas include placemaking, the history of architecture and design, popular preferences and (above all) the associations of urban form and design with well-being and health. The architectural syllabus should be shorter and more practical, and the government should consider ways of opening new pathways into the profession ... Planning has undoubtedly suffered from budget cuts over the last decade, with design and conservation expertise especially suffering. By having a more rules-based approach, by moving the democracy forward, by using clearer form-based codes in many circumstances, by limiting the length of planning applications and by investing in digitising data entry and process automation, it should be possible to free up resources. We don't pretend this profound process of re-engineering will be easy.[1]

beauty

noun [C or U]

UK /ˈbjuː.ti/ US /ˈbjuː.t̬i/

the quality of being pleasing, especially to look at, or someone or something that gives great pleasure, especially when you look at it:

This is an area of outstanding natural beauty.

The piece of music he played had a haunting beauty.

She was a great beauty (= a beautiful woman) when she was young.

9

The B Word

To *secure the home healthy, the house beautiful, the town pleasant, the city dignified and the suburb salubrious.*

Aims of the Planning Act, 1909

There are not enough chairs; part of the audience has to stand. But I only become aware of that after I have sat down. When I offer my chair, I am politely ignored. I have no business being here. The receptionist, whom I know privately, has smuggled me in, under a pretence that is mostly false. Drawings are pinned up on the walls, or rather, stuck to boards placed just in front of the walls, which themselves are cluttered with artworks. But apart from the ostentatious setting and the average age of those partaking, the ensuing ritual feels similar to that of an average studio crit.

The commissioners—all men—make their entry, shuffling past the boards, mumbling half-finished sentences like conspirators sharing the details of their imminent plot. There is the possibility to present in person too, and at least one of the teams up for review has decided to make use of the opportunity. It is customary that such presentations are given jointly by the architect and the client, and that is indeed who the man and woman next to one of the boards turn out to be. They are here to present their plans for the refurbishment of a nineteenth-century building to house a local community centre. The project, they claim, is all about the surrounding area, which has gone downhill dramatically. A beautifully designed building is needed to radically change the fortunes of the immediate neighbourhood.

'Beauty is a bit of a touchy subject at present, beyond the remit of this commission according to some...' One of the commissioners tries to steer the conversation to more neutral ground, but he is stopped dead in his tracks by the arrival of another man, immaculately dressed in a pinstriped suit, a pink shirt (with a white collar) and a purple tie. 'Touchy a subject it is', he confirms. 'But if indeed you're aiming to restore this area to its former glory, shouldn't you be talking all about conservation and preservation...?'

I never realized there was a difference. I feel intimidated.

Not so the presenters. The intervention is a welcome opportunity to correct their earlier mistake. 'Yes! Conservation and preservation! Our thoughts exactly: bringing out the beauty of the existing building!'

'We will let you know our feedback in two weeks', pinstriped man replies. 'Any other projects we need to review?'

'There is one more we should get a verdict on, Chairman', somebody points out, 'a scheme by Terry Farrell, in quite a prominent location.'

'I think we've had quite enough Terry Farrell'. And off he is. The chairman's presence has not lasted longer than ten minutes.

The Royal Fine Arts Commission

It must have been the late eighties, or early nineties perhaps—I do not remember exactly—that I attended. The setting: a large mansion on St James's Square; the occasion: a meeting of the Royal Fine Arts Commission (RFAC). The nature of my presence: a young foreign architect eager to see projects in the UK being evaluated at the highest level. The project under discussion, I now realize, was of no importance, just as I realize the importance of the project that was left undiscussed.

What is perhaps most telling in hindsight was the guarded manner in which members of the commission operated—state-sanctioned arbiters of beauty circumspect about their own competence. At the time of the meeting, the role and position of the commission were the subject of some debate. Appointed by royal warrant in May 1924 to enquire into questions of public amenity or artistic importance, the Royal Fine Arts Commission was Britain's first de facto beauty commission. In its own words: 'The Royal Fine Arts Commission is the UK's chief Government advisor whose duty it is not only to prevent blunders but to "beautify England".'[1] But by the late 1980s not all saw it that way. Nicholas Ridley, who had just taken over as secretary of the Department of the Environment, made his position—and thereby that of the government—abundantly clear: 'I really don't think there's a role for arbiters of taste. We all have our own taste, and it is not right for a publicly supported critic to be laying down standards.'[2]

For the first sixty or so years of its existence, the Royal Fine Arts Commission kept a low profile—an advisory body, which was unpaid and without formal powers—derided in the press as a 'toothless watchdog'. Things changed in 1980, when the newly instated Conservative government of Margaret Thatcher issued Circular 22/80, emphasizing the 'extremely subjective' nature of aesthetic matters and restricting state control to environmentally sensitive areas. Subsequent circulars followed, further discouraging 'aesthetic control' over the built environment.

Under Thatcher, it was the state's mission to leave as few barriers as possible. Creativity and innovation were twin pillars of the free market, and bodies like the RFAC would only get in the way. Design control was to be limited to one-off legacy or high-profile projects—not least perhaps as an effective way to deflect attention away from more questionable developments perpetrated elsewhere.

Even with its mandate steadily being eroded, the RFAC's profile was significantly raised when, in 1985, Thatcher made the flamboyant (and vocal) Norman St John-Stevas MP, later Lord St John of Fawsley, its new chair. Apart from drawing attention to an institution whose purpose was seriously in question, the appointment was also not without political risk. While loyal to the PM, St John-Stevas was critical of her liberal economic policies. A one-nation Tory who 'looked to Disraeli rather than Milton Friedman', the new chairman was part of the old establishment.[3] As the former leader of the House of Commons and minister for the arts, he was known to be a notorious social snob—a conflicted, 'paradoxical figure' who later, having been elected master of Emmanuel College Cambridge, earned the nickname 'Mein Camp'. Yet despite the stuffiness of its chair, in the 1980s and 1990s the RFAC was the only public institution to argue for the importance of beauty in the built environment and the role of the public sector in guaranteeing it.[4]

From 1985, the commission's review letters were often written directly by the chairman himself, colourful in language, talking of 'architectural disasters' as 'blots on the landscape'.

Intentional or not, the unsparing critique also seemed inspired by a carefully cultivated obliviousness of prevailing political winds. When, in the 1980s, Arup Associates' modernist scheme for the redevelopment of Paternoster Square was scrapped after the intervention of then Prince Charles, the RFAC equally rallied against the more classical alternative scheme proposed by Sir Terry Farrell. It was thought that the commission was motivated by its own aesthetic predilections. 'I think there probably is still one school of architecture represented on the Commission ... They should mix it up a bit', said Farrell.

He was backed up by London's chief planning officer, Peter Rees, who stated that 'the commission doesn't understand the City and its needs. Tradespeople tend to take a more pragmatic view about development than the landed gentry and they also have less time to have aesthetics for breakfast. The point about the RFAC is that it should be trying to improve design standards, not dictate an architectural style.'[5] Despite RFAC opposition, the Farrell scheme obtained planning permission, only to be written off by the recession in the early 1990s. When the project was reopened, a later scheme by RFAC commissioner Sir William Whitfield was posited as a stylistic compromise to ensure that development indeed happened.

With the introduction of private finance initiatives (PFI) in the 1990s, public sector cost cutting became a major concern of the RFAC. Though careful not to question the financial justifications of such initiatives, the chairman believed that it was in direct conflict with design quality, since good architecture was too often considered expendable and developers 'crammed commercial uses into every cranny' in the name of maximizing profits. In the 1995 RFAC report the chairman argued that through private finance initiatives 'too low a priority is given to design quality, by which I mean not just the outward appearance of a building but also its fitness for its purposes'.[6]

To exercise its aesthetic influence, the commission organized seminars and publications on the evaluation of architectural quality. In 1990, the commission published *Planning for Beauty*, which advocated 'the adoption by Government of a more positive stance towards design control [the term "aesthetic control" had begun to slip from common usage at this time]; the wider use of design guidelines to emphasize the visual impact of buildings and the importance of public realm concerns; and the establishment of a national network of "Architectural Advisory Panels" to relieve pressure on the RFAC and to help raise design standards locally'.[7] The report characterized a more general and widespread concern that the built environment in the UK was in a dire state—a sentiment shared by the then Prince of Wales.

In response to the report, the then-secretary of state for the environment, Chris Patten, accepted the need to redefine government design guidance and in collaboration with the Royal Town Planning Institute, the Royal Institute of British Architects and the Department of the Environment, he wrote an amendment to the advice contained in Circular 22/80. In 1992, this amendment was incorporated into government guidance as Annex A to the revised Planning Policy Guidance note 1. The annex recognized for the first time design as a material consideration in the planning of towns and cities. Design was incorporated into planning policy, in place of beauty.

Patten's successor, Secretary John Gummer, went further in raising the profile of design with his Quality in Town and Country initiative, drafted in 1994. Notable for its absence in the plan, however, was the Royal Fine Arts Commission. Lord St John of Fawsley died in 2012. The obituary in *The Independent* describes him as 'a deeply generous, cosmopolitan and civilized man, widely read and an engaged patron of the arts. An engaged and successful chairman of the Royal Fine Arts Commission until its abolition in 1996.'[8]

CABE

In *The Twilight of Sovereignty*, financier and former chairman of Citicorp Walter B. Wriston proclaimed the Information Revolution, and with it the collapse of conventional forms of democratic political power and the triumph of a new market democracy. The idea that politicians could effectively interpret the will of the people was already held to be false. Appetites were best expressed, and served, in the economy.

Good governance was a question of economics and not politics per se. There was no better gauge of public sentiments than spending. The economy was held to be preferable to a representative democracy—the only way to respond democratically to people's lives. The principles were extended to areas of society generally considered beyond economic remit, offering the world a simplified model of society in which each person is a rational agent, self-seeking and acquisitive, acting entirely in their own self-interest.

The same applied to public servants. Public duty, and the idealism implied in it, was simply an illusion. The public sector, too, was best operated as a technocratic system. Management consultants, previously mostly a feature of the private sector, made their entry, further narrowing the definition of public service as a form of organizational management, driven by targets and numbers to be measured and improved upon.

A new breed of politicians was eager to capitalize on this trend. After their narrow election defeat in May of 1992, the Labour Party made efforts to modernize. As part of their vision for the future, and in collaboration with architect and Labour peer Richard Rogers, they co-published with Penguin Books *A New London*—which served as a blueprint for the later Urban Task Force. Politicians recognized an enthusiasm for the European city and contrasted images of urban London with European examples held to be more congenial. The New London was open, clean, experimental.

Tony Blair was made leader of the Labour Party in 1994, marking the advent of New Labour, formulated in response to the New Right of Thatcher and Reagan, which was itself characterized by economic liberalism and social conservatism. New Labour likewise touted the deregulation of business, dismantling of the welfare state, privatization of state-owned industries and a restructuring of the national workforce. In the 1996 draft manifesto *New Labour, New Life for Britain,* it abolished its long-held commitment to socialism and declared its endorsement of market economics. New Labour was modelled on a centrist 'third way'. It focused its efforts on increasing electoral success, putting together focus groups to test policy ideas for swing voters. They undertook tactical voting programmes to stoke public opposition to the Conservative Party.

In May 1997, Labour won by a landslide majority. Modelling themselves on the economic policies of the Clinton administration, they ceded fiscal responsibility to bankers and markets. Labour oversaw the instantiation of a streamlined economic model, with performance targets and incentives set across the board. Each public service was given a named minister responsible for delivering and achieving those targets. Against the background of a significant housing shortage, the secretary of state for the environment and deputy prime minister, John Prescott, instigated New Labour's Urban Task Force, of which Lord Rogers of Riverside was made chair in 1998. The Urban Task Force's role was, in Rogers's own words, 'to identify causes of urban decline and establish a vision for our cities, founded on the principles of design excellence, social wellbeing and environmental responsibility'.[9] In the associated report, *Towards an Urban Renaissance*, published in June 1999, one of its recommendations was the hope for 'better quality design'. The authors were careful, however, to make the point that 'better' wasn't about beauty per se: 'A key message of the Urban Task Force was that urban neighbourhoods should be vital, safe and beautiful places to live. This is not just a matter of aesthetics, but of economics.'[10]

Prescott was a champion of design value throughout his tenure. He believed that beyond its application in achieving performance targets, reducing construction times, and maintaining standards of sustainability, good design is 'the key to respect for people, whether they be users of the building or passers-by'.[11] Under his watch all towns and villages in England were to be measured for a Community Vibrancy Index, and the quality of life in the English countryside was broken down into a series of indices, one of which even measured how much birdsong there should be.

In August 1999, and largely in response to the Urban Task Force, the Commission for Architecture and the Built Environment (CABE) was established as an executive non-departmental public body responsible for advising government on architecture and urban design.

CABE was regarded as a successor to the Royal Fine Arts Commission, which by the end of the 1990s was thought to have run out of steam. After Culture Secretary Chris Smith's review of the arts, the Royal Fine Arts Commission was an easy target for Labour: 'an undemocratic, elitist, pompously titled quango, run out of stuffy St James's Square by a Tory peer who served as a minister under Mrs Thatcher'.[12] The commission was patrician and didn't fit with the New Labour outlook. In contrast, CABE was intended to be more democratic, regional and user friendly. The remit of this new commission was expanded under its champion, John Prescott, who doubled its budget. Beyond buildings, CABE was intended to take over public space policy—to advise architects, planners and policymakers on what constitutes good urban design. According to its founding chair, developer Sir Stuart Lipton, its purpose was 'to inject architecture into the bloodstream of the nation'.

Sunand Prasad, one of the founding commissioners of CABE and RIBA's president from 2007 to 2009, also led the development of the Construction Industry Council's Design Quality Indicators. The DQIs were created to complement the existing key performance indicators for assessing construction processes, as part of the industry's Movement 4 Innovation. They were intended to assess the design quality of the finished product in its suitability to the physical, aspirational and emotional needs of a variety of end users. The authors of the DQI based their criteria on the two-thousand-year-old Vitruvian principles of *firmitas*, *utilitas* and *venustas*—which they translated as *functionality*, *build quality* and *impact*, respectively. 'Where these three qualities are considered equally there is opportunity for excellence.'[13] Of the three transliterated terms, the third is by far the most ambiguous. While the first two are to some extent material and fact-based—and, in that sense, measurable—the ways in which a building might be deemed impactful are not clear.

Perhaps the term 'impact' marked a return to beauty without overt use of the word. In an April 2001 article headed 'The Fear of Beauty Is Destroying Our Built Environment', Richard Rogers made the following admission: 'Whenever I hear the word culture I reach for my gun. Goering's words have been haunting me over the last four years, since agreeing to chair the New Labour Government's Urban Task Force', adding that 'one of the most puzzling discoveries I made during this period is that civil servants and politicians in this country will always shy away from any discussion of even the most commonplace aesthetic values. Beauty makes our public servants nervous.'[14]

When writing the Urban Task Force report he was strongly advised to refrain from using words like 'beauty', 'harmony', 'aesthetic' and even 'architecture' if he wanted the report to be taken seriously by those that mattered. Instead, he focused on certain sturdy and dependable principles such as 'planning' and 'construction'. 'Can we really believe in New Labour's commitment to our architectural environment when the word "aesthetics" continues to cause such waves down the corridors of Whitehall?' Throughout, Rogers heavily emphasizes the view that investing in architecture 'makes sound financial sense'.

He takes as an example the Georgian terraces build by Nash and Cubitt in the early nineteenth century, which continue to command high returns on units when compared to similar housing schemes. 'Good design', he says, 'adds to the bottom line: beauty pays.' But, as he explains, 'I look forward to the day when politicians don't feel that they have to justify investment in the built environment by reference to narrow utilitarian values. Roll on the day when they learn to value beauty for itself.' In his speech to the Urban Summit in October 2002, he went further: 'We flinch at the word "beauty" in public policy. But it is architectural beauty that transforms size into scale and matter into light, rhythm and colour. Why do we flinch?' Rogers volunteers the answer to his own question: 'Values cannot be reduced to meaningless performance targets—we all stand in awe in a place of beauty. And we must make sure that the new dwellings we need form beautiful building blocks of new communities, not soulless and soul-destroying suburban sprawl. We cannot repeat the mistakes of the past.'[15]

In 2002, CABE published their report *The Value of Good Design: How Buildings and Spaces Create Economic and Social Value*. Beginning with the Vitruvian triad as a sound basis for judging architecture 'now as when they were conceived', they offered a further disambiguation of good design: order; clarity of organization; expression and representation; appropriateness of architectural ambition; integrity and honesty; architectural language; conformity and contrast; orientation, prospect and aspect; detailing and materials; structure, environmental services and energy use; flexibility and adaptability; sustainability; rounding it all off with 'a final point' that a building is beautiful when 'the resulting lifting of the spirits will be as valuable [a] contribution to public wellbeing as dealing successfully with the functional requirements of the building's programme'.[16]

The word 'beauty' appeared to be making a comeback, but only as an emergent property of the sound delivery of other things. Still, when Labour won its third consecutive victory in 2005 and Rogers, motivated by new milestones such as the London 2012 Olympic bid and the immanent update of government standards for housing and sustainability, published an update to the original UTF report titled *Towards a Strong Urban Renaissance*, the mention of beauty was again conspicuously absent. In June of that year, Conservative MP Oliver Letwin, in a speech to the Centre for Social Justice titled 'Conducting Politics as if Beauty Matters', complained that 'we haven't heard much in British politics about anything to do with beauty'—citing Rogers's earlier remarks.[17]

The guide for government policy decision making at the time was the *Green Book*, a set of guidelines issued by HM Treasury on how to appraise policies, programmes and projects. The *Green Book* also provided guidance on the design and use of monitoring and evaluation before, during and after implementation. However, in doing so, it mostly focused on short-term, evidence-based cost–benefit analysis.

In 2006, CABE published its own *Value Handbook*, an online resource documenting over 400 case studies, publishing more than eighty reports, advising local authority planners to use 'value' rather than cost when making the case for good design. Examples of such values include exchange value, use value, image value, environmental value, cultural value. In the interest of design, policy advisors are encouraged to ascertain the quantifiable impacts which can be readily incorporated into the government *Green Book*.

Building Better, Building Beautiful

The 2010 general election ended in a hung parliament, the first since 1974. A new government was formed of Conservatives and Liberal Democrats—the first coalition government to emerge from a UK general election. In his speech to the Civil Service Live conference held in London in July 2010, Britain's new prime minister, David Cameron, promised to 'make government accountable to the people'. The five tools by which the then-PM argued that accountability could be achieved were: choice, competition, payment by results, elections and transparency.

Despite the Tory anti-bureaucracy line, measurement was placed once again at the heart of policy. The growing emphasis on transparency and accountability in recent years has given rise to increased expectations that public expenditure be justified in explicit terms, prompting evidence-based policymaking and the so-called cost–benefit analysis of intervention. In an austerity government, economists were routinely engaged with translating wellbeing aspects of housing in financial terms.[18]

The perception of beauty, difficult to categorize, fell across established funding boundaries. Policies that resulted in measurable value were prioritized. Numbers were what counted, and housing provision was newly regarded in infrastructural terms.

The National Planning Policy Framework from 2010 included numerous injunctions against aesthetic control: 'Planning policies and decisions should not attempt to impose architectural styles or particular tastes and they should not stifle innovation, originality or initiative through unsubstantiated requirements to conform to certain development forms or styles.'[19]

In November 2010, five months after being installed, the government announced that it would scrap funding to CABE and merge it into the Design Council. CABE went from being a publicly funded organization to sharing its operations with a charity. On the occasion, as its last feat, CABE produced *People and Places*, a report on public attitudes to beauty. As part of the report, seven essays were commissioned to tackle questions raised in the research: 'Beauty and a Love of Life' by Diana Athill; 'Beauty and Public Policy' by Glenn Parsons; 'Beauty, Localism and Deprivation' by Irena Bauman; 'Beauty, a Short History' by Alan Powers; 'Beauty, Well-being and Prosperity' by Bonnie Greer; 'The X Factor: Beauty in Planning' by Matthew Kieran; and 'Beauty: Value Beyond Measure?' by Hasan Bakhshi. Alan Powers wrote in his essay:

> The story of our thinking about beauty could be seen as a single movement from certainty to doubt. This story reflects the growing complexity of the world and the loss of religious and philosophical conviction. Thomas Hardy described this in 'Before Life and After' as 'the disease of thinking' which causes the loss of an inner conviction that, visual evidence tells us, existed 'before the birth of consciousness'. In the same way that many people believe it is better to restrict religion to personal belief and action, rather than making it a public principle, so the idea of beauty retreated long ago to become a matter of personal preference and experience—not necessarily killed by consciousness but better left understated. Politicians, planners and even architects are shy about invoking it.[20]

The results from CABE's surveys showed that respondents considered a variety of socio-environmental factors as contributing to a sense of beauty. The emotional responses to aspects of the built environment are likely informed by memories, the result being that respondents were more likely to consider older buildings more beautiful and to place a higher priority on preserving aspects of the built environment that they deemed beautiful than on constructing new buildings. This is also indicative of the values that people attach to durability, longevity and tradition.

Architecture was transferred in 2014 by Ed Vaizey, minister of state for culture and the digital economy, to the minister of state for housing and planning, Brandon Lewis, informally known as minister for architecture. In his first official statement on architecture, Lewis opined that there should be more bungalows. Ten days later, *The Independent* reported that in his own constituency, Lewis celebrated planning refusal of a bungalow scheme.[21] In January 2013 Vaizey commissioned Terry Farrell to undertake an independent national review of architecture and the built environment. The word 'beauty' did not appear once in the report.[22]

In their manifesto for the UK's 2015 general election entitled *Building a Better Britain*, RIBA sought to outline 'how architecture and the built environment can help tackle the pressing issues facing the UK, including the housing crisis, school funding, and climate change'.[23] The only use of the term 'beauty' in the document was in conjunction with the words 'outstanding' and 'natural'. The implication was that beauty is something we should protect, something intimately entwined with nature and not something that we can build.

At the general election of that year, the Conservatives won their first majority of seats since 1992. Gordon Brown's successor as leader of the Labour Party, Ed Miliband, resigned, and he was replaced by 'democratic socialist' Jeremy Corbyn, marking the death of New Labour. With the return to the Old Left as the Conservative government's prime ideological contender, a resurgence of reactionary politics seemed inevitable.

❧

For better or for worse I have been identified by the British establishment as the person who can be relied upon to defend the indefensible.[24]

Roger Scruton

In June 2018, conservative think tank Policy Exchange published *Building More, Building Beautiful: How Design and Style Can Unlock the Housing Crisis*, authored by Roger Scruton and former Labour mayor of Newham Sir Robin Wales.[25] This instigated the later Building Better, Building Beautiful government commission, which was launched in November of the same year. The commission was an independent body established to advise the government on 'how to promote and increase the use of high-quality design for new build homes and neighbourhoods ... making them more likely to be welcomed, rather than resisted, by existing communities'.[26]

Of the nine specialist advisors only two were practising architects: Sunand Prasad of DQI and Paul Monaghan. It was the appointment of Sir Roger Scruton as chair, however, that prompted a backlash. Author of *Art and Imagination*, *The Aesthetics of Architecture* and, most pertinently perhaps, *How to be a Conservative*, Scruton was widely recognized as England's most accomplished conservative since Edmund Burke, the founder of modern conservatism. His appointment as housing advisor was met with opposition from the left, owing ostensibly to his unpalatable views on homosexuality and immigration. But perhaps the main point of contention was his sense of style. According to Rowan Moore in *The Guardian*: 'The conservative philosopher who shares Prince Charles's views on architecture is surely the worst person to head the government's new commission to improve UK housing.'[27] Charles Holland of FAT

183

fame opined that 'this is the same old binary argument about traditional rather than contemporary architecture, which feels like a tedious hangover from the 1980s, a pantomime Prince Charles speech reverberating forever'.[28] And Douglas Murphy, who referred to Scruton as a 'ludicrous curmudgeon', declared that 'our housing crisis has almost nothing to do with aesthetics, modern or traditional, but rather is to do with land, wealth and exploitation. This commission is just an easy distraction from far bigger problems that the government have no intention of doing anything about.'[29]

Scruton responded by saying that the public should have the kind of architecture they would vote for, not the kind that is imposed on them by the disciples of Le Corbusier and Mies, to whom popular taste merely represented an obstacle to progress: 'Whether this is reigniting a culture war I do not know. But it means seeing things as they are and acknowledging the sovereignty of aesthetic judgment.'[30]

In a panel discussion held at Central St Martins, Scruton was asked whether he thought that the Building Better, Building Beautiful watchdog might be considered a government decoy to distract from the more pressing housing issues. Scruton candidly responded: 'I'm here in order to make it look as though something is being done. And all I know is that in so far as I've been asked to do something, is to confront this question of why people object to things being built in their neighbourhood.'[31] At a meeting at the Policy Exchange in London, Paul Finch countered by pointing out that the last year in which the UK had met an anticipated housing demand was 1978. 'A cursory glance at the statistics would expose this fantasy that if you could only design things slightly more nicely then people would be queueing up and hammering on the door of the members of their local planning committee to give it permission.'[32]

Finch attributed much of the disagreement to the 'slagging match' between modernists and classicists reignited by then the Prince of Wales in the 1980s and called instead, as per the

Architects' Journal campaign slogan, for 'more homes, better homes, whatever the style'. According to Scruton, however, the aim of the commission was to overcome popular resistance to new development proposals—assess through opinion polls the ways in which beauty mattered to the British public. 'We are beauty-oriented creatures, it is a fact that is not sufficiently taken into account', and questions about style, he said in an interview, 'will be left as open as possible'. Although he was a proponent of the classical pattern book vernacular, Scruton spoke in terms of freedom of choice and liberation from the tyranny of modernism —which he deemed a kind of bureaucracy, anti-democratic, authoritarian. His detractors seemed likewise convinced by the stuffiness, if not the tyranny, of beauty. In loyal accordance with his conservative principles, however, Scruton was not telling people to like classicism; he sought rather to remind them that in some sense they already did. 'Like the pleasure of friendship, the pleasure of beauty is curious: it aims to understand its object and to value what it finds.'[33]

Living with Beauty

The conclusions of the Building Better, Building Beautiful commission were contained in its final report *Living with Beauty*, presented on 30 January 2020, by Secretary of State Robert Jenrick and commission co-chair Nicholas Boys-Smith. Roger Scruton had died roughly two weeks earlier, but the thought and writing of the former chairman—the press release assured us —had been preserved down to the last edit. Even without that assurance, its contents left little doubt. The word 'beauty' appeared 326 times, only surpassed by 'place' (362 times). Other prominent words in the report are: 'community' (121 times), 'neighbourhood' (62 times) and 'regeneration' (24 times). And while beauty never acquired proper definition, the report's cover—with pictures of Piece Hall, a Grade I listed building in

Calderdale, and Nansledan, a then–Prince Charles–endorsed extension to the Cornish coastal town of Newquay—offered ample clue of the type of architecture the commission would like to see realized in its name. Modern architecture also featured, but only the kind limited in scale with brick façades.

Perhaps most telling of the report's chauvinistic undercurrent was the full-bleed photograph preceding the executive summary: the medieval town of Malmesbury, the burial ground of the first king of England. In combination with the map featured a few pages later—showing that the commission had visited 'every corner of England'—it became a painful manifestation of the increasingly narrow interpretation of cultural identity in post-Brexit Britain: Scotland, Wales and Ulster were left blank; 'living with beauty', it appears, is something quintessentially English.

There was mention of ugliness, too. 'Refusing Ugliness' is the flipside of 'Asking for Beauty'—two of the three pillars upon which the report is built. ('Promoting Stewardship' is the third.) Like beauty, the notion of ugliness remained ill-defined. Both terms acquired their meaning only in terms of the effects presumed to ensue in their wake. Beauty is 'everything that promotes a healthy and happy life, makes a collection of buildings into a place, and turns anywhere into somewhere, and nowhere into home'. The effects of ugliness, not surprisingly, are the opposite: 'Ugliness means buildings that are unadaptable, unhealthy and unsightly, and which violate the context in which they are placed. Such buildings destroy the sense of place, undermine the spirit of community, and ensure that we are not at home in our world.'[34] While beauty elevates, ugliness desecrates.

More concretely: The Wintles in Shropshire are beautiful; Viñoly's Walkie Talkie building is ugly. Compared to the somewhat sweaty description of beauty, the identification of ugliness feels surprisingly direct and heartfelt. One wonders which of the two came first. To what extent was the commission's idea of beauty the result of a simple inversion of what it found ugly, of a persistent bias against modern architecture, and everything else the commission—and particularly its chairman—loved to hate:

> Much of our research highlights the enormous social cost of ugliness, as well as the way in which beautiful urban textures contribute not only to the well-being of those who live and work in them, but also to a massive uplift in economic value. We should aim to spread that value from those who can afford to put beauty at the top of their personal agenda to those—including the disadvantaged and the homeless—who depend upon the wise use of planning in order to provide them with their legitimate share. Beauty is an intrinsic value; but it has social and economic value too and is indeed fundamental to the happiness and well-being of human communities.[35]

The report continued to claim that beauty offers a panacea against 'overly dense flats in small blocks', 'unaffordable homes' and 'tax disincentives to a long-term approach'. Ironically, most of the phenomena beauty was supposed to magically make disappear had been created (in part) by the economic policies of the Conservative government itself, the political patron of the commission.

More than any other planning system in Europe, the British system has relegated the initiative to build to the market. Permissions granted are less the result of regulation than they are of negotiation and that includes the notion of beauty. One of the explicit hopes of the commission was that a more institutionalized notion of beauty might help rid the British planning system of at least one of its vagaries and 'create a predictable level playing field'. Yet without a more fundamental reform of the system itself, it remains doubtful if it can.

As occurs often with persistent dilemmas, the ultimate verdict was left to the people: 'It should no longer be assumed that the people are to be led by the architects and the planners, rather than the other way round.'[36] In highlighting the democratic deficit in our built environment, the commission was hardly breaking new ground. Tom Wolfe broached this subject extensively in his *From Bauhaus to Our House*. Jane Jacobs raised the issue as early as the 1950s. Unlike the commission, however, neither contemplated the possibility of a consensual notion of beauty. Linking the two, it seems a small step from democracy to populism.

In May 2021, the government announced that the conclusions of *Living with Beauty* would be translated into a National Model Design Code (NMDC). Over a six-month period, fourteen councils would work with one or more architecture firms to set out the principles for new development. Aspects for consideration were street character, building type and façade, and environmental, heritage and wellbeing factors. One of the architects lined up for the task was Sir Terry Farrell, a prominent member of the design advisory committee of the mayor of London, his firm devoted as ever to improving design standards: 'We are committed to creating people-focused design and our team's extensive experience in community engagement and understanding of the local area will allow us to create a design code that reflects what residents want to see.'[37]

Exit

People in the room are beginning to take notice of me. I feel a tap on my shoulder. 'What did you say the nature of your presence here was?' I fail to produce a convincing answer. I'm asked to leave, urged to forget anything I may have seen or heard.

innovation
noun [C or U]
UK /ˌɪn.əˈveɪ.ʃən/ US /ˌɪn.əˈveɪ.ʃən/
(the use of) a new idea or method:
    the latest innovations in computer technology

10

Architecture without Architects

Part of our troubles results from the tendency to ascribe to architects—or, for that matter, to all specialists—exceptional insight into problems of living when, in truth, most of them are concerned with problems of business and prestige.

Bernard Rudofsky, *Architecture without Architects*

Tuesday, 17 October 2017, 3:45 p.m. It is a cold and windy afternoon. Canadian prime minister Justin Trudeau addresses a press conference in Toronto to announce a new, revolutionary form of urban development: 'Sidewalk Toronto will transform Quayside into a thriving hub for innovation and a community for tens of thousands of people to live, work, and play.'[1] The prime minister has decided to stick to the script, even if the script is still being written. His words precede similar language later used in Toronto's *Master Innovation and Development Plan*, the four-volume tome outlining the development's brand identity published two years later: 'A place where my son can ride his bike in the middle of the street and be totally safe / A city that brings out the best in me / A city that helps my mommy not be so tired... / A city that reminds me to breath [sic]... / A city that has enough room for my grandma to live with us.'[2]

Unveiled by Sidewalk Labs, a Google subsidiary company, Quayside was a mixed-use development containing some 3.5 million square metres of offices, retail and housing (35 per cent of which was pledged as affordable) as well as a primary school, on a site of roughly five hectares. The project promised to create

44,000 direct jobs and C$14.2 billion in annual economic impact by 2040, cut greenhouse gases by 89 per cent, provide 40 per cent low-income housing units and promote transportation alternatives to the car, all within an 'open digital ecosystem'.[3]

Sidewalk Toronto was to achieve this with an arsenal of tech-driven features: self-driving taxis by Waymo and Lyft, garbage robots scurrying about in underground tunnels, flexible buildings in tall wood and protective structures over outdoor spaces in order to 'double' the amount of time in which it is possible to be comfortable outside. The neighbourhood was to embody 'radical mixed use' that did away with zoning altogether, made possible by sensors that constantly monitored temperature, light, sound and structural integrity. It would have had walkable streets at an 'intimate human scale', allowing for retail to flourish. The citizens of Quayside would have had 'a highly secure, personalized portal through which each resident could access public services and the public sector'.[4]

Some 530 Torontonians showed up at the St Lawrence Centre for the Arts to hear about the Sidewalk Toronto project in November 2017. The live-streamed discussion has since been viewed by over 5,000 people online. Sidewalk Labs itself spoke of a 'robust' public consultation process, with 21,000 people engaging in person, 280,000 in online events or videos, one hundred-plus hours spent co-designing with communities, over seventy-five local expert collaborations across six advisory groups, and so on. All of this was to affirm that Sidewalk Labs Toronto 'takes its cues from the people, not lofty design principles'.[5]

Despite its noble intentions, the project has been met with unprecedented opposition from locals as well as magnates of the technology sector itself, with Blackberry CEO Jim Balsillie calling it a 'colonizing experiment in surveillance capitalism attempting to bulldoze important urban, civic, and political issues'.[6] With time, the future of the project came to look increasingly bleak. And indeed, Sidewalk Labs Toronto was aborted in May 2020, citing 'unprecedented economic uncertainty brought on by the Covid-19 pandemic'.[7]

Fifty years earlier

In a prescient echo of Sidewalk Labs' PR campaign, activist and later Toronto resident Jane Jacobs wrote in 1961 of the symbolic function of the sidewalk as the lively space where diverse citizens could take ownership of the city: 'The ballet of the good city sidewalk never repeats itself from place to place, and in any one place is always replete with new improvisations'.[8] The generational critique of repetitive, large-scale postwar modernism of which Jacobs was a leader demanded that the creation of the city should be reclaimed from the distant architect and developer and given back to the people. 'Cities have the capability of providing something for everybody, only because, and only when, they are created by everybody.'[9]

Intentional or not, Jacobs's grassroots movement against the powers of postwar architects and planners was handed a theoretical foundation a few years later, in the form of Bernard Rudofsky's 1964 exhibition at the MoMA entitled *Architecture without Architects*. The exhibition, followed by a book of the same title, introduced the viewer to 'non-pedigreed architecture', defined as 'communal architecture produced not by specialists but by the spontaneous and continuing activity of a whole people with a common heritage, acting within a community experience'.[10] Rudofsky loved sidewalks, too: 'Above all, it is the *humaneness* of this [vernacular] architecture that ought to bring forth some response in us. For instance, it simply never occurs to us to make streets into oases rather than deserts.'[11]

As a further testament to the waning confidence in architects, Christopher Alexander, professor at University of California Berkeley, wrote *A Pattern Language* in 1977, a guidebook of construction techniques for the non-professional. Alexander's book continues to be a bestseller in university bookstores. Today, a website maintained by his daughter contains pages with names such as 'The Struggle for People to be Free'.[12]

Smart everything

If the 1960s saw the onset of a renewed consciousness of the *people* as the true makers of the city, it was also the decade in which the computer first emerged as a tool for simulating and understanding the world, fuelling an attitude of unparalleled enthusiasm for the massive amounts of information contained within the environment around us. Christopher Alexander's theories about human-centred design went on to affect both the fields of urban design and software, sparking exhilaration about the potential of a relation between the two. In Silicon Valley, promoted by companies like IBM and Cisco, the discipline of urbanism met with the concept of the smart city—a concept that soon went global, taking urban conferences by storm and wooing mayors the world over. In 2011, the first Smart City Expo World Congress was held in Barcelona, bringing together 'smart economy, smart environmental practices, smart govern-ance, smart living, smart mobility, and smart people'.[13]

The enabler of the smart city is data—the more, the better. Data in the form of fibre-optic networks have allowed cities not only to have citywide Wi-Fi, but also smart water, smart lighting, smart parking management and even smart trash cans that let sanitation workers know when they are full.

But the reach of data goes much further. Today, the mobile location data sector harvests billions and billions of data from almost any conceivable mobile device, involving layers upon layers of data sellers, most of them subject to nondisclosure agreements shielding them from naming the origins of the data they compile. This data is then sold to companies that compile it into the actual models of cities.

One of the biggest names in this emerging field—Doppelgänger —belongs to Sidewalk Labs. Doppelgänger merges various patches of information relating to populations—naming the Census Bureau and 'other sources'—in order to create a synthetic yet complete database of city residents or 'virtual households'. While only simulating the inhabitants, Doppelgänger nonetheless accurately reflects their characteristics, including representative numbers of seniors, teachers, disabled people, electric-vehicle owners and so on. Armed with this simulation, policymakers and urban planners are better able to avoid tradeoffs where some community members win and some lose—in other words, they can create situations 'where everyone wins'.

But, of course, not everybody can win. The proclaimed triumph of the virtual world is also a not-so-implicit message about the acute crisis of the real one. Replica, another Sidewalk Labs subsidiary, describes an urban environment in crisis:

> The business model of the built environment is broken. Communities have long felt the strain of housing shortages, aging transit systems, and a shifting retail landscape; the Covid-19 crisis pushed them to the breaking point and exposed the shortcomings of how we plan and manage cities ... If you feel unsafe, you won't ride the subway to work, and if you don't go to work, you don't buy a cup of coffee, and if you don't buy a cup of coffee, the coffee shop closes. Before you know it, you're into a full-blown negative feedback loop that affects all parts of a place.[14]

Platforms such as Replica promise to identify the real people out there—not the supposed people dreamed up according to ethnic, gender or sexual orientation biases, but the people inhabiting the infinitely complex reality which up until now has evaded accurate representation. Indeed, Replica has taken on racism as a *casus belli*.

This is why Replica is putting together an advisory board of members focused on combating systemic, structural racism, and providing them free access to our data platform. This access will also include insights highlighting disparate access to jobs, health-care and education by race and ethnicity. For example, in the snapshot below, we capture Black residents in Chicago who use the Red line for traveling to and from work. On average, these Black residents travel nearly 25% more than White residents, cul-minating into an annual average of 125 hours of extra commuting —time spent away from their families and participating in their local community.[15]

As it turns out, data has a human face. Not the face of one specific person, but the face of *all* specific people, made fathom-able for the first time in history. The dancers in Jane Jacobs's intricate sidewalk dance can finally be 'known'. All that remains is to design and build the city for them. This is the city that we were unable to build before; the city which we were forced to rely on architects and planners to design.

Enter the algorithm

In 2008, *The Economist* estimated that 47 per cent of the work done by humans will be replaced by robots by 2030. The World Economic Forum estimated in a 2016 report that between 2015 and 2020, 7.1 million jobs will be lost around the world, as 'artificial intelligence, robotics, nanotechnology and other socio-economic factors replace the need for human employees'.[16] Google Brain co-founder Andrew Ng has simply called artificial intelligence 'the new electricity'.

Even if often regarded as one of the last bastions of the analogue, the construction sector has not been without its own considerable developments in the past decades. From its origins in 1959 at MIT, computer-aided design has taken significant strides, from the first interactive robot draftsman in 1963 to the arrival of AutoCAD in the early 1980s, allowing design to be carried out on a personal computer rather than a mainframe. Programmes such as UNISURF and CATIA, originally arising in the automotive and aeronautics industry, made it possible to visualize complex three-dimensional geometry. The 1980s also saw the arrival of the first parametric modelling software, Pro/ ENGINEER.

Advocates of parametricism such as Lars Spuybroek have promised to evoke 'an architecture of life' where 'design [would] become a form of breeding, not unlike the breeding of roses or dogs'.[17] Philippe Starck, Kartell and Autodesk have recently unveiled the 'world's first production chair designed with artificial intelligence'.[18] Christie's recently sold an AI-created artwork painted using an algorithm for US$432,000—more than forty times its original estimated selling price.[19] Visions of the algorithm's impact on the design of daily life are becoming ever more palpable, such as in AI CITY designed by the Bjarke Ingels Group, in which solar panels adjust themselves to let dewdrops reach the plants below, bedroom windows adjust their opacity to allow the natural light to wake sleepy residents, for whom an AI virtual housekeeper named Titan selects breakfast, matches their outfit with the weather, and prepares a schedule to get through the day ahead. 'After breakfast, you step into your intelligent, fully automated vehicle and begin your intercity commute, browsing global market news— recommended by an algorithm, of course!'[20]

Other architects are attempting to incorporate the power of algorithms into their design process. Jesper Staahl, architect and customer success manager at Norwegian company Spacemaker, affably reflects in his blog: 'I am not only contributing to create a tool that is used by architects but to a tool co-created by architects.'[21] Spacemaker has been developing an AI platform mainly as a means to address sustainability. A presentation on its website lays out a compelling arithmetic: 'By 2050, there will be nearly 10 billion people on earth. 90% of future global population growth will take place in cities. Which means building a new "Paris" every week. Buildings account for 40% of all carbon emissions.'[22] Spacemaker aims to make a generative design platform that draws from a ready database and is able to quickly test the impacts of concepts. It is meant to bring architects, developers, consultants and municipalities around the same table. Its website shows a team of 110 happily smiling people—'from data scientists to architects, to sailors, skiers, climbers, software engineers, designers, and many more'.[23]

On a more realistic note, the typical real-world application of algorithms to architectural design has been prosaic at best. In 2015, McKinsey Consulting identified the AEC [architecture, engineering and construction] industry as one of the least digital, and therefore least efficient, industries of the twenty-first century.

Silicon Valley

It is hardly a surprise, therefore, that the most serious effort to develop algorithmic architecture has not come from architects or designers, but again from Silicon Valley. In this respect, McKinsey's report primarily served as a wake-up call not to the construction industry but to tech, and subsequently it became a catalyst for investment communities in the latter industry to pour billions of dollars into the digitalization of building solutions.

One of the first construction-related apps to be developed for the mass market was the Procore construction management app in 2002. Created by a Bay Area executive with hands-on experience in construction sites, it is an app that allows a client or project leader to follow the work of construction teams in real time. Procore soon made headlines for its use among Hollywood celebrities and claims to have been 'breaking down the communication and data silos that have been holding the industry back'.[24]

Since then, the nascent world of property tech, or PropTech, has been booming. Silicon Valley has become a hotbed of construction technology platforms and apps developed by countless start-ups. The sector, effectively non-existent little more than a decade ago, has gone from US$20 million total investment in 2008 to approximately US$4 billion ten years later, a two-hundred-fold increase.[25]

PropTech is nurtured by numerous joint-venture consultancies that connect entrepreneurs with financial backers. The Fifth Wall, formed in 2016, is one such entity. Funded by existing US real estate industry big players, it uses the venture capital to irrigate new initiatives in the 'Built World'. Its ventures include the automation of construction equipment; 3D-printing (on Earth as well as other planets); residential property management; a marketplace for property service professionals such as electricians; a platform for buying and selling property; the design and management of premium short-stay rental property; a marketplace putting the owners of storage space (including one's parking space or attic) in touch with those needing somewhere to put their stuff; a retail foot traffic analysis platform; a mortgage exchange platform; turnkey home wellness renovations for private residents that guarantee energy savings; utilities and infrastructure AI that can 'stop incidents before they happen'; a platform for commercial real estate operations; and even a system allowing owners to 'transform their buildings into power plants'.

One company in the Fifth Wall portfolio, Homebound, claims to 'take care of every part of the building process', assisting homebuilders through financing, design, lot preparation, construction and moving in. While customers can opt to do the design work with an architect, 'you can also fast-track the design process by selecting a popular floor plan or home finish package to get a professional aesthetic without the time'. As the Homebound website states, 'we're here to get you home'.[26]

The online sales brochure gives a case study of Richard, an older gentleman whose house has recently been destroyed by wildfires. 'With Homebound's support, he made his home even better than before by upgrading to a fully updated kitchen, adding large walk-in closets, and designing a large, shaded patio at the perfect angle, finally allowing him to take advantage of his hillside home's sweeping views.' Photographs show Richard discovering his new house, or chatting with a younger woman … his daughter? A neighbour? 'Welcome home, Richard.'[27]

Construction platforms such as Homebound can be found in abundance and seem poised to change various aspects of construction methodology. ICON, a company developing 3D printing for low-cost housing, uses a 2,000-pound printer that can be brought on-site. Rival Mighty Buildings has been developing a new substance, called Light Stone Material or LSM, claimed to be a highly moldable monolithic structure that can be fashioned into non-supported elements like overhangs. Other companies such as Prescient appear to be reintroducing mass prefabrication, fully integrated into a digital BIM platform.

PropTech invites a prolific crossover of business activities, such as a former in-house Apple architect launching a mass-timber housing company or architect Bjarke Ingels teaming up with a WeWork executive and (surprise!) former Sidewalk Labs model lab head to launch Nabr, a 'design living' company.

Perhaps one of the most ambitious ventures in this regard was Katerra. Founder and CEO Michael Marks had led a company manufacturing electronic components for the likes of Microsoft, but his subsequent ambition was to streamline the construction industry the same way that he had done for electronics, with a company that integrated supply chains into an all-in-one solution for prefabricated housing components. When architects did not flock to specify Katerra products, Katerra bought an architecture office in order to specify them itself. Katerra's business activity grew to produce design software, air conditioning systems and façade glazing systems, as well as carrying out general contracting, architectural design, engineering and project management. One of Katerra's principal backers was SoftBank, which invested US$2 billion over two years.

Six years after its launch, in June 2021, Katerra filed for bankruptcy, citing the collapse of a major funder. Most analysts see beyond the public statement, though. A former employee, speaking to an American professional architects' journal, mused that 'there was a misconception that the entire industry was broken ... That's not the case. There are portions in need of repair, but there is a lot that works well. Katerra launched into reinventing the entire industry.'[28]

Smarter decisions in record time

The initial forays into digitization did, at the very least, reveal the extent to which the construction industry, even if not in critical condition, could become a lot more cost effective. Not surprisingly perhaps, Katerra's explorations were soon followed by others.

'In this video we will explore how Delve will save you time and money', says a cheerful, crisp American female voice. The oration is part of a three-minute introduction video called 'How Delve Helps Real Estate Developers Unlock Value', which Delve, also a subsidiary of Sidewalk Labs, sends out to interested parties. No longer single-mindedly focused on Toronto, Sidewalk Labs has meanwhile continued to 'build products and places to radically improve quality of life in cities for all'. Delve's mission is described as follows:

> Delve solves multi-dimensional optimization problems specific to urban design and development. First, by using machine learning and computational design, Delve generates thousands of comprehensive design options. Second, Delve evaluates the

multiple impacts these different options could have on key metrics and quality-of-life indicators. Finally, the Delve software identifies design options with the best performance and provides a detailed analysis of each to the user.[29]

Design options are evaluated according to criteria selected by the developer, such as hours of direct sunlight, proximity to public transportation, 'walkability', construction cost, unit count, as well as capital value and net profit. The client also indicates the relative importance of these criteria. Each option receives a score indicating how well it meets the weighted criteria. A chat window allows for team discussion and members can 'favourite' the designs they like best. Users can feel at ease that their liability in making decisions is minimized.

'Delve's proposals all score well and differ from each other in strategy, powered by an AI that mimics the human aesthetic insight', writes Douwe Osinga, director of engineering at Sidewalk Labs.[30] Apart from the machine learning boost that provides hundreds of alternatives at the click of the mouse, what makes Delve stand out is that it integrates financial modelling directly into the design process, measuring value and cost as a function of area, immediately outputting total project cost and value. When, in 2004, UK real estate developer Quintain Ltd. engaged Delve for a twelve-acre mixed-use development on the North East Lands site in Wembley Park, London, Delve supposedly managed to generate, evaluate and optimize 40,000 variants that increased the number of housing units while preserving quality of environment over an existing benchmark design. By the end of its eight-week engagement, Delve had produced twenty-four high-performing variants allegedly exceeding all goals across unit yield, usable built area, daylight access, sun hours on the ground and daylight impacts on neighbours. An image accompanying the project description shows apartment layouts in a 'high-performing design option'. Fifteen- to twenty-storey tower blocks snake around a block. Different unit types pepper the floors of buildings in no conceivable order, with little discernable pattern over different storeys. Several units are located in pinch points of a block and therefore have limited façade exposure in relation to their area, with some units having no façade exposure at all.

Some buildings stand side by side, the corner apartments at their ends facing each other across a gap of a few metres, if not centimetres. 'Delve allowed for the exploration of thousands of options across many dimensions of possible design choices and performance and showed Quintain that the project could achieve both higher yield while increasing quality of life.'[31]

Delve is not the only digital company to take an interest in the housing market. In a blog entry on 18 June 2019, Sundar Pichai, CEO of Google, published an announcement on the company blog:

> As we work to build a more helpful Google, we know our responsibility to help starts at home. For us, that means being a good neighbor in the place where it all began over 20 years ago: the San Francisco Bay Area … Across the region, one issue stands out as particularly urgent and complex: housing. The lack of new supply, combined with the rising cost of living, has resulted in a severe shortage of affordable housing options for long-time middle- and low-income residents … Today we're announcing an additional $1 billion investment in housing across the Bay Area.[32]

With the creation of 'at least' 15,000 homes in mixed-use developments, Google pledges to address the housing shortage in the Bay Area and San Jose by converting US$750 million worth of its properties.[33] A further US$250 million will go towards supporting developers in the creation of 5,000 affordable homes. One of the areas, North Bayshore, envisions 'Community, Nature, Innovation and Economics' as guiding principles to achieve 'Place'. Google will not develop the sites itself, however;

it is partnering with Australian company Lendlease, builder of the super-thin 432 Park Avenue skyscraper in Manhattan.

Brochures for the Google San Jose Downtown West project abound with cheerful colours and casually handwritten words and statements such as 'Welcome—we're glad you're here!' 'Let's keep the conversation going' and 'Big thanks to you!' Downtown West promises 4,000 units, six times more housing than currently projected in its zone; 15 acres of park and open space, 25,000 on-side jobs, US$200 million in community benefits and zero net new greenhouse gas emissions.[34]

Sidewalk Labs, Delve, Google … Silicon Valley tech giant Alphabet, mother company of all three, was getting involved in real estate development at precisely the right moment. Since 2010, housing prices in Mountain View, the Bay Area enclave that hosts Google's headquarters, have more than doubled, reaching a median of US$2 million in 2018. Many residents of the town are no longer able to afford to rent, much less own a house there. One article describes the living situation of one resident, working as a freelance security guard for Google, who opted for the US$800 per month of a rented camper van rather than the US$2,500 of an apartment.[35] In March 2019, legislators in Mountain View voted to ban overnight camper van squatters.

One real estate news site quoted the value of Alphabet's real estate property portfolio at US$14.5 billion in 2019.[36] Approximately one third of this portfolio is taken up by the company's two New York offices; the remaining $10 billion is comprised of various operational real estate ventures throughout the US and the world, with offices and data centres in seventy countries in 2018, as well as numerous vacant plots and buildings. In July 2018, Alphabet purchased US$820 million worth of vacant buildings in Sunnyvale, California.

More than just funding real estate on purchased lands, the Alphabet family is already setting out to disrupt the world of construction on a more fundamental level. Sidewalk Labs is currently 'exploring the development of an offsite construction company that can deliver high-quality mass timber buildings for more sustainable living and working'.[37] Its first prototype, dubbed PMX, aims to push the envelope on mass timber high-rise, reaching 35 floors. Sidewalk Labs touts prefabricated wood construction elements as a means to live up to climate goals as well as saving time and money by avoiding on-site construction. The appeal that this will hold for developers—forever eager to cut costs while simultaneously wanting to be seen doing the right thing—will prove virtually irresistible. PMX offers them the prospect of having their cake and eating it—the end to a regime of tough choices, typically voiced by architects.

Algocracy

Sociologist Aneesh Aneesh has dubbed the mode of governance that ensues in the general application of algorithms as 'algocracy'. 'Under the algocratic mode of governance, work is controlled not by telling the worker to perform a task, nor necessarily by punishing the worker for their failure, but by shaping an environment in which there are no alternatives to performing the work as prescribed.'[38] When computer programmes are able to create digital twins that are so detailed as to effectively supplant the original in validity, and when programmes have the ability to play out scenarios within the mirror world, will 'reality follow the simulacrum?'[39]

Had they been born in the twenty-first century, Jane Jacobs and Robert Moses might not have been enemies, their differences reconciled by high-resolution data collection and irrefutable algorithmic logic. Once PropTech can leverage enough computational power to successfully absorb the role of the constructor and sociologist, it will be able to claim the position of agent as well as that of critic. A tempting form of efficiency perhaps, yet pressing questions remain. In ascribing to algorithms the exceptional insight into problems of living once ascribed to architects, do we really rise above problems of business and prestige? Is the world indeed better off without architects? Is big tech the answer to Rudofsky's quest?

Appendix: The Principles of Profspeak

Profspeak is the official language of the twenty-first century. At the time of writing this book, not everyone relies on Profspeak equally yet, but its vocabulary is well on the way to becoming mainstream language. Profspeak represents the highest form of linguistic abstraction. It is English, but not really. It is what English has been made into by a global majority who do not have English as their first language and whose proficiency is a result of their job rather than their education. Profspeak is the most spoken language in the world—the way in which we have come to discuss and value our living environment, the prevalent mode of communication across professions—from business consultants to tech entrepreneurs, from healthcare professionals to building contractors, from engineers to architects.

For all its global application, Profspeak owes deeply to the idiosyncrasies of the English language, particularly to its ability to divorce words from meaning. Where traditional English—or Layspeak—still allows for a certain disambiguation, such is not the case with Profspeak. Profspeak is semantic opportunism at its best. Intentionally so. When words can carry any and all meaning, no credible disagreement can ever ensue as a result of their use. Profspeak allows us to exchange words for as long and as often as we want, while at no point having to see eye to eye. Profspeak's genius resides in its ability to facilitate consensus in the absence of agreement. With Profspeak as our lingua franca, at long last there is the possibility of world peace.

Not only does Profspeak liberate words from meaning, it also frees them from grammar. There are no conjugations, inflections or declensions; there are only nouns, verbs and adjectives. (Adverbs have been done away with altogether.) Nouns and verbs are best interchangeable. DESIGN is a verb (to design a building) and a noun (world-class design). Occasionally, the interchangeability includes the adjective, too. In Profspeak, the word GREEN is at once a noun (greenery), a verb (to make green) and an adjective (the green grass). ARCHITECT is a noun (the profession) and a verb (the activity the profession is considered to engage in). The indistinguishability, particularly between nouns and verbs, serves a purpose. It introduces a calculated ambiguity whether or not a word—as, for instance, uttered during a meeting—refers to an action or a thing—something that needs to be done, or something that has already happened. Any obligation to do work—REAL WORK, in Profspeak terms—can be infinitely deferred. Speech and work become interchangeable—talking *is* working.

The interchangeability between adjectives and nouns serves a similar purpose: to ambiguate the normative charge of words. In Profspeak, the word CREATIVE can either be a compliment (when used as an adjective) or simply a job description (when used as a noun). Flattery or observation? It's all in the ear of the hearer.

Words can be blunt, and the vocabulary of Layspeak falls well short of capturing present sensitivities. Not having evolved with time, its crude singular nouns tend to be unnecessarily offensive. A once stylistic lapse brings relief: the euphemism, disparaged in Layspeak, not so in Profspeak, whose apt use of the euphemism already verges on stylistic mastery. The architect and the craftsman find their common ground as BUILT ENVIRONMENT PRACTITIONERS (a bona-fide genderless term); brick and mortar are given a respectable make-over as REAL ESTATE VENTURES, and unoriginal ideas command respect as EVIDENCE-BASED DESIGN. In Profspeak, long words are the preferred mode of expression, eliminating the need for further explanation. In the end, these long words save time, describing at once the thing, the context in which the thing exists, the process to arrive at the thing and what follows in its wake—including the unintended by-products.

The longer the word, the better. Ideally, the relation between the word and its definition becomes the inverse. They trade places. The more the definition is emphasized, the more the original word fades into the background. Architect, craftsman, building ... one day, we may only know these terms as 'archaic formulations', belonging to an age long gone: Layspeak, just another word for old English.

Profspeak expressly welcomes change. New words and expressions are viewed as enrichments, even if they constitute a breach of stylistic or grammatical conventions. Profspeak is not an impregnable fortress guarded by aging language purists. There are no fixed rules as to what goes and what doesn't. In Profspeak, there are no mistakes, only UPDATES.

Neologisms are the bread and butter of Profspeak. In a world where language is increasingly subject to copyright, a constantly new flow of words and expressions is essential to prevent stagnation. Moreover, neologisms inspire participation, their history short enough for everyone to remember their inception. Through neologisms, living speakers are given the opportunity to become co-authors of the language they speak. Profspeak firmly believes that those who use a language have a right to shape that language. Neologisms are the sign of a living language, vital to the INTELLECTUAL HEALTH of Profspeak.

Where Layspeak guarded the integrity of language, Profspeak operates in the name of integrity full stop. Virtue is the holy grail of Profspeak, the demonstration of which can never relent. Compound words, even if (more than) occasionally tautological, are the foot soldiers of Profspeak's unequivocal crusade for morality. FORWARD PLANNING, END-STATE VISION, GOODWELL CERTIFICATION ... redundancy is Profspeak's equivalent of underlining for emphasis. All doubt is to be eliminated. In stating the obvious, compound words do not just emphasize, they are also highly efficient instruments of distinction. Consider the notion PEOPLE-FIRST DESIGN. The addition 'people-first' seems superfluous. Isn't it the business of design to put people first? Its apparent existence suggests this may not be the case. Before there was 'people-first design', there was 'design', which evidently offered no guarantee of putting people first—if it considered people at all. The introduction of the mutant branch of 'people-first design' promotes the understanding of 'design' as a hypothetical antonym. After 'people-first design', 'design' becomes 'people-last design', and all who practise it agents of evil by default. No Profspeaker, however, will ever be caught saying this. Such would be Illspeak, which the conventions of Profspeak prohibit at all times.

HUMAN-CENTRIC ARCHITECTURE, EMANCIPATORY DESIGN, SMART MOBILITY… the examples continue ad infinitum. The established disciplines invariably get the wrong end of the stick—inhumane, hierarchical and stupid by implication, as archaic as the singular words that signify them. Still, we shouldn't complain. In a final instance, even Profspeak's own neologisms aren't above suspicion. The introduction of a term like HEALTHY PLACEMAKING makes its earlier iteration, PLACEMAKING, unhealthy by default. Purges of its vocabulary are a matter of routine for Profspeak, only for the omitted entries to become part of even longer, compounded compound words.

Maturing by the day, Profspeak meanwhile allows for the translation of almost all Layspeak. Take the following sentence: 'Any architect with a certain awareness and understanding of sustainability will try to design green buildings to further improve the quality of the environment.' In Profspeak, the entire sentence can be rephrased as follows: SMART SUSTAINABILITY MINDFUL BUILT ENVIRONMENT PRACTITIONERS ARCHITECT TO GREEN GREEN GREEN. When used proficiently, Profspeak becomes pure poetry.

Is Profspeak simply another word for jargon? If jargon is the specialist language used internally within a specific profession, then Profspeak does not comply. Its vocabulary is an opportunistic, eclectic borrowing across jargons, comprising words from the digital world as well as from the medical world, from psychoanalysis as well as from the world of business, from the realm of behavioural sciences as well as that of classical studies. It incorporates cyber terms next to words from Latin or Greek.

More than a testament to jargon itself, Profspeak is a testament to the promiscuity of jargon. It encourages professionals to bond across the confines of their profession, speak the same language, bring to the table their own expertise as well as the ability to paraphrase the expertise of others. Profspeak is a fusion-mix of all specialist jargons combined, in which specialist terms acquire general implications as an added bonus. As such, Profspeak simultaneously embodies the apotheosis of jargon and its destruction. Uber-jargon or after-jargon? Profspeak defers conclusion.

The Oxford English Dictionary contains some 170,000 entries. The total number of Profspeak words is about a tenth of that, again a tenth of which allow one to get by on a regular basis. Many of its terms do not feature in the English dictionary as such. So far, the glossary of Profspeak is an appendix to the English dictionary, loosely arranged, with a commitment to alphabetical order that is perfunctory at best. Yet, over time, Profspeak may well come to replace the English language. And things won't stop there. As a substitute for conventional language, Profspeak will also increasingly act as a substitute for knowledge as we know it. Command of a thousand words or so of Profspeak will qualify anyone to participate in any meeting, attend any gathering, compose any slide deck, hold any presentation ... Profspeak has already made the boundaries between established domains of knowledge disappear. It is only a matter of time before it will make these domains disappear altogether.

No longer is there any need to know anything, all one must be capable of is speaking Profspeak. Profspeak facilitates the definitive superseding of professions by professionalism, perhaps even by its mere aura—if it doesn't already. And why not? For what other purpose did God create PEOPLEKIND but to talk? Loquor, ergo sum.

A small excerpt from the Dictionary of Profspeak is printed on the following pages.

A

AMWF, *abb*. Architect's Mental Wellbeing Foundation.

ACTION ARCHITECTURE, *noun*. a brand of architecture which may otherwise be carried out in a state of inactivity, or stupor.

ACTIVE LISTENING, *noun*. a technique of careful listening and observation of non-verbal cues, with feedback in the form of accurate paraphrasing, that is used in counselling, training and solving disputes or conflicts.

ACTUALIZATION, *noun*. realization of the intangible; the act of making real, but not really (*the actualization of potential*).

ADHOCRACY, *noun*. improvised democracy; a form of democracy and 'making do'—which may be considered characteristic of democracy in general.

ADULTING, *noun*. the practice of behaving in a way characteristic of a responsible adult, especially the accomplishment of mundane but necessary tasks.

AFFINITY DIAGRAM, *noun*. (management) tool that attributes coherence to otherwise random ideas and data by grouping them into families. (See also 'groupthink'.)

AGRITECTURE, *noun*. portmanteau of 'agriculture' and 'architecture', applying the former to the latter.

AHA EFFECT, *noun*. 1. the common human experience of suddenly understanding a previously incomprehensible problem or concept, also known as 'the eureka effect' or the 'aha moment'. 2. the state of elation brought about by the illusion of a new discovery, common to the unwitting plagiarist.

ANACHRONOMETRICS, *noun.* neologism denoting an act of temporal displacement in which one seizes on the future or past as a point of comparison to emphasize differences.

ANTICIPATORY DESIGN, *noun.* the design of structures or material objects people did not know they needed.

ARCHITECT, *verb.* 1. to design and configure (a software programme or system) (*few software packages were architected with Ethernet access in mind*). 2. the activity architects are considered to engage in.

ARCHIPRENEUR, *noun.* 1. compound word of 'architect' and 'entrepreneur', typically combining the worst of the two typologies. 2. split personality.

ARCOLOGY, *noun.* 1. portmanteau of 'architecture' and 'ecology': a branch of architecture dedicated to the creation of integrated, densely populated, environmentally conscious human habitats. 2. a divination of desert fathers, sometimes with unwanted consequences.

ARTWASHING, *noun.* 1. the use of art to legitimize otherwise fraught operations. 2. the kind of washing one cannot help but think makes things dirtier at the same time.

ASTROTURFING, *noun.* the deceptive practice of presenting an orchestrated marketing or public relations campaign under the guise of unsolicited comments from members of the public.

ATAXOPHILIA, *noun.* a love of mess or disorder.

ATAXOPHOBIA, *noun.* a fear of mess or disorder.

AUTOPHOBIA, *noun.* the fear of being on one's own (also known as 'monophobia').

AUTOPOESIS, *noun.* compound of αὐτο ('self') and ποίησις ('creation'), indicating a system capable of reproducing and maintaining itself by creating its own parts and eventually further components.

B

BACK-END DEVELOPMENT, *noun.* that which is furthest from the front; the tail end of a project, process or investment.

BETA LAUNCH, *noun.* the knowing release of an unfinished (software) product as a way to identify potential flaws before releasing a finished version.

BLUE-SKY THINKING, *noun.* thinking that is not grounded in or in touch with the realities of the present.

BOOSTERISM, *noun.* the keen promotion of a person, organization or cause.

BOTTOM UP, *adjective.* proceeding from the bottom of a hierarchy upwards. *noun.* (plural) drinking game.

BRAND, *verb.* 1. mark with a branding iron. 2. assign a brand name to. 3. literally, to burn.

BRANDING, *noun.* 1. the action of marking with a branding iron. 2. the action of describing someone or something as having a particular bad or shameful quality. 3. the promotion of a particular product or company by means of advertising and distinctive design.

BRANDSCAPE, *noun.* the range of brands available in the market or a specific market segment, especially considered collectively as a cultural phenomenon.

BRANDSCAPING, *noun.* the organization of physical space as an extension or representation of a brand.

BREADCRUMB, *noun.* 1. small fragment of bread. 2. series of connected pieces of information or evidence. 3. hierarchical series of hyperlinks displayed at the top of a web page, indicating the page's position in the overall structure of the website.

BREADCRUMBING, *noun.* 1. the act of sending out flirtatious but non-committal social signals (i.e., 'breadcrumbs') in order to lure a romantic partner in without expending much effort. 2. leading someone on.

BREADCRUMBER, *noun.* someone who engages in the act of breadcrumbing.

BREATHWORK, *noun.* a New Age term for various breathing practices in which the conscious control of breathing is said to influence a person's mental, emotional or physical state, with a claimed therapeutic effect.

BRUTALISM, *noun.* architectural style celebrating the beauty of bare building materials and structure, prevalent in the United Kingdom during the 1950s and '60s.

BRUTALIST, *adjective.* rough; heavy handed. *noun.* an adherent or practitioner of brutalism.

BUCKET TESTING, *noun.* (sometimes referred to as A/B testing or split testing) method testing two versions of a website against one another to see which performs better on specified key metrics such as clicks, downloads or purchases.

BUILT ENVIRONMENT PRACTITIONER, *noun.* architect.

C

CSR, *abb.* corporate social responsibility.

CTA, *abb.* call to action.

CACOPHILIA, *noun.* 1. the love of ugliness. 2. the love of things and people that are stupid, vulgar and worthless.

CASE STUDY, *noun.* 1. the use or analysis of a single example in order to illustrate a thesis or principle. 2. perfect alibi for generalizing.

CASUALIZATION, *noun.* the transformation of a workforce from one employed chiefly on permanent contracts to one engaged on a short-term or casual basis.

CATALYST, *noun.* 1. a substance that increases the rate of a chemical reaction without itself undergoing any permanent chemical change. 2. a person or thing that precipitates an event.

CELEBRATE, *verb.* 1. to acknowledge (a significant or happy day or event) with a social gathering or enjoyable activity. 2. honour or praise publicly.

CEREBRATE, *verb.* to think deeply about something; ponder.

CENTRALIZE, *verb.* 1. concentrate (control of an activity or organization) under a single authority. 2. bring (activities or processes) together in one place.

CHAKRA, *noun.* (in Indian thought) each of seven centres of spiritual power in the human body.

CHANGE AGENT, *noun.* a person who aims to transform (an organization, an institution or a society) by inspiring and influencing others.

CHROMOPHOBE, *noun.* someone with a persistent fear of, or aversion to colour.

CHUNKING, *noun.* 1. divide into chunks. 2. (in psychology or linguistic analysis) group together connected items or words so that they can be stored or processed as single concepts. 3. (of data) divide into separate sections.

CIRCLE BACK, *verb.* to come back to; to consider for discussion again at a later time.

CIRCULAR DESIGN, *noun.* 1. the creation of round objects. 2. products and services that no longer have a life cycle with a beginning, middle or end.

CIRCULARITY, *noun.* 1. (of things) the state or quality of being in the shape or form of a circle. 2. (of rhetoric) the act of constantly returning to the same point or situation. 3. (of products) re-entry into the supply chain after expiration.

CLAUSTROPHILIA, *noun.* an unusual taste for confined places.

COLLECTIVE ACTION, *noun.* action taken together by a group of people to achieve a common objective.

COLLECTIVE ACTION PROBLEM, *noun.* a problem, inherent to collective action, posed by disincentives that tend to discourage joint action by individuals in the pursuit of a common goal.

COLOUR-CALMING, *noun.* the application of colour in psychotherapy.

COMMUNITY, *noun.* 1. a group of people living in the same place or having a particular characteristic in common. 2. the condition of sharing or having certain attitudes and interests in common. 3. American television sitcom created by Dan Harmon.

COMMUNITY-BASED SOLUTIONS, *noun.* 1. solutions of the community by the community for the community. (See 'top down' and 'bottom up'.) 2. locally produced substance mixtures for intravenous or respiratory intake.

COMMUNITY ENGAGEMENT, *noun.* the act or process of involving the community in helping the community.

COMMUNITY ENHANCEMENT, *noun.* the outcome of community engagement, if successful.

CONCEPT, *noun.* an abstract idea (*structuralism is a difficult concept*).

CONCEPTING, *noun.* in advertising, the act of generating concepts, usually with the aim to sell a commodity (*our team is concepting a whole new line of body products*).

CONCEPTUAL, *adjective.* 1. on the level of ideas. 2. justification of insufficient depth or elaboration of work conducted at a given stage (*it's not actually something; it is conceptual*).

CONCILIARIST, *noun.* 1. someone who believes in the resolution of conflicts by people being open to the viewpoint of others, not least that of the conciliarist. 2. an advocate of conciliarism, a reform movement in the Catholic Church from the fourteenth to sixteenth centuries.

CONCRETE JUNGLE, *noun.* see 'verdurelessness'.

CONFIDENTIAL BENEFITS CONSULTATION, *noun.* the act of seeking or providing advice on how to get the most with the least effort and the largest element of surprise.

CONSCIOUSNESS REVOLUTION, *noun.* drastic change, not of things themselves but of the way they are thought about, commonly used to describe the 'counterculture' in the US of the 1960s and '70s and the associated rise of feminist, environmental and racial equality movements.

CRAFTIVISM, *noun.* blend of the words 'craft' and 'activism': activism centred on practices of craft.

CREATIVE, *adjective.* the quality of being imaginative or having original ideas. *noun.* a person whose job involves creative work.

CREDENTIALISM, *noun.* belief in or reliance on academic or other formal qualifications as the best measure of a person's intelligence or ability to do a particular job.

CRITICALITY, *noun.* 1. a state of critical urgency. 2. (physics) the point at which a nuclear reaction is self-sustaining. 3. (academia) the business of being a critic.

CROSS-MODAL, *noun.* 1. (mobility) a journey involving two or more forms of transport. 2. (neuroscience) the interaction between two or more different sensory modalities, such as that between vision and hearing in speech perception.

D

DEALIGNMENT, *noun.* (political science) antonym of 'realignment': a trend or process whereby a large portion of the electorate abandons a previous political affiliation without developing a new one to replace it.

DECISION FATIGUE, *noun.* the deteriorating quality of decisions that tends to occur after long sessions of decision making.

DECLUTTER, *verb*. to remove unnecessary items from an untidy or overcrowded place.

DERACINATE, *verb*. 1. to uproot, to remove or separate from a native environment or culture. 2. to remove racial or ethnic characteristics or influences.

DERACINATION, *noun*. the process of deracinating.

DE-RISK, *verb*. (business) to take steps to make certain ventures less risky or less likely to involve a financial loss.

DESIGN-LED INTERVENTION, *noun*. intervention in which design is not an afterthought.

DESIGN FOR LIFE, *noun*. 1. furniture design company. 2. song by the Manic Street Preachers.

DESIGN RESEARCH, *noun*. 1. conducting preliminary studies and analysis preceding the act of designing itself. 2. procrastination.

DESIGN SPRINT, *noun*. time-constrained time period during which a selected group of people must develop a design concept. (See also 'pressure cooker'.)

DESIGN THINKING, *noun*. the cognitive process involved in the act of designing.

DESIGN THOUGHT, *noun*. the occasional by-product of design thinking.

DESIGN VALIDATION, *noun*. testing process to see if a design product performs as intended. (See also 'greenlight'.)

DEVELOPMENT QUANTUM, *noun*. square metres.

DEVIATIONISM, *noun*. departure from accepted party policies or practices (esp. from Orthodox Communism).

DIGITAL LIFE, *noun*. 1. the traceable and untraceable history of a person's use of the internet. (See also 'online footprint'.) 2. research programme at MIT.

DRIVER FOR CHANGE, *noun*. problem.

DRUNK TESTING, *noun*. the testing of products, websites or software by people in an inebriated state to see if they are accessible enough to be used even after excessive alcohol intake.

E

ECO-ANXIETY, *noun*. the distress caused by climate change.

ECO-NATIONALISM, *noun.* a synthesis of nationalism and green politics.

ECOTHERAPY, *noun.* therapeutic treatment which involves doing outdoor activities in nature—also referred to as nature therapy, forest therapy, forest bathing, grounding, earthing, Shinrin-Yoku or Sami Lok.

ELITE OVERPRODUCTION, *noun.* the condition of a society producing too many elite members to be absorbed into the power structure.

EMANCIPATORY DESIGN, *noun.* design with a specific focus on benefiting people disadvantaged because of disability, gender or race.

EMERGENCY PREPAREDNESS, *noun.* the level of preparation made to ensure one's safety before, during and after an emergency or natural disaster.

EMOTIONAL CAPITAL, *noun.* the accumulated feelings and beliefs held by an organization and its employees (*having fun on the job builds emotional capital*).

EMOTIONAL INFRASTRUCTURE, *noun.* the attachment felt by employees to their organizations, particularly in times of challenge (*emotional infrastructure is a key intangible element for any company to thrive*).

EMOTIONAL INTELLIGENCE, *noun.* the capacity to be aware of, control and express one's emotions and to handle interpersonal relationships judiciously and empathetically (*emotional intelligence is the key to both personal and professional success*).

ENCOUNTER GROUP, *noun.* (American) a group of people who meet to gain psychological benefit through contact with one another.

END STATE VISION, *noun.* goal.

ENGAGEMENT RATE, *noun.* metric used to measure the average number of interactions of social media content.

ENGINEER, *verb.* 1. to lay out or design a work of construction. 2. to apply certain skills to make something happen (*to engineer a business deal*).

EQUITABLE DESIGN, *noun.* design aimed at groups that have been historically underrepresented, taking into consideration gender, sexuality, race, ethnicity, nationality and abilities. (See also 'emancipatory design'.)

ETHICALLY RESPONSIVE DESIGN, *noun.* design in accordance with certain moral principles, used interchangeably to reflect the moral principles of the designer, the customer or both (*ethically responsive design means working hard to design great products alongside our beliefs*).

EVIDENCE-BASED DESIGN, *noun.* 1. design based on the application of knowledge and insights generated by precedents. 2. panacea against the whims of architects.

F

FAULT TOLERATION, *noun.* the ability of a system to continue its intended operation when part of the system fails.

FLIPPED LEARNING, *noun.* pedagogical approach in which direct instruction moves from the classroom to the student's homes, freeing up time to engage interactively in the subject matter during class time.

FLOTSAM, *noun.* 1. the wreckage of a ship or its cargo found floating on or washed up by the sea. 2. people or things that have been rejected or discarded as worthless. (See also 'jetsam'.)

FLOURISHING, *noun.* the art of knowing how to do well.

FOLLOWER GROWTH, *noun.* the number of new followers gained on a social media platform over time.

FORWARD PLANNING, *noun.* planning (pleonasm).

FRANKENSTEINING, *noun.* combining in one output or form the products of several origins, not necessarily in aesthetic agreement.

FREE-MARKET URBANISM, *noun.* 1. planning doctrine that tries to reconcile free-market policies and the associated deregulation of planning policies with the notion of urban planning. 2. planning against the odds.

FRONT-END DEVELOPMENT, *noun.* that which is closest to the front; the initiation of a project, process or investment. 2. (real estate) development considered pioneering or innovative.

FRONT-END DEVELOPER, *noun.* a (real estate) developer professing to be up to speed with the latest trends.

FULL-STACK DESIGNER, *noun.* a designer competent in every stage of the design process.

FUNIFY, *noun.* 1. to make something that is not fun, fun. 2. mobile app.

FUTURE-PROOFING, *noun.* the act of anticipating in the present whatever eventualities might occur in the future (*this approach allows you to future-proof your applications*).

FUTURITY, *noun.* 1. the future time (*the tremendous shadows which futurity casts upon the present*). 2. a future event. 3. renewed or continuing existence (*the snowdrops were a promise of futurity*). 4. (US) a horse race.

G

GBCI, *abb.* Green Business Certification Inc.

GAME CHANGER, *noun.* an event, idea or procedure that effects a significant shift in the current way of doing or thinking about something (*a potential game changer that could revitalize the entire industry*).

GAZE PATH, *noun.* the path our eyes take when reading and processing information from a screen or in print.

GENDER HACKING, *noun.* 1. feminine hacking ethic, more explicitly political in motivation, meant to counter the prevailing hacking ethic of 'frontier masculinity'. 2. an illicit way of establishing a person's gender.

GLOBULAR, *adjective.* 1. globe-shaped, spherical. 2. composed of globules.

GOODWELL, *noun.* township in Oklahoma.

GOODWELL CERTIFICATION, *noun.* certificate obtained by employers upon being compliant with certain standards regarding engaged, equitable and humane workplaces.

GO-TO EXPERT, *noun.* individual whose expertise is sought and rewarded. (See also 'thought leader'.)

GRACEFUL DEGRADATION, *noun.* the ability of a system to maintain functionality when portions of that system break down.

GREEN, *verb.* to render living environments and also artefacts, such as a space, lifestyle or brand image, into more environmentally friendly versions of themselves.

GREENLIGHT, *verb.* to approve; to give permission.

GREENWASH, *verb.* to legitimize otherwise fraught endeavours by making them appear green or environmentally conscious.

GROUPTHINK, *noun.* the practice of thinking or making decisions as a group, resulting typically in unchallenged, poor quality decision making (*there is always a danger of groupthink when there is no clear hierarchy*).

GROWTH CENTRE, *noun*. 1. a place, real or virtual, for the fostering of economic growth. 2. a centre of economic, social and cultural activities in rural areas, where people exchange ideas regarding improved methods of agricultural production.

GUERRILLA GARDENING, *noun*. a(n activist) form of gardening using land that the gardeners have no legal right to, generally abandoned sites or areas neglected by their legal owner.

GUERRILLA TESTING, *noun*. the gathering of feedback to a design or prototype by taking it into the public domain and asking random passersby for their thoughts.

GURU, *noun*. 1. a Hindu spiritual teacher. 2. an influential teacher or popular expert (*a management guru*). 3. online freelance hiring agency.

H

HCI, *abb*. human computer interaction.

HAPPINESS INDEX, *noun*. index measuring the feeling of happiness in terms of psychological wellbeing, health, work–life balance, community, social support, education, arts and culture, environment, governance and material wellbeing—more specifically, everything.

HAPPINESS LADDER, *noun*. see 'happiness index'.

HAPPY BY DESIGN, *adjective*. word play promoting the theory that well-designed buildings or cities have the ability to make people happy. 3. book by Ben Channon.

HAPPY-HOME HACK, *noun*. 1. illegal entry of an unsuspecting (usually suburban) home. 2. (derogatory) interior designer.

HEALING ENVIRONMENT, *noun*. a physical setting that supports people through the stresses imposed by illness and bereavement.

HEALTH ARCHITECTURE, *noun*. 1. the art of designing buildings that promote a healthy balance between physical, emotional, cognitive and spiritual wellbeing. 2. the type of architecture typically applied to medical facilities.

HEALTH-RELATED BEHAVIOUR CHANGE CAMPAIGN, *noun*. organized course of action to get people to adopt healthier habits.

HEALTHY LIFESTYLE EXPERIENCE, *noun.* enjoying zucchini instead of pasta, eating copious amounts of salad, working out and posting it all on social media.

HEDONISTIC SUSTAINABILITY, *noun.* (neologism) 1. the admixture of environmental ecology and fun, two commonly thought incompatible phenomena. 2. organized fun for the ecologically aware. 3. the means by which unsustainable attitudes are allowed, unpardonably, to continue.

HIPSTER, *noun.* (informal) 1. a person who follows the latest trends and fashions, especially those regarded as being outside the cultural mainstream. 2. a subculture that embodies a particular ethic of consumption that seeks to commodify the idea of rebellion or counterculture.

HUMAN-CENTRIC DESIGN, *noun.* atypical approach to design where products adjust to people instead of the other way round.

HUMAN-ORIENTED DESIGN, *noun.* see 'human-centric design'.

I

IDEATION, *noun.* the formation of ideas or concepts, especially by 'ideas persons' or 'creatives'. (See also 'paranoid ideation'.)

IMAGINEERING, *noun.* the devising and implementing of a new or highly imaginative concept or technology.

IMMERSIVE ENVIRONMENT, *noun.* a simulation that fills the user's visual field, giving the sensation of physical presence.

IMPACT GENERATION, *noun.* the doing of something that generates an impact.

INCLUSIVE DESIGN, *noun.* design that permits use by as many people as possible, regardless of age, race, religion, gender or disability.

INCLUSIVE DESIGN OFFICER, *noun.* One with a proven background in implementing inclusive design. Commonly a self-description.

INCLUSIVITY, *noun.* The practice or policy of including people who might otherwise be excluded or marginalized, such as those who have physical or mental disabilities and members of minority groups.

INCREMENTAL PLANNING, *noun.* 1. the breaking down of an overall plan into intermediate stages which might be regarded as finite in themselves. 2. planning with no intention to ever finish.

INFLUENCER, *noun.* (alt spelling: influenza) 1. a person or thing that influences another. 2. a person with the ability to influence potential buyers of a product or service by promoting or recommending the items on social media.

INFORMAL, *adjective.* 1. friendly; unofficial. 2. idiom suitable for everyday language. 3. book by Cecil Balmond.

INFORMALITY, *noun.* the state or quality of being informal.

INTEGRATED DESIGN, *noun.* an approach to design which brings together specialisms usually considered separately.

INTEGRATIVE DESIGN, *noun.* an approach to design which brings together people usually considered separately.

INTELLECTUAL HEALTH, *noun.* the ability to use one's brain without getting into trouble.

INTELLIGENT HOME, *noun.* 1. a home that thinks for itself and does not need to be set straight when doing so.

INTENTIONALITY, *noun.* to be about something, or about nothing, if that is the intention.

INTERCONNECTEDNESS, *noun.* the state of being connected with each other (*the interconnectedness of all things in the universe*).

INTERCONNECTION, *noun.* a mutual connection between two or more things (*the complex interconnections between people's lives*).

INTERCONNECTIVITY, *noun.* the state or quality of being interconnected (*this network has great interconnectivity*).

INTERSUBJECTIVITY, *noun.* (philosophy) the relation between people's cognitive perspectives.

J

JAM SESSIONING, *noun.* a method of designing whereby multiple parties or specialists come together to offer their 'live' contribution, not necessarily with preparation.

JARGON, *noun.* 1. special words or expressions used by a profession or group that are difficult for others to understand. 2. (archaic) a form of language regarded as barbarous, debased or hybrid.

JARGONEER, *noun.* a keen promotor of the use of jargon.

JARGONIZE, *verb.* to turn (conventional language or expressions) into jargon.

JARGONIST, *noun.* somebody in the habit of jargonizing.

JEOFAIL, *verb.* official or legal acknowledgement of a mistake.

JETSAM, *noun.* 1. the wreckage of a plane or its cargo found scattered across land or floating on sea. 2. people stranded at airports as a result of cancelled flights or immigration policies. (See also 'flotsam'.)

JOBBING, *adjective.* (British) the state of being employed to do occasional pieces of work, rather than on a regular or permanent basis (*a jobbing architect has to take any work he can get*).

JOBBERY, *noun.* theft of one's job.

JOBSWORTH, *noun.* the effect of a certain political or economic decision measured in the number of jobs it creates.

JUMBOISM, *noun.* an admiration for large things.

JUXTAPOSITIVITY, *noun.* the state or quality of juxtaposition.

K

KAW *abb.* Keep Austin Weird.

KPI *abb.* key performance indicator.

KARMA, *noun.* 1. the sum of a person's actions in this and previous states of existence, viewed as deciding their fate in future existences. 2. luck (good or bad), viewed as resulting from one's actions.

KAROSHI, *noun.* (Japanese) death caused by overwork or job-related exhaustion (*karoshi victims*).

KEY DRIVER, *noun.* motive.

KEYNOTE, *noun.* 1. (music) the note on which a key is based. 2. a typically meaningless address at an even more meaningless conference.

KEYSTONE, *noun.* 1. a central stone at the summit of an arch, locking the whole together. 2. the central principle on which all else depends. 3. the initial stage of a broken promise (*job growth remains the keystone of the government's policy*).

KICKSTARTER, *noun.* 1. a device to start an engine by the downward thrust of a pedal. 2. something that provides an impetus to start or resume a process. 3. crowdfunding site.

KILLSWITCH, *noun.* a safety mechanism used to shut off machinery in case of emergency (also known as an 'emergency stop', 'emergency off' and as an 'emergency power off').

KINESIOLOGY, *noun.* the study of the mechanics of body movements.

KITCHEN SINK, *adjective.* (of art forms) characterized by great realism in the depiction of drab or sordid subjects.

KOINONIPHOBE, *noun.* someone with an irrational fear of rooms.

KOINONIPHILE, *noun.* 1. someone with an irrational love of rooms. 2. museum director.

L

LABELLING *noun.* 1. attach a label to something or somebody. 2. assign to a category.

LABELLING EFFECT, *noun.* the presumed effect of labelling as a self-fulfilling prophecy.

LABELLING THEORY, *noun.* theory that posits that the behaviour of individuals is determined or influenced by the terms or categories used to describe or classify them.

LAGOM, *noun.* (Swedish) in moderation.

LATENCY PERIOD, *noun.* 1. (medical) the interval between when an individual or host is infected by a pathogen and when they become infectious. 2. (design) the time that elapses between having an idea and realizing that it is a good idea.

LEARNABILITY, *noun.* the quality of being learnable.

LEFTWINGERY, *adjective.* 1. views, opinions, principles or behaviour characteristic of those who are politically left wing. 2. sinisterness.

LEGACY CREATION, *noun.* the act of procuring the legacy of something or somebody likely not to have one otherwise.

LENTICULAR, *adjective* 1. shaped like a lentil, especially by being biconvex (*lenticular lenses*). 2. relating to the lens of the eye.

LIFESTYLISM, *noun.* the appropriation of something as a lifestyle without regard to its underlying tenets or meaning.

LIFESTYLIST, *noun.* someone who adopts the superficial trappings of a political ideology or movement without being dedicated to the cause.

LIVEABILITY, *noun*. (alt. 'livability') 1. survival expectancy; viability (of poultry and livestock). 2. suitability for human living.

LIVED-IN, *adjective*. showing evidence of age or fray; tired.

LOCALITY, *noun*. place.

LOGORRHOEA, *noun*. 1. a tendency to extreme loquacity. 2. loose-lippedness.

LOW-MAINTENANCE NATURE, *noun*. (pleonasm) nature not needing much attention or effort.

M

MVP *abb*. minimum viable product.

MBArchI *abb*. mindfulness-based architecture intervention

MBSR *abb*. mindfulness-based stress reduction

MACHINE LEARNING, *noun*. the use and development of computer systems that are able to learn and adapt without following explicit instructions, by using algorithms and statistical models to analyse and draw inferences from patterns in data.

MACRO BREAK, *noun*. instruction to the computer to suspend the execution of a particular task.

MATERIALITY, *noun*. 1. the measure of how relevant a piece of information is when taking a decision. 2. the stuff things are made of.

MEGALOMANIA, *noun*. 1. obsession with the exercise of power. 2. delusion about one's own power or importance (typically as a symptom of manic or paranoid disorder).

MEGALOPHILIA, *noun*. the love of all things large.

MEGALOPOLIS, *noun*. a very large, heavily populated city or urban complex.

MEGALOPOLITICS, *noun*. the politics associated with governing a very large, heavily populated city or agglomeration.

MENTAL HEALTH CHAMPION, *noun*. someone who champions the cause of mental health.

MENTAL HEALTH FIRST AIDER, *noun*. someone qualified to give help during the initial stages of a mental health crisis.

MENTAL HEALTH LITERACY, *noun*. knowledge about mental disorders, which helps aid their recognition, management and prevention.

MENTAL HEALTH PARITY, *noun.* the equal treatment of mental health conditions to other illnesses or disorders.

MENTAL WELLBEING, *noun.* the state of feeling comfortable, healthy or happy—with oneself and one's life in general.

METABOLIC LANDSCAPE, *noun.* 1. the interpretation of a landscape as the outcomes of metabolic processes akin to that of the human body. 2. medical term (*the single-cell metabolic landscape of human tumors*).

MICROAGGRESSION, *noun.* commonplace daily verbal or behavioural slight, significant enough to be a nuisance, not enough to warrant rebuttal (unless in the form of a similar microaggression).

MICRO-BREAK, *noun.* short, voluntary and impromptu respites in the workday, including discretionary activities such as having a snack, chatting with a colleague, stretching or working on a crossword puzzle.

MINDFULNESS, *noun.* 1. a mental state achieved by calmly acknowledging and accepting one's feelings, thoughts and bodily sensations. 2. Buddhism without Buddha.

RIGHT MINDFULNESS, *noun.* awareness of the present moment as it is.

WRONG MINDFULNESS, *noun.* awareness of the present moment as it is not.

MINDFULNESS PRACTITIONER, *noun.* someone who makes a living out of practices of mindfulness.

N

NARRATIVE-DRIVEN DESIGN, *noun.* design that takes the 'post' out of post-rationalization.

NATURE INCORPORATION, *noun.* 1. making nature part of things it is not usually considered part of (*nature incorporation into architecture*). 2. manufacturer of 'hyflo-supercel powder'.

NEEDFINDING, *noun.* 1. the process of identifying the need for a particular design or product. 2. book by Dev Patnaik.

NETWORK, *noun.* 1. an arrangement of intersecting horizontal and vertical lines. 2. a group or system of interconnected people or things. *verb.* to interact with others to exchange information and develop professional or social contacts.

NETWORKER, *noun.* a person who networks.

NETWORKEE, *noun.* a person who is being networked.

NEW-AGEISM, *noun.* 1. adherence to New Age practices and beliefs. 2. a recurring form of discrimination based on a person's age.

NON-PLACE, *noun.* a place without inspiring the sense of one.

NON-VISUAL DESIGN, *noun.* a waste of time.

NOSOCOMEPHOBIA, *noun.* a fear of hospitals.

NUDGE ARCHITECTURE, *noun.* architecture of which the point can be freely ignored.

NYCTOPHILIA, *noun.* an extreme or irrational love of darkness.

NYCTOPHOBIA, *noun.* an extreme or irrational fear of darkness.

O

OBJECTIVISM, *noun.* 1. the tendency to emphasize what is external to or independent of the mind. 2. a philosophical system developed by Russian-American writer Ayn Rand, positing that moral truths exist independently of human knowledge or perception of them.

OCCUPATIONAL THERAPY, *noun.* therapy based on engagement in meaningful activities of daily life: being well by being busy.

OCCUPATIONAL THERAPIST, *noun.* someone who practises occupational therapy.

OFFICIALDOM, *noun.* 1. (derogatory) the officials in an organization or government department, considered as a group. 2. bureaucracy.

OFFICIALESE, *noun.* the verbose writing style associated with official documents.

OFFTREND, *adjective.* at odds with a given trend. (See also 'ontrend'.)

ONBOARDING, *noun.* the action or process of integrating a new employee into an organization or familiarizing a new customer or client with one's products or services (*after the initial onboarding is complete, continue to offer new hires relevant training and development opportunities*).

ONLINE FOOTPRINT, *noun.* the traces one leaves when browsing the internet. (See also 'digital life'.)

ONTREND, *adjective.* in line with a given trend. (See also 'offtrend'.)

OPEN SOURCING, *noun.* the act of openly collaborating on a single product, typically enabled and enhanced by the availability of digital technology.

OPEN SOURCE DESIGN, *noun.* design applying the method of open sourcing.

ORGANICITY, *noun.* the state of being organic.

ORTHOCRACY, *noun.* (architecture) the rule of the ninety-degree angle.

OTHER, *verb.* to disadvantage a certain culture or class of individuals by overemphasizing their apartness or difference; alienate.

OTHERNITY, *noun.* exhibition project in the Hungarian Pavilion during the 2021 Venice Architecture Biennial.

P

PAO, *abb.* physical activity opportunities.

PCT *abb.* person-centered therapy.

PARANOID-CRITICAL METHOD, *noun.* surrealist technique developed by Salvador Dalí.

PARANOID IDEATION, *noun.* psychotic disorder symptom involving transient, stress-related paranoia, characterized by the experience of feeling threatened, persecuted or conspired against.

PARTNER, *verb.* do it to them before they do it to you. (See 'trust issues'.)

PASTORALIZATION, *noun.* the act or process of making pastoral.

PEOPLE-FIRST DESIGN, *noun.* design that puts people first (antonym of people-last design).

PERSONAL ENERGY EXPENDITURE, *noun.* the total amount of energy a person uses in acknowledging the existence of others.

PLACEMAKING, *noun.* (neologism) an approach to the design of public space which (cl)aims to transform non-places into places. (See 'non-place'.)

PLACE-STAKING, *noun.* the reserving of places by marking or bounding them with stakes.

PLACE-TAKING, *noun.* the act of claiming a place as one's own (usually preceded by a form of place-staking, not seldom in the name of placemaking).

PLAZA BONUS, *noun.* the additional floors allowed in a building by zoning laws as a reward for creating an adjacent plaza.

PLURALISTIC WALKTHROUGH, *noun.* (computing) multiangled inspection of a piece of software or website in an effort to optimize the human–computer interface.

POLITICAL CORRECTNESS, *noun.* the avoidance of forms of expression or action that are perceived to exclude, marginalize or insult groups of people who are socially disadvantaged or discriminated against.

POLITICAL CORRECTNESS GONE MAD, *noun.* Harvard.

PRECARIAT, *noun.* 1. portmanteau of 'precarious' and 'proletariat': people whose employment and income are insecure, especially when considered as a social class.

PREDICTIVE CITY, *noun.* city to which predictive abilities are ascribed due to the implementation of digital technology.

PRESENTISM, *noun.* 1. the anachronistic introduction of present-day ideas and perspectives into depictions or interpretations of the past. 2. an irrational prejudice towards Christmas.

PRESSURE COOKER, *noun.* 1. an airtight pot in which food can be cooked quickly under steam pressure. 2. a highly stressful situation or assignment (*an academic pressure cooker which turns young people into depressives*).

PROGRESSIVISM, *noun.* support for or advocacy of social reform.

Q

QI, *abb.* quite interesting.

QUALITY TEAM, *noun.* forget it!

QUANTIFIED SELF, *noun.* the cultural phenomenon of self-tracking with technology.

QUANTUM LEAP, *noun.* an abrupt change, sudden increase or other dramatic advance.

QUIDDITY, *noun.* 1. the inherent nature or essence of someone or something. 2. a distinctive feature; a peculiarity.

R

RMT, *abb.* regenerative massage therapy.

REAL WORK, *noun.* work that is real, unlike work that is not.

REBRANDING, *noun.* branding, for when branding hasn't worked the first time.

REDLINING, *noun.* 1. the act of driving a car at or above the rated maximum revolutions per minute of its engine. 2. discriminatory practice in which services are withheld from potential customers who reside in neighbourhoods classified as 'hazardous' to investment.

REGIONALLY INFLECTED, *adjective.* given a particular shape or twist by the region (*the design is one of the most important examples of regionally inflected modernism of the late twentieth century*).

RELIGIOSITY, *noun.* strong religious feeling or belief.

RESILIENCE, *noun.* 1. the capacity to recover quickly from difficulties; toughness. 2. the ability of a substance or object to spring back into shape; elasticity.

RESTORATIVE ENVIRONMENT, *noun.* an environment or natural setting which can help overcome emotional or physical stress.

RESTORATIVE SPACE, *noun.* 1. space designated to help overcome emotional or physical stress. 2. (archaic/obsolete) home.

REWILDING, *noun.* 1. the act of restoring an area of land to its natural uncultivated state, used especially with reference to the reintroduction of species of wild animal that have been driven out or exterminated.

S

SJW *abb.* social justice warrior.

SSOT, *abb.* single source of truth.

SAFETYISM, *noun.* the piety preached by those for whom 'running with scissors' is a moral as well as physical danger.

SAFE SPACE, *noun.* A space made unsafe for those deemed undesirable or old-hat.

SATISFACTION THRESHOLD, *noun.* the minimum level of satisfaction required to feel satisfied about something or someone.

SCIENCE-BASED TARGET, *noun.* a target for which there is scientific evidence to support that it is worth pursuing.

SELF-ACTUALIZATION, *noun.* the state of having reached one's full potential; the condition allowed to ensue after basic material requirements have been fulfilled.

SELF-COMPASSION, *noun*. self-pity made socially acceptable.

SELF-HEALING, *noun*. curing oneself without the help of a doctor or the use of pharmaceuticals.

SIMPLEXITY, *noun*. complexity made simple; simplicity made complex.

SLEEP INCORPORATION, *noun*. a common habit of employees to have small naps to compensate for long working hours.

SLEEP SUPPORT, *noun*. 1. professional help in the overcoming of sleep disorders 2. brand of melatonin.

SMART EVERYTHING, *noun*. the state in which all human tasks will have been replaced by digital appliances or devices.

SOCIABILITY, *noun*. the quality of being sociable.

SOCIAL TRUST, *noun*. the concept of 'trust' applied more widely to a larger group or society as a whole.

SPECIALNESS, *noun*. 1. the state of something or someone being special, distinct. 2. idiosyncrasy given the benefit of the doubt.

SPIRIT-TO-SPIRIT, *adjective*. likeminded.

STATUS ANXIETY, *noun*. the tension or fear of being perceived as 'unsuccessful' by society in materialistic terms.

STAYCATION, *noun*. a holiday spent at home, or in one's home country.

STIGMATIST, *noun*. 1. someone in the habit of stereotyping others on the basis of perceivable social, mental or physical characteristics. 2. a person whose body is marked by religious stigmata.

SUCCESSFUL BUILDING, *noun*. a building compliant with a certain measure of success, either because it is award winning, world class, innovative, sustainable, creative, beautiful, fosters a sense of place and wellbeing, or all at once.

T

TBL *abb*. triple bottom line.

TASK FLOW, *noun*. diagram representing the various steps of a task. (See 'workflow'.)

TED, *abb*. Technology, Entertainment, Design: American media organization that posts talks online for free distribution.

TEDify, *verb*. compress (or extend) a presentation to last exactly seventeen minutes and thirty seconds.

THOUGHT LEADER, *noun.* individual ascribed the quality of 'thought leadership'; an authority in a specific field whose expertise is sought and rewarded. (See also 'go-to expert'.)

THOUGHT SHOWER, *noun.* the spontaneous generation of new ideas during a group discussion, predicated on the statistical axiom that the larger the number of ideas, the larger the probability of a good one. (See also 'jam sessioning'.)

TOKENISM, *noun.* the practice of making only a perfunctory or symbolic effort.

TOTEMISM, *noun.* belief in which humans are thought to have kinship or a mystical relationship with a spirit-being, such as an animal or plant.

TOP DOWN, *adjective.* 1. proceeding from the top of a hierarchy downwards. 2. One of two states of a convertible car.

TRANSFORMATIVE POLITICS, *noun.* fiction.

TRENDING, *adjective.* currently popular or widely discussed online.

TROLL, *noun.* 1. an ugly creature depicted as either a giant or a dwarf. 2. a person who makes a deliberately offensive or provocative online post. 3. a line or bait used in trolling for fish.

TROLLING, *noun.* 1. to make a deliberately offensive or provocative online post with the aim of upsetting someone or eliciting an angry response from them. 2. carefully and systematically searching an area for something.

TRUE INTENT STUDY, *noun.* a survey intercepting a live visitor of a particular site or app asking why they are visiting.

TRUST ISSUES, *noun.* 1. an innate inability to trust people or the outcome of their actions. 2. insufficient trust between people taking part in a common endeavour. (See also 'partner'.)

TRUTH SYSTEM, *noun.* (information technology) system to ensure that members of an organization rely on the same information or data when making decisions. (See also 'SSOT'.)

T-SHAPED DESIGNER, *noun.* someone with a deep, specific knowledge within their field (represented by the vertical stem in a capital 'T') as well as a certain level of experience in numerous fields related to their own (represented by a shorter, horizontal crossbar on the top).

U

UGC, *abb.* user-generated content.

USP, *abb.* unique selling point.

UNDERSTATED LUXURY, *noun.* luxury without the obvious emphasis or embellishment of such.

UNEDIFYING, *adjective.* (especially of an event taking place in public) distasteful; unpleasant (*the unedifying sight of the two leaders screeching conflicting proposals*).

UNPUTDOWNABLE, *adjective.* 1. (of a book) so engrossing that one cannot stop reading it. 2. Oliver Wainwright while working at OMA.

UNREGENERATE, *verb.* the process of regeneration in reverse.

UPCYCLE, *verb.* reuse (discarded objects or material) in such a way as to create a product of higher quality or value than the original.

UPLEVEL, *verb.* elevate somebody or something beyond current capabilities or perceptions.

UPSCALE, *verb.* make bigger.

UPSTART, *noun.* Gareth Keenan in *The Office.*

URBAN, *adjective.* 1. in, relating to, or characteristic of a town or city. 2. music radio format coined by radio DJ Frankie Crocker; term used by rappers. 3. politically correct substitute term for 'black'.

URBAN ACUPUNCTURE, *noun.* small-scale interventions in a city in the hope to transform the larger context.

URBAN MYTH, *noun.* untrue story.

URBAN PLANNING, *noun.* the technical and political process of planning cities.

URBANISM, *noun.* the study or 'science' of planning cities.

URBANITE, *noun.* city dweller.

URBANITY, *noun.* 1. urban life 2. refinement of manner.

URBANOLOGY, *noun.* a branch of sociology that has taken it upon itself to deal with the fall out of urban planning.

URBANOLOGIST, *noun.* Richard Florida.

UTILITARIANISM, *noun.* (philosophy) doctrine that actions are right if they are useful or for the benefit of a majority.

V

VANCOUVERISM, *noun.* 1. Vancouver's global liveability ranking packaged and marketed as a universal planning doctrine; a concerted pledge for other cities to follow Vancouver's example. 2. book by Larry Beasley.

VANGUARDISM, *noun.* 1. the actions or beliefs of those who lead a certain field. 2. (Leninism) a strategy whereby the most class-conscious and politically 'advanced' sections of the proletariat or working class form organizations in order to draw larger sections of the working class towards revolutionary politics and serve as manifestations of proletarian political power opposed to the bourgeois.

VEGETATIVE PROPAGATION, *noun.* asexual reproduction.

VERBIAGE, *noun.* excessively lengthy or technical speech or writing.

VERDURELESSNESS, *noun.* the absence of (lush green) vegetation (*the estate was in a sad state of verdurelessness*). (See 'concrete jungle'.)

VIEW-BASED URBANISM, *noun.* urbanism practised with apt consideration for the optics which ensue in its wake.

VISUAL DESIGN, *noun.* design.

VITAL, *adjective.* 1. essential. 2. lively.

VITALITY, *noun.* the quality of being vital.

VITALISM, *noun.* the theory that the origin and phenomena of life are dependent on a force or principle distinct from purely chemical or physical forces.

VITALITARIANISM, *noun.* doctrine that actions are right if they inspire the greatest possible vitality.

VULGARIZATION, *noun.* 1. the act or process of making something vulgar. 2. the act or process of making something better known and understood by ordinary people; popularize.

W

WALKABLE NEIGHBOURHOOD, *noun.* Notting Hill.

WALLPAPER, *verb.* 1. to cover the walls of (a room) with wallpaper. 2. indiscriminately subject different things to the same treatment.

WANDERLUST, *noun.* a strong desire to travel.

WELL AP, *abb.* WELL-accredited professional.

WELL BUILDING STANDARD™, *noun*. performance-based system for measuring, certifying and monitoring features of the built environment thought to impact human health and wellbeing, such as air, water, light and comfort.

WELL v2™, *noun*. WELL Building Standard version 2.

WELLBEING, *noun*. the state of being comfortable, healthy or happy—with oneself and with life in general.

WELLNESS, *noun*. the active pursuit of the state of being comfortable, healthy or happy.

WELLNESS ARCHITECTURE, *noun*. 1. the organized promotion of physical and mental wellbeing. 2. the type of architecture typically applied to wellness facilities.

WELLNESS OPTIMIZATION, *noun*. creation of the best possible conditions to pursue the state of being in good health.

WISDOM 2.0, *noun*. 1. event series exploring the application of ancient wisdom in modern life. 2. book by Soren Gordhamer.

WORK FEVER, *noun*. 1. frantic urge to work. 2. high temperature brought on by the thought of work.

WORKFLOW, *noun*. the stages through which a piece of work passes from initiation to completion.

WORLD CLASS, *adjective*. 1. ranking among the world's best; outstanding. 2. attracting or comprising world-class players or performers. 3. (informal) being a notorious example of its kind.

WOW FACTOR, *noun*. 1. (informal) a quality or feature that is extremely impressive. 2. the ability to inspire a state of exaltation, commonly attributed to being 'world class'.

X

X, *verb*. to cross out single letters of type.

X-ING, *noun*. the activity of crossing out single letters of type.

X-ER, *noun*. member of Generation X.

X-CHASER, *noun*. adept at mathematics, finding the value of X.

XENAGOGUE, *noun*. one who conducts/appeals to strangers/foreigners.

XENIATROPHOBIA, *noun*. an abnormal fear of foreign doctors.

XENIZATION, *noun*. the act of travelling as a stranger.

XENOCRACY, *noun.* a government formed by foreigners.

XENOFEMINISM, *noun.* 1. feminist movement that promotes the use of technology to abolish gender. 2. book by Helen Hester.

XENOGLOSSY, *noun.* the ability to speak a language you have not actively learned.

XENOMANIA, *noun.* the intense enthusiasm for anyone or anything foreign.

XERISCAPE, *noun.* a garden or landscape created in a style that requires little or no irrigation or other maintenance.

Y

YAWN, *abb.* young and wealthy but normal.

YIELD, *verb.* 1. produce or provide (a natural, agricultural or industrial product). 2. give way to arguments, demands or pressure. *noun.* 1. the amount produced. 2. the total earnings from an investment.

YIELDING, *adjective.* 1. (of a substance or object, not hard or rigid) giving way under pressure. 2. (of a crop, soil, etc.) producing a yield; productive.

YIELD SPREAD, *noun.* the delta between the quoted rates of return on two different investments.

YOYO, *noun.* a volatile market.

YUPPIE 2.0, *noun.* see 'hipster'.

Z

ZAG, *noun.* a sharp change of direction. *verb.* to make a sharp change of direction.

ZIG, *noun/verb.* see 'zag'.

ZAGGER, *noun.* someone who, when given the option to zig, zags.

ZIGGER, *noun.* someone who, when given the option to zag, zigs.

ZIGZAG, *noun.* a line or course having abrupt alternate right and left turns. *adjective.* having the form of a zigzag; veering alternately to right and left. *adverb.* so as to move right and left alternately. *verb.* have or move along in a zigzag course.

ZOOM, *noun.* 1. camera shot that changes smoothly from a long shot to a close-up or vice versa. 2. video communications platform.

ZOOM FATIGUE, *noun*. tiredness of excessive use of video communications (not limited to the use of 'Zoom' as a platform per se).

ZOOM READINESS, *noun*. 1. (of a room) the absence of embarrassing decorations or family photos. 2. (of a zoom caller) having oneself positioned in such a way as not to reveal that one is semi-clothed.

Acknowledgements

This book owes a special debt of gratitude to Leo Hollis for being at once critical, encouraging and patient; to Jacqueline Tellinga for her support, moral and otherwise; to Alex Retegan, Hans Larsson, Matthew Bovingdon-Downe and Adam Kouki for helping to make its chapters excellent, innovative, creative, sustainable and beautiful; and to the Cambridge Online Dictionary of English for being a valuable anchor whenever words got the better of their meanings.

Notes

Introduction

1 Paul Tostevin, '8 Things to Know about Global Real Estate Value', savills.com, July 2018.
2 Sonia Sykra, 'How Does Construction Impact the Environment?', gocontractor.com, 21 June 2017.

1. Tears and Love

1 Herbert Muchamp, 'The Miracle In Bilbao', nytimes.com, 7 September 1997.
2 Celestine Bohlen, 'The Guggenheim's Scaled-Back Ambition; A Museum Director's Risk-Taking Approach Gets a New Look in Hard Times', nytimes.com, 20 November 2001.
3 Interview with Juan Ignacio Vidarte, the-report.com, 1 October 2001.
4 Previous locations considered by the Guggenheim were Salzburg and Punta della Dogana in Venice. See Hannah McGivern, 'Twenty Years On: How the Guggenheim Bilbao Came of Age', theartnewspaper.com, 24 November 2017.
5 *Impact of the activities of the Guggenheim Museum Bilbao on the economy of the Basque Country 1997–2000*, prensa.guggenheim-bilbao.eus, 12 January 2001.
6 'The Bilbao Effect', forbes.com, 20 February 2002.
7 Tom Jacobs, 'Branding Bilbao: A Cultural Investment That Paid Off', psmag.com, 14 June 2017.
8 Richard Tomkins, 'Happy Birthday Globalization', ft.com, 6 May 2003.
9 Annie Bennet, 'Aviles Awaits the Niemeyer Effect', moochingaroundspain.com, 3 April 2011.
10 Benjamin Forgey, 'Beyond Bilbao: Revisiting a Special Effect', washingtonpost.com, 20 October 2002.
11 Bruce Murphy, 'New Addition Leaves Art Museum Mired in Debt', philanthropynewsdigest.org, 30 July 2003.

12 'Denver Art Museum', designbuild-network.com, 21 March 2005.

13 Elisabeth Merrill, 'Zaha Hadid's Center for Contemporary Art and the Perils of New Museum Architecture', researchgate.net, September 2019.

14 Dorothy Spears, 'When the Final Touch Is the Exit Door', nytimes.com, 12 March 2018.

15 Department of Culture, Media and Sport, *Better Public Buildings*, October 2000.

16 Jonathan Glancey, 'War and Peace and Quiet', theguardian.com, 22 April 2002.

17 See phaeno.de.

18 Quoted in Andrew Ayers, 'The €255.4-million Question: Is It a Masterpiece That Future Generations Will Cherish?', architectural-review.com, 27 August 2015.

19 Interview with Peter Eisenman, bombmagazine.org, 1 October 2011.

20 Quoted in Giles Tremlett, Spain's Extravagant City of Culture Opens Amid Criticism', theguardian.com, 11 January 2011.

21 Ibid.

22 Suzanne Daley, 'A Star Architect Leaves Some Clients Fuming', nytimes.com, 24 September 2013.

23 Giles Tremlett, 'Architect Santiago Calatrava Accused of "Bleeding Valencia Dry"', theguardian.com, 8 May 2012.

24 Interview with Santiago Calatrava, architecturalrecord.com, 27 June 2012.

25 Rowan Moore, 'The Bilbao Effect: How Frank Gehry's Guggenheim Started a Global Craze', theguardian.com, 1 October 2017.

26 Matt Chaban, 'Frank Gehry Really, Really Regrets His Guest Appearance on The Simpsons', observer.com, 9 May 2011.

27 *Impact of the Activities of the Guggenheim Museum Bilbao.*

Data, p. 28–29

1 See burjkhalifa.ae.

2 Katie Warren, 'The World's Skinniest Skyscraper Is Almost Complete. I Toured Its First Luxury Condo—Take a Look Inside the NYC Tower That's 24 Times as Tall as It Is Wide', businessinsider.nl, 11 August 2020.

3 Niall Patrick Walsh, 'World's Tallest Modular Buildings Completed', archdaily.com, 3 July 2019.

4 Associated Press in Changsha, 'Chinese Construction Firm Erects 57-Storey Skyscraper in 19 Days', theguardian.com, 30 April 2015.

5 See hitachi.com.

6   See atlasobscura.com.

7   See klm.com.

8   See guinnessworldrecords.com.

9   See guinnessworldrecords.com.

10 Christopher Klein, '10 Things You May Not Know About the Eiffel Tower', history.com, 30 March 2020.

11 Roberto A. Ferdman, 'The World's New Largest Building Is Four Times the Size of Vatican City', qz.com, 3 July 2013.

12 See boeing.com.

13 Leah Dolan and Megan C. Hills, 'Designs Unveiled for The World's Largest Single-Domed Greenhouse', edition.cnn.com, 12 May 2021.

14 KPF, 'KPF-Designed MGM COTAI Achieves a GUINNESS WORLD RECORDS™ Title', kpf.com, 23 April 2019.

15 See guinnessworldrecords.com.

16 Jon Dioffa, 'World's Largest and Most Expensive Family Home Completed', inhabitat.com, 15 October 2010.

17 See apis-cor.com.

18 Oliver Smith, 'World's Longest Building: Prora on the Island of Rugen in Germany Is a Former Nazi Resort', traveller.com.au, 20 November 2018.

19 Emely Acobo, 'Jinping Underground Laboratory, China—The World's Deepest Underground Laboratory', re-thinkingthefuture.com.

20 What Are the Biggest Underground Structures?', groundworks companies.com, 2 October 2020.

21 Kara Williams, 'Take A Plunge into The World's Deepest Swimming Pool, Complete with A Sunken City', travelawaits.com, 23 July 2021.

22 See guinnessworldrecords.com.

23 Alice Young, 'The 10 Most Expensive Buildings in The World', constructionglobal.com, 10 June 2016.

24 See guinnessworldrecords.com.

25 AD Editorial Team, 'Bloomberg's New European Headquarters Rated World's Most Sustainable Office Building', archdaily.com, 10 October 2017.

26 Rosamond Hutt, 'This Warehouse Is One of the World's Greenest Industrial Buildings', weforum.org, 19 August 2019.

27 Renee Ghert-Zand, 'MKs May Turn the Air Blue, but Knesset Is Earth's Greenest Parliament', timesofisrael.com, 8 April 2015.

28 Megan Willett-Wei, 'This staircase and Plant-Filled Building Is Designed to Be the Healthiest Workplace in the World', business insider.com, 5 November 2015.

29 See atlasobscura.com.

2. Officially Amazing

1 Jeff Schofield, 'Case Study: Capital Gate, Abu Dhabi', *CTBUH Journal*, Issue II, 2012.
2 'Farthest Leaning Church Tower', guinnessworldrecords.com, 17 January 2007.
3 National Geographic Channel, 'The Leaning Tower of Abu Dhabi Documentary', *Megastructures*, 5 April 2010.
4 Jeff Schofield and Pierre Martin Dufrense, *18 Degrees: Capital Gate —Leaning Tower of Abu Dhabi: The Ultimate Diagrid*, Basel: Bikhäuser, 2016.
5 Ibid.
6 U+A, 'Capital Gate', ua-intl.com.
7 Schofield, 'Case Study'.
8 Quoted in RMJM, 'The Capital Gate ADNEC', archello.com.
9 Quoted in RMJM, 'RMJM: Exclusive Hospitality Design Projects', rmjm.com, 12 April 2008.

Data, p. 45

1 See en.innovative-architecture.de.
2 See archdesignaward.com.
3 See akdn.org.
4 See architectureprize.com.
5 See worldarchitecture.org.
6 See architecturedesignaward.com.
7 See aia.org.
8 See alvaraalto.fi.
9 See currystonefoundation.org.
10 See dedalominosse.org.
11 See citedelarchitecture.fr.
12 See pritzkerprize.com.
13 See architecture.com.au.
14 See architecture.com.
15 See tamayouz-award.com.
16 See architecture.com
17 See internationalarchitectureawards.com.
18 See paawards.com.
19 See architectural-review.com.
20 See culture.ec.europa.eu.
21 See leafawards.arena-international.com.

3. Everyone a Winner

1 Tom Dyckhoff, 'The Malling of Our Cities', thetimes.co.uk, 10 January 2007.

2 Edwin Heathcote, 'Carbuncle Cup: Award Mocks Ugly Buildings but Doesn't Stop Them', ft.com, 16 September 2016.

3 Liz Walder, *History, Design, and Legacy: Architectural Prizes and Awards: An Academic Investigation of the Royal Institute of British Architects' (RIBA) Royal Gold Medal*, Cardiff: Wordcatcher Publishing, 2019, 24.

4 See pritzkerprize.com.

5 Quoted in Y-Jean Mun-Delsalle, 'Created In 1979, Jay Pritzker's Prize Is Still Architecture's Highest Honor, forbes.com, 13 March 2016.

6 See architecture.nd.edu.

7 See w-awards.architectural-review.com.

8 'A Decade of Design Awards: We Look Back Through the Years', wallpaper.com, 14 January 2014.

9 In 2017, both magazines were sold off to Metropolis Group, who also owns *Property Week*.

10 'ASA Ruling on AI Global Media Ltd t/a Build', asa.org.uk, 22 August 2018.

4. Crisis? What Crisis?

1 Bloomberg, 'Bloomberg's New European Headquarters Rated World's Most Sustainable Office Building, October', Bloomberg. com, 1 October 2017.

2 Foster + Partners, 'Bloomberg's New European Headquarters Rated World's Most Sustainable Office Building', fosterandpartners.com, 2 October 2017.

3 Steven Levy, 'One More Thing Inside Apple's Insanely Great (Or Just Insane) New Mothership', wired.com, 16 May 2017.

4 Oliver Wainwright, 'Bloomberg HQ: A £1bn Building That Looks Like a Regional Department Store', theguardian.com, 25 October 2017.

5 Lloyd Alter, 'Please Stop Calling the New Bloomberg HQ the World's Most Sustainable Office Building. It's Not', treehugger. com, 11 October 2018.

6 Christopher Schnaars, Hannah Morgan, 'In US Building Industry, Is It Too Easy to be Green?', eu.usatoday.com, 24 October 2010.

7 Quoted in Bloomberg, 'Bloomberg's New European Headquarters'.

8 David Gottfried, *Explosion Green: One Man's Journey to Green the World's Largest Industry*, New York: James Publishing, 2014, 31.

9 See breeam.com.

10 'Why Choose BREEAM', www.breeam.com.

11 See usgbc.org.

12 Hans Carl Von Carlowitz, *Sylvicultura Oeconomica*, Leipzig: 1713, 105.

13 See Ulrich Grober, 'Deep Roots—A Conceptual History of "Sustainable Development" (Nachhaltigkeit)', *Discussion Papers / WZB, Wissenschaftszentrum Berlin für Sozialforschung*, Berlin: WZB, 2007, 22–24.

14 Gifford Pinchot, *Breaking New Ground*, Washington, DC: Island Press, 1988, 319.

15 Gifford Pinchot, 'The Forest. Forest-Policy Abroad—III', *Garden and Forest* 4 (152), 1891, 35.

16 Pinchot, *Breaking New Ground*.

17 Archibald MacLeish, 'A Reflection: Riders on Earth Together, Brothers in Eternal Cold', nytimes.com, 25 December 1968.

18 Edward Goldsmith, *Blueprint for Survival*, London: Tom Stacey Ltd, 1972, 1.

19 Ibid., 5.

20 Donella H. Meadows, Club of Rome, *The Limits to Growth*, New York: Pan Books, 1972, 142.

21 Ibid., 158.

22 Peter Passell, Marc Roberts and Leonard Ross, 'The Limits to Growth', nytimes.com, 2 April 1972.

23 World Commission on Environment and Development, *Our Common Future*, New York: Oxford University Press, 1987, 7.

24 Ibid., 46.

25 United Nations, *Agenda 21*, 1992, 40.4.

26 Livio D. DeSimone and Frank Popoff with World Business Council for Sustainable Development, *Eco-efficiency: The Business Link to Sustainable Development*, Cambridge: MIT Press, 1997, 89.

27 Hendrik A. Verfaillie and Robin Bidwell, *Measuring Eco-efficiency: A Guide to Reporting Company Performance*, 2000, 2.

28 See gbci.org.

29 Michael Green, '2019 Social Progress Index: Measuring Real Things That Matter', skoll.org, 18 September 2019.

30 Somini Sengupta, 'Global Action Is 'Very Far' From What's Needed to Avert Climate Chaos', nytimes.com, 26 February 2021.

31 WMO, 'Climate Change Threatens Sustainable Development', public.wmo.int, 22 September 2021.

32 Billy Nauman, '"Green Bubble" Warnings Grow as Money Pours into Renewable Stocks', ft.com, 19 February 2021.

33 Bjarke Ingels, 'Hedonistic Sustainability', ted.com, May 2011.

5. All WELL

1 WHO Regional Office for Europe, 'Biological Effects of Man-made Mineral Fibres', EURO Reports and Studies 81, Copenhagen 1983.

2 Sumedha M. Joshi, 'The Sick Building Syndrome', *Indian Journal of Occupational and Environmental Medicine* 12(2), 2008, 61–64.

3 TSSA, 'Sick Building Syndrome', tssa.org.uk.

4 Ake Thorn, 'Case Study of a Sick Building: Could an Integrated Biopsychosocial Perspective Prevent Chronicity?', *European Journal of Public Health* 10(2), June 2000.

5 George Augustus Sala, 'The Health Exhibition: A Look Around', in *Illustrated London News* 85, 2 August 1884, 94.

6 Philip and Leah Lovell, *Diet for Health by Natural Methods: Together with Health Menus and Recipes; Complete Instructions for the Cure of the Sick Without the Use of Drugs*, Los Angeles: Times-Mirror Press, 1927. Quoted in Beatriz Colomina, *X-ray Architecture*, Zurich: Lars Müller Publishers, 2019.

7 Richard Neutra, 'Steel Construction with Plaster', *California Plasterer*, 1929. Quoted in Beatriz Colomina, *X-ray Architecture*, Zurich: Lars Müller Publishers, 2019.

8 Frank Macfarlane Burnet, *Natural History of Infectious Diseases*, New York: Cambridge University Press, 1962, 3.

9 See Clare Cooper Marcus and Marni Barnes, *Healing Gardens: Therapeutic Benefits and Design Recommendations*, New York: Wiley, 1999; M.T. Southwell and G. Wistow, 'Sleep in Hospital at Night—Are Patients' Needs Being Met?', *Journal of Advanced Nursing* 21(6), 1101–9; Roger S. Ulrich, Robert F. Simons et al., 'Stress Recovery During Exposure to Natural and Urban Environments', *Journal of Environmental Psychology* 1(3), 1991, 201–30.

10 John Baptista van Helmont, *Oriatrike, or Physick Refined,* London: Printed for Lodowick [Lloyd], [1662], 526.

11 David Sackett, William M. Rosenberg et al., 'Evidence Based Medicine: What It Is and What It Isn't', *BMJ*, 312, 71.

12 Kirk Hamilton, 'Four Levels of Evidence-Based Practice', *Healthcare Design* 3(4), 2003, 18–26.

13 Kerstin Sailer, Andrew Budgen et al., 'Evidence-Based Design: Theoretical and Practical Reflections of an Emerging Approach in Office Architecture', *Undisciplined! Design Research Society Conference 2008*, Sheffield Hallam University, Sheffield, UK, 16–19 July 2008.

14 Kirk Hamilton, 'Four Levels of Evidence-Based Practice'.

15 Susanne Colenberg, Tuuli Jylhä, Monique Arkesteijn, 'The Relationship Between Interior Office Space and Employee Health and Well-being—A Literature Review', *Building Research and Information* 49(3), 2021.

16 Ibid., 9.

17 See globalwellnessinstitute.org.

18 Ibid.

19 See Urban Land Institute, *Building Healthy Places Toolkit: Strategies for Enhancing Health in the Built Environment*, 2015.

20 Quoted in Patrick Sisson, 'Can the Right Home Make You Live Longer?', curbed.com, 15 October 2019.

21 Ibid.

22 Quoted in Samantha Sharf, 'This Ex-Goldman Trader and His $800 Million Startup Hope You'll Pay Extra for Real Estate That Aces a 'Wellness' Test', forbes.com, 11 April 2019.

23 See wellcertified.com.

24 Delos Living LCC, *Investing in Human Health: The Science behind Darwin Home Wellness Intelligence*, 2019, 4.

25 Rachel Hodgdon, 'Lead by Example: Cultivating Wellness in the Workplace', resources.wellcertified.com, 3 September 2019.

26 Eleftherios Zakaris and Crystal Rosen, 'Climate Change, Human Health and the Built Environment, an EMEA Roundtable', resources. wellcertified.com, 8 February 2022.

27 Paul J. Rosch, 'The Quandary of Job Stress Compensation', *Health and Stress: The Newsletter of the American Institute of Stress*, March 2001.

28 Nadia Wood and Chi Lam, *Preparing and Architecting for Machine Learning: A White Paper*, 9 April 2020, 4.

29 See v2.wellcertified.com.

30 Paul Scialla, 'Paul Scialla On Human Friendly Building Standards', youtube.com, 26 August 2016.

31 See v2.wellcertified.com.

32 See standard.wellcertified.com.

33 Oliver Heath, 'CBRE Madrid: The Benefits of WELL Building in Practice', blog.interface.com, 4 May 2018.

34 Deepak Chopra, 'How to Stay Well', youtube.com, 2 June 2016.

35 Samantha Sharf, 'This Ex-Goldman Trader and His $800 Million Startup'.

36 Ibid.

37 Already in 2006, in Swedish medical journal *Läkartidningen*, doctor Robert Walinder spoke of '(pseudo) medical diagnoses from actors outside the health sector', voicing concern over a trend in which perceived anxieties on the part of employees or residents are amplified by surveys with leading questions conducted by consultancy firms that do not have the medical competency required.

Data, p. 103

1 *Monocle*, 'Quality of Life Survey, top 25 cities', monocle.com, 21 June 2019.

6. Vancouver™

1 Mercer, 'Vienna Tops Mercer's 21st Quality of Living Ranking', mercer.com, 13 March 2019.

2 Roberta Ryan and Yvette Selim, 'Livable Sydney. Livable for Whom?', *Livable Cities from a Global Perspective*, New York: Routledge, 2018.

3 Mohamad Kashef, 'Urban Livability Across Disciplinary and Professional Boundaries', *Frontiers of Architectural Research* 5(2), 2016, 239–53.

4 Jane Austin, *Mansfield Park*, New York: W.W. Norton & Company, 1998, 166.

5 Lewis Mumford, *From The Ground Up: Observations On Contemporary Architecture, Housing, Highway Building, and Civic Design*, San Diego: Harcourt Brace Jovanovic, 1956, 219.

6 Jane Jacobs, *The Death and Life of Great American Cities*, New York: Vintage Books, 1961, 14.

7 Quoted in Donald Gutstein, *Vancouver Ltd.*, Toronto: Lorimer, 1975.

8 Ibid.

9 Quoted in Rod Mickleburgh, 'Visionary Mayor Art Phillips Remade Vancouver', theglobeandmail.com, 24 April 2013.

10 Harry Lash, *Planning in a Human Way: Personal Reflections on the Regional Planning Experience in Greater Vancouver*, Ottawa: Ministry for Urban Affairs, 1976, 45.

11 Ibid., 54.

12 Ibid., 54.

13 Greater Vancouver Region, *The Livable Region 1976/1986: Proposals to Manage the Growth of Greater Vancouver*, 1975, 4.

14 Greater Vancouver Regional District, *Creating Our Future: Steps to a more Livable Region*, 1990, 9.

15 City of Vancouver, *Administrative Report*, 31 October 2006, 4.

Data, p. 123

1 See pps.org

2 Fred Kent, 'Transformative Times: Earth Day 1970, Placemaking, and Sustainability Today', pps.org, 21 April 2010.

3 Ibid.
4 Lynda H. Schneekloth, Robert G. Shibley, Placemaking: The Art and Practice of Building Communities, New York, Chichester, Brisbane, Toronto, Singapore: Wiley, 1994.
5 See placemakers.nl.
6 See placemakingplus.com.
7 See cnu.org.
8 Urban Land Institute, Creative Placemaking. Sparking Development with Arts and Culture, 2020.
9 See artscape.ca.
10 Holly Moskerintz, 'ULI Advances Placemaking: A Value to Real Estate', nar.realtor, 11 December 2018.
11 See digital-placemaking.org.
12 Delaware County Planning Department, Tactical Placemaking. Planner's Portfolio 12, September 2017, delcopa.gov.
13 Nicola Dempsey, 'We need to talk about place-keeping!', place-keeping.org, 10 November 2013.
14 See jocowenarchitects.com.
15 Ben van Berkel. Quoted in UNStudio, 'UNStudio Report: Architecture and Urban Design Critical to Helping Build Communities Post-Corona', unstudio.com, 22 July 2021.
16 See markoandplacemakers.com.
17 See streetdots.co.uk.
18 Hans Karssenberg, Developing Our Cities Around Community and Place, thecityateyelevel.com.
19 Savills, Spotlight Development: The Value of Placemaking, 2016, savills.co.uk.

7. Here nor There

1 See en.wikipedia.org.
2 See pps.org.
3 Neal Peirce, 'Planning for Public Spaces as if People Mattered', Washington Post, 12 May 1978.
4 Quoted in Barbara Palmer, 'Fred Kent. The Doctor of Place', PCMA Convene, November 2008.
5 Kathy Kiefer, 'Earth Day—'What Is It?', kathykieferblog.wordpress.com, 16 April 2015.
6 Fred Kent, 'Transformative Times: Earth Day 1970, Placemaking, and Sustainability Today', pps.org, 21 April 2010.
7 See 'Lindsay Triangle', nycgovparks.org.
8 Palmer, 'Fred Kent. The Doctor of Place'.
9 Elizabeth Giddens, 'Impresario of the Village Green', nytimes.com, 30 September 2007.

10   Martin Gottlieb, 'Conversations/Fred Kent; One Who Would Like to See Most Architects Hit the Road', nytimes.com, 28 March 1993.

11   The Aspen Institute, 'AIF 09: In Conversation with Frank Gehry', youtube.com, 13 July 2009.

12   Lynda H. Schneekloth, Robert G. Shibley, *Placemaking: The Art and Practice of Building Communities*, New York: John Wiley & Sons, 1995.

13   Ibid.

14   Kathleen Madden, Andrew Schwartz, Project for Public Spaces, *How to Turn a Place Around. A Handbook for Creating Successful Public Spaces*, New York: Project for Public Spaces, 2000.

15   Quoted in Glenn Collins, 'Bryant Park Braces for a Tidal Wave of Traffic', nytimes.com, 5 June 2008.

16   Paul Goldberger, 'ARCHITECTURE VIEW; Bryant Park, An Out-of-Town Experience', nytimes.com, 3 May 1992.

17   Collins, 'Bryant Park Braces for a Tidal Wave of Traffic'.

18   Quoted in bryantpark.org.

19   Alison Gregor, 'Bryant Park Office Rents Outperform the Rest of Midtown', nytimes.com, 2 October 2012.

20   See downtowndetroit.org.

21   JC Reindl, 'Ilitch Organization to Get $74m Bonus for Hitting Arena District Goal', eu.freep.com, 11 May 2019.

22   Michael Jackman, 'The District Detroit: The City of Today, Tomorrow!', metrotimes.com, 3 March 2015.

23   John Gallagher, 'Downtown Detroit Sales Prices Rise to "Insane" Levels', eu.freep.com, 23 April 2016.

24   Quoted in Rod Meloni, 'Dan Gilbert to Unveil Plans for Reinventing Downtown Detroit with Development Strategy', clickondetroit.com, 27 March 2013.

25   Ibid.

26   Ben Austen, 'The Post-Post-Apocalyptic Detroit', nytimes.com, 11 July 2014.

27   Ibid.

28   See discoverygreen.com.

29   See downtownpittsburgh.com.

30   See rosekennedygreenway.org.

31   See downtownseattle.org.

32   Rick Snyder, 'A Special Message from Governor Rick Snyder: Community Development and Local Government Reforms', 21 March 2011.

33   See sfplanning.org.

34   'Regeneration and Placemaking: Shape Meaningful Places We All Value', jll.co.uk.

35 Urban Land Institute, 'Creative Placemaking. Sparking Development with Arts and Culture', 2020.

36 Jane Jacobs, 'Downtown is for People', *Fortune*, 1958.

8. Rule Bohemia!

1 Department of Communications and the Arts (Australia), *Creative Nation: Commonwealth Cultural Policy*, webarchive.nla.gov.au, 30 October 1994.

2 Jonathan Gross, *The Birth of the Creative Industries Revisited. An Oral History of the 1998 DCMS Mapping Document*, kcl.ac.uk, 2020, 9.

3 Department for Digital, Culture, Media & Sport, *Creative Industries Mapping Documents 1998*, gov.uk, 9 April 1998.

4 Quoted in Gross, *The Birth of the Creative Industries Revisited*, 6.

5 Ibid., 12.

6 Ibid., 6.

7 Hasan Bakhshi, Ian Hargreaves and Juan Mateos-Garcia, 'A Manifesto for the Creative Economy', April 2013, media.nesta.org.

8 Gross, *The Birth of the Creative Industries Revisited*, 19.

9 Richard Florida, *The Rise of the Creative Class, Revisited*, New York: Basic Books, 2011, 38–39.

10 Ibid., 39.

11 Richard Florida, 'Bohemia and Economic Geography', *Journal of Economic Geography*, 2, 2002, 64.

12 Florida, *The Rise of the Creative Class*, 135.

13 Alec MacGillis, 'The Ruse of the Creative Class', prospect.org, 18 December 2009.

14 Ross Atkin, 'A Tale of Cool Cities', csmonitor.com, 8 October 2003.

15 Kim Margolis, 'Young Dayton Adults Strive to Help the City Thrive', *Dayton Daily News*, 30 April 2010.

16 coolcities.com.

17 Rana Florida, 'Watch CREATE: Detroit's Inaugural Ideas Fest on City Building', huffpost.com, 9 July 2015.

18 Shinan Govani, 'Richard and Rana Florida's Long Journey to Baby Mila', thestar.com. 26 November 2015.

19 Donald Bonk, 'Richard Florida: Iconic Thoughts on Pittsburgh', pittsburghquarterly.com, 19 August 2020.

20 See Jamie Peck, 'Struggling with the Creative Class', *International Journal of Urban and Regional Research*, 20 December 2005; Steven Malanga 'The Curse of the Creative Class', city-journal.org, 2004; and MacGillis, 'The Ruse of the Creative Class'.

21 'LSE Events, Prof. Richard Florida, The New Urban Crisis', youtube.com, 11 October 2017.

22 Oliver Wainwright, '"Everything Is Gentrification Now": but Richard Florida Isn't Sorry', theguardian.com, 26 October 2017.

23 MacGillis, 'The Ruse of the Creative Class'.

24 Department for Digital, Culture, Media and Sport, *Creative Industries Mapping Documents 1998*.

25 Walter Isaacson, *Steve Jobs: The Exclusive Biography*, London: Little, Brown, 2011, 463.

26 Office Snapshots, 'Pixar Headquarters and the Legacy of Steve Jobs', officesnapshots.com, 16 July 2012.

27 Robert Iger, *The Ride of a Lifetime*, New York: Random House, 2019, 150.

Data, p. 167

1 The Building Better, Building Beautiful Commission, Living with Beauty. Promoting Health, Well-being and Sustainable Growth, January 2020, 1–5.

9. The B Word

1 Royal Fine Art Commission, *Records of the Royal Fine Art Commission*, 1924.

2 Ibid.

3 Dennis Kavanaugh, 'Lord St-John of Fawsley: Flamboyant Politician Who Fell Foul of Margaret Thatcher', independent.co.uk, 6 March 2012.

4 Matthew Carmona and Andrew Renninger, 'The Royal Fine Art Commission and 75 Years of English Design Review: The Final 15 years, 1984–1999, *Planning Perspectives* 32(4), 2017, 581.

5 Quoted in Amanda Ballieu, 'Architecture: The Mandarins Meet Their Match: When the Royal Fine Art Commission Decrees, Governments Defer. But in Paternoster Square It Is Being Spurned (CORRECTED)', independent.co.uk, 3 February 1993.

6 Carmona and Renninger, 'The Royal Fine Art Commission'.

7 Royal Fine Art Commission, *Records of the Royal Fine Art Commission*.

8 Kavanaugh, 'Lord St-John of Fawsley'.

9 Richard Rogers, 'Lord Rogers' Speech to the Urban Summit Today', theguardian.com, 31 October 2002.

10 Urban Task Force, *Towards an Urban Renaissance*, London: E & FN Spon, 1999, 5.

11 Quoted in Sebastian Macmillan (ed.), *Designing Better Buildings: Quality and Value in the Built Environment*. London: Taylor & Francis, 2004, 2.

12 James Fischer, 'Architecture: The Country's Architectural Enforcer', independent.co.uk, 20 August 1998.

13 dqi.org.uk.

14 Richard Rogers, 'The Fear of Beauty is Destroying our Urban Environment', independent.co.uk, 2 April 2001.

15 Rogers, 'Lord Rogers' Speech'.

16 Commission for Architecture & the Built Environment (CABE), *The Value of Good Design: How Buildings and Spaces Create Economic and Social Value*, 2002.

17 Oliver Letwin, *Conducting Politics as if Beauty Matters*, conservative-speeches.sayit.mysociety.org, 6 June 2005.

18 See Gabriel M. Ahlfeldt and Nancy Holman, 'Distinctively Different: A New Approach to Valuing Architectural Amenities', *SERC Discussion Paper 171*, 2005.

19 Department for Communities and Local Government, *National Planning Policy Framework*, 27 March 2012, 15.

20 Alan Powers, 'Beauty, a Short History', *People and Places*, 15 November 2010.

21 Andrew Lainton, 'Brandon Lewis Celebrates Defeat of Bungalows Scheme', independent.co.uk, 29 August 2014.

22 See *The Farrell Review of Architecture and the Built Environment*, farrellreview.co.uk, August 2014.

23 RIBA, *Building a Better Britain*, architecture.com, July 2014.

24 Roger Scruton, 'On Defending Beauty', spectator.org, May 2010.

25 Scruton later confessed: 'I haven't written one page of it'.

26 See Ministry of Housing, Communities and Local Government, *Living with Beauty: Report of the Building Better, Building Beautiful Commission*, gov.uk, 30 January 2020.

27 Rowan Moore, 'Would You Trust Roger Scruton to Design Your New Home?', 25 November 2018.

28 Quoted in India Block, 'UK's New Commission for Beautiful Buildings Is "Tedious Hangover from 1980s" Say Architects', dezeen. com, 6 November 2018.

29 Ibid.

30 Ibid.

31 Quoted in Ella Jessel, 'Beauty Watchdog Could Be Government Decoy, Admits Scruton', architectsjournal.co.uk, 25 January 2019.

32 Quoted in Ella Jessel, '"Stop Being Defensive and Build What British People Want", Kit Malthouse Tells Architects', architectsjournal. co.uk, 20 November 2018.

33 Roger Scruton, *Beauty*, Oxford: Oxford University Press, 2009, 31.

34 Ministry of Housing, Communities and Local Government, *Living with Beauty: Report of the Building Better, Building Beautiful Commission*.

35 Building Better, Building Beautiful Commission, *Living with Beauty. Promoting Health, Well-being and Sustainable Growth*, January 2020, 22.

36 @JoeShalam, twitter.com, 30 January 2020, 6:14 PM.

37 Vaughn Horsman. Quoted in Tom de Castella, 'Farrells and PRP Help Councils Draw Up New Design Codes', architectsjournal. co.uk, 24 August 2021.

10. Architecture without Architects

1 Justin Trudeau, 'Announcing Sidewalk Toronto: Press Conference Live Stream', youtube.com, 17 October 2017.

2 Sidewalk Labs, *Master Innovation and Development Plan*, 2019, Volume 0, slideshare.net, 9.

3 See sidewalklabs.com.

4 Quoted in Herman van Bosch, 'Google's Sidewalk Labs Takes the Lead in "Smart City" Development in Toronto. Smart City Hub', smartcityhub.com.

5 See sidewalklabs.com.

6 Quoted in Leyland Cecco, '"Surveillance Capitalism": Critic Urges Toronto to Abandon Smart City Project', theguardian.com, 6 June 2019.

7 Quoted in Eleanor Gibson, 'Sidewalk Labs Abandons Toronto Smart City During Pandemic', dezeen.com, 7 May 2020.

8 Jane Jacobs, *The Death and Life of Great American Cities*, New York: Vintage Books, 1961, 50.

9 Ibid., 138.

10 Bernard Rudofsky, *Architecture without Architects: An Introduction to Non-Pedigreed Architecture,* New York: Museum of Modern Art, 1962.

11 Ibid., 15.

12 See patternlanguage.com.

13 Boyd Cohen, 'What Exactly Is a Smart City?', fastcompany.com, 19 September 2012.

14 Replica, 'A New Way to Plan and Manage Cities', replicahq.medium. com, 16 September 2020.

15 Ibid.

16 Klaus Schwab and Richard Samans, 'Preface', in *The Future of Jobs Employment, Skills and Workforce Strategy for the Fourth Industrial Revolution,* World Economic Forum, January 2016.

17 Lars Spuybroek, *The Architecture of Continuity*, Rotterdam: V2 Publishing, 2008, 71.

18 Sebastian Jordahn, 'Philippe Starck, Kartell and Autodesk Unveil "World's First Production Chair Designed with Artificial

Intelligence"', dezeen.com, 11 April 2019.

19 Natashah Hitti, 'Christie's Sells AI-Created Artwork Painted Using Algorithm for $432,000', dezeen.com, 29 October 2019.

20 See terminusgroup.com.

21 Jesper Staahl, 'Architects and Our Tools: A Return from User to Creator', spacemakerai.com, 29 March 2021.

22 See spacemakerai.com.

23 Ibid.

24 See app description at apps.apple.com.

25 Louisa Xu, 'Modernizing Real Estate: The Property Tech Opportunity', forbes.com, 22 February 2019.

26 See homebound.com.

27 Ibid.

28 Daniel Davis, 'Katerra's $2 Billion Legacy', architectmagazine.com, 18 June 2021.

29 See sidewalklabs.com.

30 Quoted in Stephen Cousins, 'Generative City Design Gets the Google Treatment', ribaj.com, 9 November 2020.

31 See sidewalklabs.com.

32 Sundar Pichai, '$1 Billion for 20,000 Bay Area Homes', blog.google, 18 June 2019.

33 See realestate.withgoogle.com.

34 See *Downtown West's Social Infrastructure Plan*, Spring 2021.

35 Alistair Barr, 'An RV Camp Sprang up Outside Google's Headquarters. Now Mountain View Wants to Ban It', bloomberg.com, 21 May 2019.

36 Mark Maurer, 'Map: A Look at Google's Growing Empire', therealdeal.com, 21 Mar 2018.

37 See sidewalklabs.com.

38 Aneesh Aneesh, 'Technologically Coded Authority: The Post-Industrial Decline in Bureaucratic Hierarchies', *Conference: International Summer Academy on Technology Studies*, Deutschlandsberg, 2002, 8–9.

39 Aneesh, 12.

Index